Besides being ___ of genius T. S. Eliot was a many-s. ___ etters and his work requires and rewards approaches from a variety of ___ view. In this *Companion* an international team of leading Eliot scholars contribute specialized studies of the different facets of his work to build up a carefully coordinated and fully rounded introduction.

Five chapters are devoted to his poetry and drama. These cover his entire output in verse, bringing out the most significant features, clarifying what is problematic, and showing where the interest lies for readers now. Taken together these chapters constitute a complete account of Eliot's poems and plays from several distinct points of view. Written by critics and teachers with a deep understanding and appreciation of his work, a wide knowledge of previous and current Eliot studies, and well acquainted with the interests and needs of students, they will make even Eliot's most difficult verse at once more approachable and more intelligible.

The preceding seven chapters present and assess the major aspects and issues of Eliot's life and thought. The subtle inter-relations of the life and the work are sensitively revealed. There is new information about Eliot's American roots, and new insight into what he made of England. A philosopher argues for a new and more discerning placing of Eliot as a philosopher. The meaning and intent of his literary and social criticism, and the special political problems of the latter, are searchingly scrutinized. A study of the nature and evolution of Eliot's religious sense affords a quite new insight into its shaping presence in all his work. Later chapters place Eliot's work in a series of historical perspectives. One examines his borrowings from his predecessors, while another registers his impact on later twentieth-century poets. A wide-ranging exploration of what tradition meant in the context of modernism, is followed by an investigation of the way in which -isms and authors are constructed by critics and critical fashions, and of how Eliot has figured in this process.

There are two practical aids: a chronological outline giving the principal dates and facts of Eliot's life and works; and an expert review of the whole field of Eliot studies supplemented by a helpful listing of the most significant publications. *The Cambridge Companion to T. S. Eliot* is designed to enhance the enjoyment and advance the understanding of Eliot's work among both new readers and those already familiar with it by bringing together the best current intelligence on the full range of his writings.

THE CAMBRIDGE
COMPANION TO
T. S. ELIOT

Cambridge Companions to Literature

THE CAMBRIDGE
COMPANION TO
T. S. ELIOT

EDITED BY
A. DAVID MOODY

CAMBRIDGE
UNIVERSITY PRESS

Published by the Press Syndicate of the University of Cambridge
The Pitt Building, Trumpington Street, Cambridge CB2 1RP
40 West 20th Street, New York, NY 10011–4211, USA
10 Stamford Road, Oakleigh, Melbourne 3166, Australia

First published 1994
Reprinted 1996

Printed in Great Britain at the University Press, Cambridge

A catalogue record for this book is available from the British Library

Library of Congress cataloguing in publication data

The Cambridge Companion to T. S. Eliot / edited by A David Moody.
p.   cm. – (Cambridge Companions to Literature)
Includes index.
ISBN 0 521 42080 6 (hardback) – ISBN 0 521 42127 6 (paperback)
1. Eliot, T. S. (Thomas Stearns), 1888–1965 – Criticism and interpretation.
I. Moody, Anthony David. II. Series.
PS3509.L43Z64728 1994
821'.912–dc20 93–43558 CIP

ISBN 0 521 42080 6 hardback
ISBN 0 521 42127 6 paperback

CONTENTS

CONTRIBUTORS

CHARLES ALTIERI's books include *Painterly Abstraction in Modernist American Poetry* (1989), *Canons and Consequences* (1990), and *First Persons* (1994). He now teaches at the University of California at Berkeley.

JEWEL SPEARS BROOKER is the author of *Mastery and Escape: T. S. Eliot and the Dialectic of Modernism* (1993), co-author of *Reading "The Waste Land": Modernism and the Limits of Interpretation* (1990), and editor of *The Placing of T. S. Eliot* (1991) and of *Approaches to Teaching Eliot's Poetry and Plays* (1988). Professor of Literature at Eckerd College in Florida, Dr. Brooker has also taught at Columbia University and at Doshisha University in Japan. She served as President of the T. S. Eliot Society from 1985 to 1988.

HARRIET DAVIDSON teaches twentieth-century literature and theory at Rutgers University. She is the author of *T. S. Eliot and Hermeneutics: Absence and Interpretation in "The Waste Land"* (1985) and of articles on modern and contemporary poetry.

ROBIN GROVE teaches literature at the University of Melbourne, where his interests include Renaissance poetry and drama, the nineteenth-century novel, and courses in cultural theory from the Pauline epistles to Barthes. Originally trained as a musician, he is active both as a performer and critic, and is dance-reviewer for the national daily *The Australian*. His recent work includes studies of Wordsworth, Herbert, and Austen, *The Early Poetry of T. S. Eliot* (1993), and *Emily Brontë's "Wuthering Heights"* (1994).

CLEO MCNELLY KEARNS is the author of *T. S. Eliot and Indic Traditions: A Study in Poetry and Belief* (1987), and of articles on modern literature, religion, and literary theory. She has taught at Rutgers University, the University of Strathclyde, and Princeton Theological Seminary, and is currently Associate Professor of Humanities at New Jersey Institute of Technology.

ix

JOHN KWAN-TERRY formerly with the Department of English Language and Literature at the National University of Singapore was at the time of his death in late 1993 Professor and Dean of the School of Arts at the Nanyang Technological University. He published on contemporary American and British poetry, East–West comparative literature, translation, Chinese painting and poetry, prosody, the new literatures, and literacy issues.

JAMES LONGENBACH is Joseph H. Gilmore Professor of English at the University of Rochester. He is the author of several books about modern poetry, including *Modernist Poetics of History: Pound, Eliot, and the Sense of the Past* (1987) and *Wallace Stevens: The Plain Sense of Things* (1991).

ALAN MARSHALL teaches English and American literature at the University of York. He has published poems, articles on George Oppen and Edward Thomas, and is currently completing a book on modern American poetry.

TIMOTHY MATERER's books include *Vortex: Pound, Eliot and Lewis* (1979) and he edited *The Selected Letters of Ezra Pound to John Quinn, 1915–24* (1991). His essay "Occultism as Sign and Symptom in Sylvia Plath" was awarded the 1991 *Twentieth Century Literature* Prize in Literary Criticism.

J. C. C. MAYS is Professor of English and American Literature at University College, Dublin. He has written on Joyce, Beckett, and other Irish writers, and his edition of Coleridge's poems and plays will appear shortly in the Bollingen *Collected Coleridge*.

A. DAVID MOODY's books include *Thomas Stearns Eliot: Poet* (1979 – new edition, 1994) and he edited *"The Waste Land" in Different Voices* (1974). He is Professor of English and American Literature at the University of York and is currently studying Ezra Pound.

JAMES OLNEY is Henry J. Voorhies Professor of English at Louisiana State University and Editor of *The Southern Review*. His books include *Metaphors of Self: The Meaning of Autobiography* (1972) and *Autobiography: Essays Theoretical and Critical* (1980).

JEAN-MICHEL RABATÉ, born in 1949, formerly at the University of Dijon, is now Professor of English at the University of Pennsylvania. He has published books on Ezra Pound, Samuel Beckett, James Joyce, Thomas Bernhard, and aesthetic theory. His most recent publications include *James Joyce* (Paris, 1992) and *La Penultième est morte* (1993).

PETER DALE SCOTT is a former Canadian diplomat, now a poet, writer, researcher, and English Professor at the University of California, Berkeley. His most recent books include *Crime and Cover-Up* (1977, reissued 1993), *The Iran-Contra Connection* (in collaboration, 1987), *Coming to Jakarta: A Poem About Terror* (1989), *Cocaine Politics* (in collaboration, 1991), *Listening to the Candle: A Poem on Impulse* (1992) and *Deep Politics and the Death of JFK* (1993).

BERNARD SHARRATT is Reader in English and Cultural Studies and chair of the Communications and Image Studies degree program at the University of Kent at Canterbury, England. His publications include *Performance and Politics in Popular Drama* (co-edited, 1980), *Reading Relations: Structures of Literary Production: A Dialectical Text/Book* (1982), *The Literary Labyrinth: Contemporary Critical Discourses* (1984), and essays on Skelton, Milton, Coleridge, Morris, Tressell, Foucault, Williams, and the cultural study of time.

RICHARD SHUSTERMAN is Professor of Philosophy at Temple University, Philadelphia. He is author of *The Object of Literary Criticism* (1984), *T. S. Eliot and the Philosophy of Criticism* (1988), and *Pragmatist Aesthetics: Living Beauty, Rethinking Art* (1992). He has edited *Analytic Aesthetics* (1989), and co-edited *The Interpretive Turn: Philosophy, Science, Culture* (1991).

ERIC SIGG is the author of *The American T. S. Eliot: A Study of the Early Writings* (1989), and *California Public Gardens: A Visitor's Guide* (1991). He works as an attorney in Los Angeles.

PREFACE

In 1919 when he was helping to bring about the modernist revolution T. S. Eliot wrote (not without a sense of irony) of "the existing monuments" of literature, and of how they would have to be rearranged when "the new (the really new) work of art" appeared among them. Over the succeeding twenty-five years it was his own poetry and criticism, from "Gerontion" and *The Sacred Wood* through to *Little Gidding*, which came to dominate the imaginary museum of literature in English. It was declared the Age of Eliot, thus according him the status of a classic in his own lifetime. He had created as only the greatest writers have done both the really new works of art and the critical taste for them. That age and its taste have passed – F. R. Leavis and the American New Critics who made Eliot's literary canons prevail are invoked now only to explain, or to explain away, the phenomenon of Eliot's success. For a time after his death in 1965 Eliot himself seemed in danger of becoming simply another monument, frozen in a fixed idea of his achievement. But there is too much life in his work for the accepted ideas to contain it; and a new generation of readers, coming to it in the frame of mind of this end of the century, are finding that there is much in it which answers to current preoccupations. This is no longer the age of Eliot, but Eliot is none the less a poet for our time.

The seventeen contributors to this *Cambridge Companion to T. S. Eliot* are drawn from various countries and belong to various critical schools or to none. But they have in common a regard for Eliot as a notable contemporary, one with a past certainly that must be taken into account, and with a future as well. They have in common also a freedom from modish jargon and from preset ideas of what is to be said about him. The animating concern is for what Eliot's works have to offer their readers now, and for whatever there may be of enduring value in them. There is no attempt, therefore, to give an account of "the critical heritage" – though we are all of course beneficiaries of it. But rather than adopting a historical approach which would explain where we have got to with Eliot by tracing the developments of opinion and judgment, each chapter enters directly into some aspect or part of his work, in the conviction that for readers the best place to start from, and indeed the only sure place, is wherever we happen to find ourselves. A live intelligence operates always in the here and now – in "the present moment of the past," as Eliot put it.

Intelligence of course needs to be informed, and the *Companion* not only provides much relevant information, but also indicates, in the full review of Eliot studies, how more may be found as it is required. We have not tried to tell the reader everything he or she may want to know. Our aim has been to present Eliot's major works and the main issues arising in them, and to situate them in their appropriate contexts. There are chapters therefore on his thought and theory as philosopher, literary critic, and social philosopher, and on his religious development. One third of the *Companion* is devoted to his practice as a poet and playwright. There are chapters on how his personal experience and his American and English backgrounds enter into his work. And finally there are chapters on some of the historical perspectives in which it has its place.

Under our examination of his many sides from our diverse points of view Eliot appears more various, less readily formulated and pinned down, than some of his critics have thought. Behind even his more dogmatic statements there is to be found a persistent skepticism and pragmatism; and his verse, far from closing off the exploration of experience with affirmations of faith, proves to be unceasingly committed to "the intolerable wrestle / With words and meanings." Moreover, his writing, and especially his poetry, requires of the reader not submission and assent but active and critical participation in the process of interpreting experience and creating value. It is a body of work which has much to offer in a time of uncertainty, not least in its demonstration that a wise not-knowing is the opposite of know-nothingness. This is the Eliot, various, subtle, and rewarding, we would open to a plurality of readers.

A.D.M.

c. 1668	Andrew Eliot emigrates from East Coker in Somerset, England, to the Massachusetts Bay Colony.
1834	William Greenleaf Eliot graduates from Harvard College and moves to St. Louis, Missouri to found a Unitarian Church there.
1888	Thomas Stearns Eliot born September 26 in St. Louis, seventh and youngest child of Henry Ware Eliot and Charlotte Champe Stearns Eliot, and grandson of William Greenleaf Eliot.
1898	Attends Smith Academy, St. Louis, a school founded by his grandfather.
1905	First published poems in *Smith Academy Record*. Graduates from Smith and in the Fall enrols at Milton Academy, Milton, MA, to prepare for Harvard.
1906	Commences at Harvard.
1907	Publishes poems in *Harvard Advocate* – also in 1908, 1909, 1910.
1909	Receives A.B. at Harvard. He had taken courses in Greek, Latin, German, French and English language and literature, history, Florentine painting, and philosophy.
1910	Graduates and composes the Class of 1910 Ode. Receives M.A. In his M.A. year he studied with Irving Babbitt and George Santayana. In October to Paris for a year attending lectures at the Sorbonne, hearing Bergson at the Collège de France, and taking private lessons with Alain-Fournier. Meets Jean Verdenal.
1911	Returns to Harvard Graduate School to read for doctorate in philosophy. Takes courses in Indic Philology, Sanskrit and Indian Philosophy. Completes "Prufrock," "Portrait of a Lady," "Preludes" and "Rhapsody on a Windy Night."
1912	Appointed Assistant in Philosophy. Meets Emily Hale.
1913	Participates in Josiah Royce's seminar on the problem of interpretation. Reads F. H. Bradley's *Appearance and Reality* and decides to write his dissertation on Bradley's epistemology.

1914   Meets Bertrand Russell. Awarded Harvard traveling fellowship to study philosophy for a year at Oxford – principally reads Aristotle with Harold Joachim. Meets Ezra Pound in London.

1915   Marries Vivienne Haigh-Wood on June 26. Visits parents and Harvard in August. "Prufrock" and other poems of 1911–12 published. Takes job as teacher at High Wycombe Grammar School.

1916   Becomes Junior Master at Highgate Junior School. Doctoral dissertation accepted at Harvard. Begins reviewing for periodicals and giving university extension lecture courses – continues with the latter until 1918 only.

1917   In March enters the Colonial and Foreign Department of Lloyds Bank in the City of London. *Prufrock and Other Observations* published. Becomes Assistant Editor of *The Egoist*. Writes some poems in French and others in quatrains.

1919   "Tradition and the Individual Talent" published in *The Egoist*.

1920   New collection of poems (containing "Gerontion") published in February, and *The Sacred Wood* in November.

1921   Suffers breakdown, takes three months leave from Lloyds Bank, goes to Margate to rest then to Lausanne where he completes the drafting of *The Waste Land*.

1922   *The Waste Land* published in the first number of *The Criterion*, which is to be Eliot's quarterly until he brings it to an end in 1939.

1925   Leaves bank to go into publishing with Faber & Gwyer (later Faber & Faber). *Poems 1909–1925* (includes "The Hollow Men").

1926   Gives Cambridge Clark Lectures, on metaphysical poetry. Publishes *Sweeney Agonistes* (in *Criterion*).

1927   Is baptized and confirmed in the Church of England, and becomes a naturalized British citizen. Publishes *Journey of the Magi*.

1928   *A Song for Simeon* and *For Lancelot Andrewes: Essays on Style and Order*.

1929   *Dante* and *Animula*.

1930   *Ash-Wednesday*, *Marina* and a translation of *Anabase* by St.-J. Perse.

1931   Publishes two poems later collected as "Coriolan."

1932   *Selected Essays 1917–1932*. In Fall to Harvard as Charles Eliot Norton Lecturer.

1933   Completes Charles Eliot Norton Lectures at Harvard, published as *The Use of Poetry and the Use of Criticism* (1933), and gives the Page-Barbour Lectures at the University of Virginia, published as *After Strange Gods* (1934). Separates from his wife.

1934   Writes the words for *The Rock: a Pageant Play*.

1935   *Murder in the Cathedral* first performed, in Canterbury Cathedral.

1936   *Collected Poems 1909–1935* (first appearance of *Burnt Norton*).

1939   *The Family Reunion* first performed. Publishes *The Idea of a Christian Society* (lectures given at Corpus Christi College, Cambridge), and *Old Possum's Book of Practical Cats.*

1940   *East Coker.*

1941   *The Dry Salvages.*

1942   *Little Gidding.*

1947   Awarded honorary doctorates by Harvard, Yale, and Princeton. Vivienne Eliot dies.

1948   Penguin Books publish *Selected Poems* in an edition of 50,000 copies. *Notes Towards the Definition of Culture.* Awarded Order of Merit and Nobel Prize for Literature.

1949   *The Cocktail Party* first performed at the Edinburgh Festival.

1952   *The Complete Poems and Plays* published in USA.

1953   *The Confidential Clerk* first performed at the Edinburgh Festival.

1957   Marries Valerie née Fletcher. Collects a dozen lectures mainly of the 1940s and 1950s in *On Poetry and Poets.*

1958   *The Elder Statesman* first performed at the Edinburgh Festival.

1963   *Collected Poems 1909–1962.*

1964   Awarded US Medal of Freedom.

1965   Dies January 4. His ashes later interred as he had wanted in the west end of the parish church of East Coker.

ABBREVIATIONS

ASG	*After Strange Gods* (London: Faber & Faber; New York: Harcourt, Brace, 1934)
AW	*Ash-Wednesday*
BN	*Burnt Norton*
CC	*The Confidential Clerk*
C & C	*Christianity and Culture* (New York: Harcourt, Brace, 1960) [Contains *ICS* and *NTDC*]
CP	*The Cocktail Party*
DS	*The Dry Salvages*
EC	*East Coker*
EAM	*Essays Ancient and Modern* (London: Faber & Faber; New York: Harcourt, Brace. 1936)
ES	*The Elder Statesman*
FR	*The Family Reunion*
4Q	*Four Quartets*
ICS	*The Idea of a Christian Society* (London: Faber & Faber, 1939, 1982; New York: Harcourt Brace, 1940)
KE	*Knowledge and Experience in the Philosophy of F. H. Bradley* (London: Faber & Faber; New York: Farrar, Straus, 1964)
Letters I	*The Letters of T. S. Eliot*, vol. I, Valerie Eliot (ed.) (London: Faber & Faber; San Diego: Harcourt Brace Jovanovich, 1988)
LG	*Little Gidding*
MC	*Murder in the Cathedral*
NTDC	*Notes Towards the Definition of Culture* (London: Faber & Faber, 1948; New York: Harcourt, Brace, 1949)
PP	*On Poetry and Poets* (London: Faber & Faber; New York: Farrar, Straus & Cudahy, 1957)
SE (1950)	*Selected Essays* (New York: Harcourt, Brace, 1950) – second American edition which does not include "John Marston."
SE (1951)	*Selected Essays* (London: Faber & Faber, 1951) – third English edition.

SW (1920)   *The Sacred Wood* (London: Methuen, 1920; New York: Knopf, 1921)
SW (1928)   *The Sacred Wood* (London: Methuen, 1928; New York: Knopf, 1930)
TCC   *To Criticize the Critic* (London: Faber & Faber; New York: Farrar,
            Straus & Giroux, 1965)
UPUC   *The Use of Poetry and the Use of Criticism* (London: Faber & Faber;
            Cambridge, MA.: Harvard University Press, 1933)
WL   *The Waste Land*
WL Drafts   *"The Waste Land": a facsimile and transcript of the original drafts
            including the annotations of Ezra Pound*, Valerie Eliot (ed.) (London:
            Faber & Faber, New York: Harcourt, Brace, 1971)

Note: Unless otherwise specified, all quotations from Eliot's poetry and plays are taken from the editions published by Faber & Faber and Harcourt Brace. Since the pagination of the English and American editions of Eliot's books sometimes differs readers are asked to notice which edition is being referred to.

I

JAMES OLNEY

Where is the real T. S. Eliot? or, The Life of the Poet

For some years we had no full, formal biography of T. S. Eliot, and this seemed, to many people, at the very least odd. For – as those many people viewed it – Eliot was, after all, the dominant figure in English letters for a good part of the twentieth century, and a biography, like being interred in the Poets' Corner of Westminster Abbey, would constitute mere public acknowledgment of such status in the literary world. The reason why there was no *Life of T. S. Eliot* for a considerable time is well known to literary scholars though, I think, imperfectly understood by them, their explanation going something like this: acting on motives that all potential biographers and indeed everyone in the scholarly world seemed to feel free to question, Eliot declared that he wanted no *Life* written, and he inserted a clause to this effect into his will; and those responsible for his estate (primarily his widow, acting as executor of his will) successfully prevented a biography by making access to the materials necessary for writing a *Life* difficult if not impossible. When I say that this explanation though well known has been imperfectly understood I mean first that, as an explanation, it seems to me a little too easy and too simple in the case of someone of Eliot's generally acknowledged subtlety and complexity, and second that critics, having accepted this suspiciously easy answer, have then either ignored or misconstrued the principled objection that Eliot held to being the subject – perhaps one might better say the object – of biographical treatment. The whole problem lies, I believe, in what we understand by the deceptively simple word "life," or "*Life*": for what Eliot was resisting, in one sense at least, was the transformation, effected by someone else, of his lower-case, unitalicized, lived life into an upper-case, italicized, written *Life*. But we must ask ourselves what *do* we mean in this instance by "*Life*," to what does the word refer and where do we locate that referent? To put the matter simply, what I believe was at issue for Eliot – and it is still a vital issue – is what I shall term "the Life of the Poet," which is a life played out *in the poetry*. This sense of a life, a written life, is radically different from what we understand when we pick up a book that purports to be the *Life* of a general or a statesman or a Hollywood celebrity; it is radically different also from the *Life*, as written by someone else, of a person who for biographical purposes is, as it were, only incidentally a poet. And as the life I am speaking about is played out in the poetry – in the whole body of poetry, the poet's entire œuvre – only the poet can write a "Life of the Poet": such a "Life" *is* the poetry, and the poetry has for its entire and sufficient subject the enacted or embodied "Life of the Poet."

We would do well, I think, to take a closer look not only at the term "Life" in our formulaic title, *The Life of XY*, but at the other side as well, the name of the poet, for this term has a potency about it and a potential for confusion or misunderstanding as great as and comparable to that of the word "Life." What is conjured up for us when we say "Shakespeare," "Eliot," "Yeats," "Whitman," "Dickinson," "Hopkins?" Is it not the poet-as-poet rather than the poet as individual man or woman? The name "Hopkins," for example, is a kind of shorthand designation for the entire poetic achievement of the man known to literary history as Gerard Manley Hopkins; it calls up for us a whole body of work, an œuvre, a career. If this is true for Hopkins, who was virtually unpublished and unknown as a poet in his lifetime – without a career it might almost seem, although in hindsight we now can see that that was certainly not the case – how much truer it would be for a highly visible and public poet like Yeats or Eliot, where the relationship of identity among the name, the public persona, and the body of work is always before us. With this correspondence between a name and an œuvre firmly in mind one receives a distinct jolt upon finding Yeats, in *The Cat and the Moon*, referring to "that strange 'Waste Land' by Mr. T. C. Eliot" or again when one comes upon this entry in Hopkins's diary of 1864: "Tuncks is a good name. Gerard Manley Tuncks. Poor Tuncks."[1] "T. C. Eliot" and "Tuncks" can never be for us as readers what "T. S. Eliot" and "Hopkins" are. In a similar way, Emily Dickinson demonstrated a sure sense of her poetic identity when she signed herself in letters to Thomas Wentworth Higginson not as "Emily Dickinson" but simply and with authorial flourish as "Dickinson." Or again it is pertinent to observe that the name "Walt Whitman" referred (and refers) not to a man but to a poetic persona. Before the first edition of *Leaves of Grass* there literally was no "Walt Whitman" but only Walter Whitman of Brooklyn, New York; the Poet, whose Life is recorded so fully in *Leaves of Grass*, did not come into existence until midway through the first of the poems, later to be known as "Song of Myself" – "Walt Whitman, an American, one of the roughs, a kosmos . . ." Eliot never names himself in his poems,[2] as Whitman and Yeats ("I, the poet William Yeats" and "Under bare Ben Bulben's head / In

Drumcliff Churchyard Yeats is laid") do, but his name is sufficiently inscribed across the body of his work and in the consciousness of all readers of poetry in this century. We refer now to "Eliot" or "Whitman," to "Dickinson," "Hopkins," and "Yeats," and know pretty well what we mean, signifying by any one of these names a distinctive swerve of style and personality (what Hopkins finds in Henry Purcell: "so arch-especial a spirit"), a particular poetic voice whose subject is both autobiographical and impersonal, a life which begins in this individual poet's life but becomes in the end no less than the "Life of the Poet." "This," as Dickinson writes, "was a Poet – It is That / Distills amazing sense / From ordinary Meanings . . ." Dickinson herself, Hopkins, Whitman, Yeats, or Eliot – "This was a Poet," whose Life is recorded across the entire body of the poetry.

We now know, for what they are worth, all the biographical details of Eliot's life, at least all those that are recordable: his childhood in St. Louis with summer holidays on the Northeast coast of the United States; his education at schools in St. Louis, at Milton Academy, at Harvard, a year in Paris, back at Harvard for graduate study and at Oxford for further graduate study and writing of the dissertation; his meeting with Ezra Pound and sudden marriage to Vivien Haigh-Wood in London; his work as a schoolmaster, as an Extension Lecturer, and in the foreign department of Lloyd's Bank; the publication of *Prufrock and Other Observations* and his very rapid consolidation of a position at the center of literary life in London, culminating in 1922 with the publication of *The Waste Land* and the founding of *The Criterion*; his move in 1925 into publishing at Faber and Gwyer (later Faber and Faber) where he spent the rest of his life, gradually becoming the preeminent man of letters of his time; his formal conversion to Christianity and his taking of British citizenship, both in 1927; the Charles Eliot Norton lectures at Harvard in 1932–33 and formal separation from his wife; the end of *The Criterion* in 1939 and a gradual turn, at the time of composing *Four Quartets* and later, from poetry to drama; death of Vivien Eliot in 1947, reception of the Nobel Prize in 1948, remarriage to Valerie Fletcher in 1957, and Eliot's own death in 1965. Throughout this public career of some fifty-five years there were frequent, regular publications: lectures and criticism, individual poems and collections, drama – the visible production of a professional man of letters. These biographical details are all there now, immensely fleshed out in the biographies by Peter Ackroyd and Lyndall Gordon, as a kind of given: they are public property, public knowledge. They are a version of what we can get in *Who's Who*, and of course we must know these details of the life in some way, but it is not clear to me that they get us much forward in the reading of the Life of the Poet. We can be sure that the major emotional events of Eliot's life – some referred to above and some not – are all there in the poems, but so thoroughly transformed into the emotion of the particular poem that they are hardly recognizable and can scarcely be traced back to the life, at least in any one-to-one way. It is the emotion of the poem that makes the poetry quick with life, and I believe we would look in vain trying to find that "significant emotion," as Eliot calls it, in any biography. This is why, though Eliot scholars will and should go on reading any *Lives* of Eliot that may appear, they should expect to find the real T. S. Eliot not there but rather in the Life of the Poet that he was himself responsible for imagining, projecting, recalling, and writing.

Coming a bit closer to where we can locate the "real T. S. Eliot," I want to keep W. B. Yeats also in view, for towards the end of his own poetic career, as he was partly consciously and partly unconsciously closing the curve of his Poet's Life, Eliot was clearly affected and I think deeply influenced both by Yeats's sense of what it is to be a poet and by the example of the poet that Yeats provided in his life and his work – affected and influenced to the degree that he not only wrote one of his finest critical pieces as the Yeats memorial lecture of 1940, but also allowed phrases, ideas, and attitudes of the older poet to enter his own poetry of the time. Eliot is famous, of course, for his allusions, his quotations and his stealings from other poets, but no poet it seems to me ever quite dominated his moral and artistic imagination at a single, given moment the way Yeats did when Eliot was writing his Yeats lecture and the last three of the *Four Quartets*; and the substance of what Eliot has to say about Yeats's "development" in his lecture reads like nothing so much as exhortation to himself to have what he calls the "exceptional honesty and courage" to live out the life of the poet to the end as Yeats had very recently been so exemplary in doing. Other poets were more important to Eliot over the long haul than Yeats ever was – Dante is the obvious one to cite – but it is a matter of some moment that Yeats, who had triumphantly concluded his Life of the Poet with his death in 1939 and posthumous publication of his *Last Poems* in the same year, should have been so present to Eliot when he came to present his lecture in 1940 and to publish *East Coker* in 1940, *Dry Salvages* in 1941, and *Little Gidding* in 1942, for though the end of Eliot's life and the conclusion of his Life of the Poet did not coincide as they did for Yeats (but Yeats, in this regard, is very rare among poets), nevertheless we can see, especially in retrospect, that in the *Four Quartets* generally, in the last three poems more specifically, and in *Little Gidding* most specifically, Eliot was consciously bringing to a culmination the Life of the Poet that he had begun some thirty years earlier with "The Love Song of J. Alfred Prufrock." What was it in Yeats that so appealed to Eliot at this decisive moment in his career? Speaking for a younger generation of poets, Eliot writes that it was not Yeats's ideas or his attitudes and not even his style that was so important but rather it was "the work, and the man himself as poet, [that] have been of the greatest significance." Yeats had a tremendous influence, Eliot says, "but the influence of which I speak is due to the figure of the poet himself, to the integrity of his passion for his art and his craft" (*PP* [New York], p. 296). Most extraordinary in Yeats was the "continual development" exhibited in his work (which we see, of course, as Eliot saw it, only from the terminus of *New Poems* [1938] and *Last Poems and Two Plays* [1939]), and behind that continual development, Eliot says, was "character: I mean the character of the artist as artist" (*PP* [New York], p. 299), discernible in every Life of the Poet, and it produces, according to Eliot, a superior impersonality in the work, the impersonality "of the poet who, out of intense and personal experience, is able to express a general truth; retaining all the particularity of his experience, to make of it a general symbol" (*ibid.*). This sense of Yeats's achievement, supreme in our time in Eliot's view, this sense of his playing out the Life of the Poet in his poetry from beginning to end, makes him the figure of the poet for Eliot, something akin to the archetype of the Poet in Yeats's own terms, able to communicate in "tongues of flame" from beyond the bourne of death in the person of the "familiar compound ghost" who inhabits briefly not only the streets of London in *Little Gidding* but more significantly Yeats's Thirteenth Cone or Sphere, the realm of the *daimones* and the great, exemplary dead. So very present was Yeats to Eliot when he was writing the last three *Quartets* that we find echoes throughout *East Coker*, *Dry Salvages*, and *Little Gidding* of such late Yeats poems as "A Prayer for Old Age," "An Acre of Grass," "What Then?," "The Spur," "Are You Content," "The Apparitions," "Man and the Echo," "The Circus Animals' Desertion," and the play *Purgatory* as well as echoes of earlier poems like "Three Things," "Sailing to Byzantium" and "Byzantium," "All Souls' Night," and Yeats's translation of Swift's epitaph.

I go into the Yeats connection less fully indeed than I could but more fully than an essay on T. S. Eliot's real life might ordinarily seem to demand for two reasons: first, in reading Yeats backwards from the point of final development to the earliest beginning, Eliot is following a Yeatsian principle of poetic structuring (called by Yeats, in the different context of *A Vision*, "the *Dreaming Back*") and he is simultaneously teaching us how to read any body of work, including Yeats's and his own, which composes in the end a Life of the Poet; and second, the idea of the poet that Eliot sees enacted in the life and the work of W. B. Yeats has been better formulated by Yeats himself in "A General Introduction to My Work" than by any other writer I can think of. To put it simply, what I see Eliot doing in *Four Quartets*, the culmination of his career, and more particularly in *Little Gidding*, the culmination of the culmination of his career, the point from which he can dream back over his entire life as a poet and draw it all up into present consciousness of a career and a destiny, is exactly what Yeats says the poet as poet – not as cranky individual but as poet – always does. This way of reading a poet backwards is particularly appropriate, I believe, in the case of a public poet like Yeats or Eliot who has from the beginning quite consciously projected his career forward. It is to read a poet not biographically, from the dates and events yielded to us by history, but autobiographically, from the poet's own imagining of what he will be and do and from his own memory of what he has been and done, all as recorded in the poems that are summary milestones on the way to being and doing. As readers we all do read poets backwards, perhaps not always thinking of what we are doing, but I would like to propose it as a principle of reading at least for a certain kind of poet, Yeatsian and Eliotic; moreover, in adopting this as a principle of reading we would be doing nothing other than poets do themselves, forever reading themselves backward then forward, rather than the other way around. This is what Yeats does in his great summary poems, those personal–impersonal public performances that so strikingly mark his career as poet – the introductory rhymes to *Responsibilities* ("Pardon that for a barren passion's sake, / Although I have come close on forty-nine, / I have no child, I have nothing but a book"[3]), "Easter 1916," "A Prayer for my Daughter," "To be Carved on a Stone at Thoor Ballylee," "The Tower" ("It is time that I wrote my will"), "Among School Children" ("A sixty-year-old smiling public man"), "A Dialogue of Self and Soul," "The Municipal Gallery Revisited," "Under Ben Bulben," "The Circus Animals' Desertion," and many that I have left out; it is what Eliot does in *his* great summary poems too – "The Love Song of J. Alfred Prufrock" (it may seem odd to call the first poem in *Collected Poems* a summary poem, but looking back I think we must recognize it as such), "Gerontion," *The Waste Land*, *The Hollow Men*, *Ash-Wednesday*, *Burnt Norton*, *East Coker*, *The Dry Salvages*, and *Little Gidding*. The list for Eliot is sparer as the naming of himself is virtually non-existent and those facts no doubt mark a temperamental difference in the two poets, but I think for either of them each of these poems comes at a crucial, transitional moment in the career, each of them is both summary and projection, "is," as Eliot puts it in *Little Gidding*, "an end and a beginning, / Every poem an epitaph," a dreaming back and also an initiation and a commencement. Every one of these summary poems constitute the real Life of the Poet and taken all together they comprise the Autobiography of the Poet – not just *a* poet, though that too, but *the* poet, a figure that includes but transcends any individual poet.

"A poet," Yeats says, speaking of what I have just called "the poet – and he states this as "The First Principle" in "A General Introduction for My Work" – "A poet writes always of his personal life, in his finest work out of its tragedy, whatever it be, remorse, lost love, or mere loneliness; he never speaks directly as to someone at the breakfast table, there is always a phantasmagoria."[4] There is a temptation, to which I shall yield in imagination if not in fact, to edit Yeats's prose at this point, suggesting that a "however" should come after the semi-colon, for the latter part of the sentence qualifies sharply what might seem to be a loose romantic tendency in the first clause; moreover, thus edited, Yeats's description of the poet's subject matter is brought into line with what Eliot had to say, nearly twenty years earlier, about the "impersonality" of the poet. Indeed Yeats might be imagined to be delivering in 1937 an implied, prevenient condemnation of an Eliotic sort of the kind of writing that two or three decades later would be known as "confessional poetry." Although Eliot could not have been aware of Yeats's "General Introduction" essay at the time that he was writing and delivering his memorial lecture on Yeats, he nevertheless seems almost to echo Yeats's phrasing when, discussing Yeats's later work, he speaks of the "second impersonality . . . of the poet who, out of intense and personal experience, is able to express a general truth." And thinking only of "Prufrock," "La Figlia che Piange," *The Waste Land*, "Marina," *Little Gidding*, and Eliot's drama in general, what better description could we have of Eliot's poetic practice than "A poet writes always of his personal life, in his finest work out of its tragedy, whatever it be, remorse, lost love, or mere loneliness"? Reading these words – "remorse, lost love, or mere loneliness" – one has the eerie sense that Yeats is deliberately describing Eliot's nearly obsessive subject matter, or conversely the eerie sense that Eliot must have written his poetry to the dictates of an essay that he could not have known. "Even when the poet seems most himself," Yeats goes on, continuing both his line of thought and the "breakfast table" figure of speech, "he is never the bundle of accident and incoherence that sits down to breakfast; he has been reborn as an idea, something intended, complete. A novelist might describe his accidence, his incoherence, [the poet] must not; he is more type than man, more passion than type." As in many of his poems (I think, for example, of "Leda and the Swan" or "Among School Children") Yeats comes a long way in the brief compass of these sentences, all the way from the poet's "personal life" to the idea of the poet, "more type than man, more passion than type" and more archetype than either man or passion. The poet, for Yeats and for Eliot as well, is someone who exists only in his poetry and as his poetry. "He is part of his own phantasmagoria," Yeats says, "and we adore him because nature has grown intelligible." He is, as poet, capable of what Eliot terms "an expression of *significant* emotion, emotion which has its life in the poem and not in the history of the poet" (*SE* [1951], p. 22), and it is there, in the poem and in the *Collected Poems*, not in the history of the poet, that we must seek the Life of the Poet. Writing to John Gould Fletcher, Eliot said, "I think there is an important distinction between the emotions which are in the experience which is one's material and the emotion in the writing – the two seem to me very different" (*Letters* I, p. 410). The shift from the plural "emotions" of life to the singular "emotion in the writing" is altogether relevant, implying the transformation of multiple, disordered emotions into the ordered and significant emotion of the poem. I do not mean, nor would either Yeats or Eliot mean, that the personal element ever ceases to be important. On the contrary, it is the very impetus that brings the poetry about and it is there as nodes of intensity in the finished poem; but it must not remain merely personal or it will not have entered into the poem at all. The poet, Yeats says, write "out of" (in one example) lost love, and in the first instance it is no doubt – it *must* be – a personal, specific lost love, but this personal experience becomes in the poem a thematic element – the theme of lost love – that speaks not to the poet alone but to all of us. Taken in the beginning from the life of the poet, it becomes finally, in and through the poetry, a part of the Life of the Poet, and at that point it avails us little as readers to worry about the name of the lost love.

What, then, is the Life of the Poet as written by T. S. Eliot? I have already suggested that it is to be found in the entire volume of *Collected Poems* but within that volume there are a number of transitional poems that record major events in Eliot's life and at the same time mark significant stages in the Poet's Life. I will glance at only a very few such passages. These transitional moments are always double, and in a double sense: they are poems of setting out but they are also poems of summary of what has gone before, so that later poems regularly take up into themselves earlier poems; and they are poems of heightened self-consciousness as the poet, observing everything, forever observing, includes himself in the observation. The title of the first volume – *Prufrock and Other Observations* – is altogether significant; and I would suggest that were the title not so unwieldy a later volume could well be called *The Waste Land and Other Observations, Including Observation of Prufrock and Other Observations.* "So I assumed a double part," the speaker of *Little Gidding* tells us as he encounters the familiar compound ghost, but this is far from the first time the poet has assumed a double part. The first time is in the first line of the first poem in *Collected Poems*: "Let us go then, you and I . . ." And is this setting out not more than the beginning of a particular poem? Is it not also the setting out upon or the commencement of the Life of the Poet? Lest it be said that Eliot could not have been aware that he was setting out upon a Life of the Poet at this point in his career, I should respond in advance, first, that this gives far too little credit to Eliot's self-consciousness, his subtlety and his ambition, and, second, that poets of sufficient stature – the stature of Yeats or Eliot, let us say – have always shown themselves at every stage aware of the Life they were writing. And the curious fact that, as he wrote to his brother Henry in September 1916, "I often feel that 'J. A. P.' is a swan song" (*Letters* I, p. 151), merely points up more dramatically Eliot's own sense that "Prufrock" was both beginning and end, an entire poetic career wrapped up in a single poem. That he knew what he was doing and knew what he had done becomes obvious, I think, when Eliot repeats the invocation to urban night walking and observation in the familiar compound ghost scene of *Little Gidding*, thus in his final poem beginning all over again and in so doing recalling his original beginning in his first poem. Moreover, Eliot thought of *Little Gidding*, too, as his "swan song" (the valedictory note is strong throughout Eliot's career) – and this time he was right. And what do we have as subject matter, in the end as in the beginning, but Yeats's "remorse, lost love, or mere loneliness," elements that are at once both personal and thematic? The only thing that relieves the loneliness, which we must judge from the poetry was a lifelong experience for Eliot (at least until his second marriage, but that occurred well after the conclusion of the Life of the Poet), is the split into "you and I" or into speaker and compound ghost. Such a split, which permits the poet to render his observations and at the same time to record the story of himself observing, is everywhere characteristic of Eliot who, thus doubled, becomes (in Yeats's term) "part of his own phantasmagoria."

I am not aware that anyone has proposed a specific experience in Eliot's "personal life" (to adopt Yeats's term) or in "the history of the poet" (Eliot's own term) behind "La Figlia che Piange," but that there must have been some undefined personal experience that generated the poem we can be sure from its emotional pressure and the intensity of affect achieved in it. And we may judge the same thing from the number of times Eliot visits and revisits the theme of "Figlia" – a kind of compound of all three of Yeats's themes, "remorse, lost love, or mere loneliness" – earlier in "Prufrock" and "Portrait of a Lady" (where a man abandons a woman but is very uncertain whether he "should . . . have the right to smile"), later in "Gerontion," *The Waste Land* (where surely the Hyacinth Girl is none other than "la figlia che piange" – "Her hair over her arms and her arms full of flowers" in the earlier incarnation, "Your arms full, and your hair wet" in the later), "Marina" (where "Figlia" is reversed and the girl – now a daughter – is recovered), "Eyes that last I saw in tears," *Burnt Norton,* and even *Little Gidding* in the "gifts" that the familiar compound ghost discloses are "reserved for age . . . / As body and soul begin to fall asunder" (in "Figlia": "As the soul leaves the body torn and bruised"). That Eliot intended "La Figlia che Piange" to be present to the reader of *Little Gidding* is confirmed by the response he made to John Hayward who questioned why Eliot speci-fied "autumn weather" in an early version of the conclusion of the fami-liar compound ghost passage: "'Autumn weather' only because it *was* autumn weather – it is supposed to be an *early* air raid – and to throw back to Figlia che piange."[5] This puts something of a burden on the reader's memory to recall the phrase "autumn weather" from a poem of some thirty years earlier, but Eliot's remark is clear indication that he wished all his poems to be seen as interlocked emotional moments in a consciousness that changed and developed but that was also continuous from beginning to end.

What I take to be the two emotional cathexes of *The Waste Land,* both of which are undoubtedly personal in origin – the Hyacinth Girl passage and the line "By the waters of Leman I sat down and wept" – are also, while not surrendering the poignancy of personal experience, fully thematic, as well as recurrent, and thus something much more than merely or limitedly personal. It is as futile as it is pointless to seek a biographical reference for the Hyacinth Girl, for she exists now neither in the history of the poet nor in her own history but in the poem itself. An analogy for what happens in this instance might be found in cookery: When cooks make a meat stock, simmering bones, meat, aromatics, and vegetables together for six or seven hours, the various elements lose their distinctive flavors, giving them up to the single essence of the stock; as food, the meat and vegetables become uninteresting and non-nourishing, their savors being entirely absorbed in the concentrated, rich stock. Just so the Hyacinth Girl – hers is another realm of existence now from the particular and individual, from the historical and biographical. "What every poet starts from is his own emotions," Eliot declares in "Shakespeare and the Stoicism of Seneca," sounding more than a little like the Yeats of "A General Introduction for my Work," and he continues, after a comparison of the emotions from which Dante and Shakespeare started, still in a Yeatsian vein: "Shakespeare, too, was occupied with the struggle – *which alone constitutes life for a poet –* to transmute his personal and private agonies into something rich and strange, something universal and impersonal" (*SE* [1951], p. 137; italics added) – into, we might say, a stock of sapid density in which it is not possible to distinguish the separate emotions or the separate ingredients from which the poet like the cook starts.

It is somewhat different with "By the waters of Leman I sat down and wept" – but only somewhat. I observed earlier that the Life of the Poet is the entire subject matter for a poet like Eliot who so clearly envisioned being a poet as a career and a destiny and marked the stages of the poet's life with a series of retrospective–prospective poems that take up into themselves earlier poems and more or less consciously look ahead to later poems. In this line Eliot is still engaged in what "alone constitutes life for a poet" but he has made that poetic process the subject of the poem in progress (as, of course, he does also in the final sections of each of the *Four Quartets*). He is recording himself as poet and describing the point he has reached in his career more directly than in the Hyacinth Girl passage but both constitute self-conscious, self-reflexive moments in the poet's life. The "waters of Leman" line is on the one hand sharply personal, alluding to Eliot's nervous breakdown and his treatment in Lausanne on Lac Leman (as such it is not unlike Whitman's great line in "Song of Myself": "I am the man, I suffer'd, I was there"); and it is on the other hand, as Eliot would have it be, "something universal and impersonal" through its echo of the Psalm that laments the exile of the Hebrew people. And like the "O City city" passage later in "The Fire Sermon" it shows the poet in a certain relationship to his material, being both inside and outside the poem, mourning a spiritual collapse and dislocation both on the shores of Lac Leman and the banks of the Thames. When Ezra Pound wrote to Eliot of *The Waste Land* that "[t]he thing now runs from April . . . to shantih without [a] break" (*Letters* I, p. 497) he was expressing the feeling of most subsequent readers of the poem; but one must remark how far from "his own emotions" the poet has come, without ever leaving them behind, in the stretch from April to shantih. "April is the cruellest month" has the poet starting out again, as in "Prufrock," at the beginning of a poem subsuming a career, and "Shantih shantih shantih" surely does the same at the end: like "Prufrock" and *Little Gidding* this must have seemed to Eliot another "swan song." But *The Waste Land* is subsuming in another way as well, for surely Chaucer, with the General Prologue to the *Canterbury Tales*, is present in the first lines of the poem so that *The Waste Land* bears to Chaucer and to the English literary tradition that had its beginning in his poem, the same relationship that Eliot argues exists between an individual talent and tradition in his essay of 1919. What Eliot implies with the commencement of *The Waste Land* is that as Chaucer was the first great individual talent in the English tradition, so, as of 1922, the poet of this poem is the last, the most recent individual talent in that same line. The story recorded here is thus not Eliot's personal story or not that only, and it is not even limited to the story of Eliot-as-poet; it is the story of the poet back to Chaucer, back even to

Homer, Eliot suggests, summed up in this story of the poet "reborn as an idea, something intended, complete."

T. S. Eliot's life was lived in the first instance *for* the poetry and in the second instance *in* the poetry. Once more Yeats provides the gloss. Writing to Katharine Tynan in September 1888 – and I emphasize the date, for Yeats would have been only twenty-three years old and at the very beginning of his career, yet he could see his destiny spread out before him much as Adam sees the whole history of humankind played out at the end of *Paradise Lost* – Yeats says of *The Wanderings of Oisin and other Poems*, "I am not very hopeful about the book. Somewhat inarticulate have I been, I fear . . . Yet this I know, I am no idle poetaster. My life has been in my poems. To make them I have broken my life in a mortar . . . I have seen others enjoying, while I stood alone with myself – commenting, commenting . . ." Surely it was something of the same that Eliot meant, from the opposite end of the career, well after he had concluded his Life of the Poet with *Little Gidding*, when he told his second wife that "he felt he had paid too high a price to be a poet." It is not ours to count the cost, however. All we can say or need say as readers is that it was by breaking their lives in a mortar that Yeats became YEATS and Eliot became ELIOT. The real significance of that act is not only that in it the life of the poet is transformed into the Life of the Poet but also that through it the Life of the Poet enters into and becomes the Life of Poetry. And the Life of Poetry in turn enters into and confers significance upon the lives of readers. This is where we can find the real T. S. Eliot, and he has been there all the while.

NOTES

1 Humphry House and Graham Storey (eds.) *The Journals and Papers of Gerard Manley Hopkins* (London: Oxford University Press, 1959), p. 48.
2 Or when he does it is with obvious irony as in "Mr. Eliot's Sunday Morning Service" or in "How unpleasant to meet Mr. Eliot!" It is one thing to proclaim yourself "Walt Whitman, a kosmos, of Manhattan the son," or "the poet William Yeats," quite another to put "Mr." so "nicely" and "precisely" before the name.
3 Eliot cites this poem as the first in which Yeats achieved his mature voice: "But it is not fully evinced until the volume of 1914, in the violent and terrible epistle dedicatory of *Responsibilities*, with the great lines

> *Pardon that for a barren passion's sake,*
> *Although I have come close on forty-nine . . .*"

Eliot stops the quotation there but I believe that the final two lines of the poem –

> *I have no child, I have nothing but a book,*
> *Nothing but that to prove your blood and mine –*

had been firmly established in his mind for more than twenty years. Writing to

John Quinn in January 1919 about the importance of publishing a volume in America to show his parents that he was right in choosing the literary life in London against their opposition, Eliot says, "This book is all I have to show for my claim – it would go toward making my parents contented with conditions – and towards satisfying them that I have not made a mess of my life, as they are inclined to believe" (*Letters* I, p. 266). In either case a "book is all I have to show" to the ancestors "to prove your blood and mine."

4 "A General Introduction for My Work," *Essays and Introductions* (London: Macmillan, 1961), p. 509. As a footnote explains, this essay, dated 1937, was "written for a complete edition of Yeats's works which was never produced."

5 Quoted in Helen Gardner, *The Composition of "Four Quartets"* (London: Faber and Faber, 1978), p. 184.

2

ERIC SIGG

Eliot as a product of America

There are many Americas. Which were Eliot's? Born into a family whose ancestors came to Massachusetts in the seventeenth century and whose members had more recently settled in a distant region, T. S. Eliot combined a New England cultural memory with midwestern experience. Although his grandparents reached Missouri in the 1830s, the family carefully maintained its New England connection. Indeed, after the patriarch, Rev. William Greenleaf Eliot, died in 1887, the poet's family began to gravitate back to Massachusetts. In the 1890s Eliot's father purchased a house on Cape Ann where his family could retreat from sweltering St. Louis summers. Soon after her husband died, Eliot's mother moved to the Boston area, as would all but her youngest child. A century after his grandparents arrived, none of Eliot's immediate family remained in St. Louis.

Partly southern and partly midwestern, located in the center of a vast continent but poised on a great inland waterway, St. Louis marked Eliot's childhood imagination. During Missouri winters he yearned for the firs, red granite, and blue ocean of coastal New England. Yet as he summered there, limestone bluffs full of fossil shellfish near the "long dark river" drew his memory back to the Mississippi. Even opening his mouth to speak, drawling like a southerner during boyhood visits to Boston, reminded Eliot of his double origins. In fact, his father was born and bred in St. Louis, and his mother and both paternal grandparents were born or raised south of the Mason–Dixon line. Yet Eliot also knew that his family, for reasons that reach deep into American history and into their past, considered themselves socially superior to the southerners they met in St. Louis.[1]

Besides differing landscapes, Missouri and Massachusetts signified distinct cultures. In both places branches of the Eliot family had gained some influence, but it had not come to them by way of a great fortune. Although far from disadvantaged, T. S. Eliot's patrimony descended less from wealth – the family history is studded with sudden, disastrous financial reversals –

than from the prestige of religion, learning, and public service. Eliot transformed this moral inheritance by translating it into art.

Eliot often – and not always fairly – criticized his family's Unitarianism. It shades our understanding of Eliot's jaundiced view of Milton, for example, to learn that Rev. Eliot considered him a Unitarian.[2] Yet Eliot must have known how deeply Unitarianism affected him. Expressing the Unitarian scorn for evangelical enthusiasm, Rev. Eliot wrote that well-educated, practical people rejected "sudden, miraculous conversion, wrought by divine power, independently of the human will . . . by which the sinner of yesterday is the saint of to-day." Requiring steady, lifelong effort, true regeneration relied on human agency rather than trusting solely to divine intervention. "It is at once arrogant and dangerous to claim direct and extraordinary guidance. It is virtually to claim inspiration, and that which begins in humility ends in pride."[3]

T. S. Eliot applied this gradualism, its seriousness and deliberation, to literary art. "Tradition and the Individual Talent" argues that acquiring tradition demands the same conscious labor that Unitarians insisted upon for regeneration. Speaking of an artist's "continual self-sacrifice" to craft and history and of "a continual surrender of himself as he is at the moment to something which is more valuable," Eliot used his grandfather's values and vocabulary. Whether religious regeneration or poetic creation, "inspiration" raised the suspicion in both grandfather and grandson of something quick, cheap, and temporary.[4] If their similar means pursued differing ends, both honored what only hard work could earn. Thus did Eliot transfer the family temper of "great difficulties and responsibilities" from cultivating the soul to writing poems.

Their far-flung family connections – to American presidents, Harvard scholars, and literary figures such as Noah Webster, the Lowells, Henry Adams, Melville, Hawthorne, Louisa May Alcott, Whittier, and many others – could have entitled the Eliots to assume a somewhat proprietary relationship to American society, even aside from their religion. Rev. Eliot's recent biographer has called him "the progenitor of what became the single most important family in American Unitarian history."[5] During the nineteenth century, Unitarianism gave the American core culture many of its values: rationalism, ecumenism, social tolerance, progress, reform, and optimism. A list of those who affiliated with Unitarianism at some time during their lives helps measure the influence. It would include historians and intellectuals: Adams, Prescott, Motley, Parkman, Palfrey, Bancroft, Ticknor, and James Freeman Clarke; and authors Emerson, Holmes, Longfellow, Bryant, Melville, James Russell Lowell, Edward Everett Hale, Thomas Wentworth Higginson, and Horatio Alger. Even in the modernist generation, Unitarian

Percival (1571–1665) m. Rebecca Lowle (d. 1645)

John Lowell (1595–1647) m. Margaret

John Lowell (1629–1694) m. Naomi (Torrey) Sylvester

Ebenezer Lowell (1675–1711) m. Elizabeth Shailer

Rev. John Lowell (1704–1767) m. Sarah Champney (d. 1756)

John Lowell (1743–1802) m. Rebecca (Russell) Tyng (d. 1816)

Rev. Charles Lowell (1782–1861) m. Harriet B. Spence (d. 1850)

Rev. Robert T.S. Lowell (1816–1891) m. Maria Duane

JAMES RUSSELL LOWELL (1819–1891) *Poet, diplomat*

R.T.S. Lowell II (1860–1887) m. Kate B. Myers

R.T.S. Lowell III (1887–1950) m. Charlotte Winslow

ROBERT LOWELL (1917–1977) *Poet*

Stephen Greenleaf (1628–1690) m. Elizabeth Coffin (1634–1678)

Tristram Greenleaf (1667/68–c. 1741) m. Margaret Piper (b. 1668)

Nathaniel Greenleaf (1691–1775) m. Judith Coffin (1693–1769)

Sarah Greenleaf (1721–1807) m. Joseph Whittier (1716–1796)

John Whittier (1760–1807) m. Abigail Hussey (1779–1857)

JOHN GREENLEAF WHITTIER (1807–1892) *Poet, editor*

William Gerrish (1617–1687) m. Joanna Lowe (1609–1677)

Capt. Stephen Greenleaf (1652–1743) m. Elizabeth Gerrish (1654–1712)

Rev. Daniel Greenleaf (1679–1763) m. Elizabeth Gookin (1681–1762)

Mercy Greenleaf (1719–1793) m. John Scollay

Priscilla Scollay m. Thomas Melvill (1751–1832)

Allan Melville (1782–1832) m. Maria Gansevoort (1791–1872)

HERMAN MELVILLE (1819–1891) *Novelist, poet*

William Greenleaf (1724–1803) m. Mary Brown (1727–1807)

Elizabeth Greenleaf (1749–1841) m.

This skeletonized chart, omitting some spouses and dates, sets forth T.S. Eliot's links to a few of his literary relatives. Sources, further links to many other authors, and a discussion exploring family history and its influence on Eliot's work and life will appear in a forthcoming essay, "T.S. Eliot and the New England Literary Family" by Eric Sigg.

T. S. ELIOT'S LITERARY RELATIVES

Andrew Eliott (1627–1703),
from East Coker, Somerset,
arrived Beverly, Mass., c. 1670

Rev. William Smith
(1706–1783)
m. Elizabeth Quincy
(1722–1775)

—

drew Eliott
50–1688)
Mary Shattuck
55–1710)

William Eliott
(d. 1721/22)
m. Mary Browne

Judith Eliot
m. Thomas Cox
(b. 1685)

Mary Smith
(1741–1811)
m. Richard Cranch
(1726–1811)

ABIGAIL SMITH
(1744–1818)
m. JOHN ADAMS
(1735–1826)
Second US President

drew Eliott
83–1749)
Ruth Symonds
76–1760)

Judith Cox
m. Jonathan Phelps

Rachel Phelps
m. Daniel Hathorne

Hon. William Cranch
(1769–1855)
m. Anna Greenleaf
(1772–1843)

JOHN QUINCY
ADAMS
(1767–1848)
Sixth US President

. Andrew Eliot
18–1778)
Elizabeth Langdon
21–1795)

Nathaniel Hathorne
(1775–1808)
m. Elizabeth Manning

CHARLES FRANCIS
ADAMS
(1807–1886)
Legislator, diplomat

nuel
ot
48–1784)

NATHANIEL
HAWTHORNE
(1804–1864)
Novelist

HENRY ADAMS
(1838–1918)
Historian, author

liam Greenleaf Eliot
81–1858)
Margaret Greenleaf Dawes
89–1875)

Rev. William Greenleaf Eliot m. Abigail Adams Cranch
1811–1887)   (1817–1908)

Henry Ware Eliot, Sr. (1843–1919)
m. Charlotte Stearns (1843–1929)

THOMAS STEARNS ELIOT (1888–1965)
Poet, critic, editor, dramatist

backgrounds influenced William Carlos Williams, e. e. cummings, and Conrad Aiken.

As the latter list suggests, by preaching a concept of duty so high and serious it might seem to become almost crushing, Unitarianism could also foment iconoclasm and rebellion. Although Eliot at first sidestepped family morality in the name of art, he urged the claims of art with the same seriousness as his relatives advocated religious and social duty. Instead of philanthropy or reform, culture supplied the initial forum for his ambition. In a March 29, 1919, letter to his mother, Eliot candidly justified his life in London in terms of gaining power and influence. Interestingly, that he proposed to rely on literary and cultural, rather than religious, means to this end seems not to have posed a problem. Only later, once he had consolidated a nearly unprecedented literary authority, would Eliot's criticism widen into moral and social discourse and thus resume the primordial gravity of his heritage.

If Eliot dismantled Unitarian theology to his satisfaction, he left its ethic largely undisturbed. From the vast Vedantic literature, for instance, Eliot chose the fable of the thunder not because it was new and strange, but because it was familiar. Resembling the Sanskrit *datta*, or "give," the radical change produced by Unitarianism taught "self-denial" and "self-sacrifice," according to Rev. Eliot. "It requires us to live for others, not only by separate acts of kindness, but by going about to do good." Rev. Eliot had in mind something like *dayadhvam* or "sympathize" when he equated a grasp of the gospel with the power to see beneath "the incrustations of sin," there to recognize "the glorified divine humanity which constitutes every immortal soul." *Damyata* – "control" – means self-control, both in the Upanishads and in Unitarianism. The most perfect regeneration, declared Rev. Eliot, required "the lesson of self-control . . . so early learned that it becomes like the alphabet of life." *Datta, dayadhvam, damyata*, in other words, restate key parts of the Unitarian code – "give, sympathize, control" – that Eliot grew up with. The coincidence allowed him to end *The Waste Land* with an exotic phrasing of household values.[6]

Up to a point, Eliot in youth seemed prepared to follow the pattern his background set forth. The power of that background, merging family, regional, and cultural factors, took its most concrete form between 1906 and 1916, when Eliot was associated with Harvard University. There his relatives Charles William Eliot, Samuel Eliot Morison, and Charles Eliot Norton achieved prominence. The web of Eliot's relation to Harvard, however, also had a deeper, more durable significance. His later complaints notwithstanding, Eliot's time at Harvard furnished a sum of intellectual capital – Dante, Laforgue, Sanskrit, Bradley – that he drew on for the rest of his life. He also relied on its resources as he wrote his first mature poetry.

The college's social exclusivity had intensified at the turn of the century. Only the right preparatory school, fashionable lodgings, and the "hallmark" of acceptance by Boston society, Morison observed, could place a freshman "on the right side of the social chasm." Eliot entered from the Milton Academy, lived on the Mt. Auburn Street "Gold Coast," and contributed to *The Advocate*. He followed his interests, his choice of courses (languages, history, literature, and philosophy, but little science or mathematics) perhaps fueling his later critique of the elective system. Unlike many Harvard students of his day, however, he was not lazy. Recovering from the low grades of a first semester crisis, he accelerated his course, finished in three years, took a master's degree in his fourth, and won a fellowship year abroad. A lack of interest in popularity marked Eliot's most revealing departure from undergraduate mores. "Above all," Morison counseled, college men had to "eschew originality."[7] At just that point Eliot quietly ceased to conform. He had already started work toward achieving private, adult goals.

Indulging a taste for picturesque, declining districts, Eliot visited North Cambridge, Dorchester, and Roxbury, giving their names to a series of short poems, some of which survive as parts of "Preludes." As if testing for quality, he also sampled Boston society, paying customary calls on hostesses who welcomed undergraduates into their drawing rooms. Alerted by the moral intensity of his own home and his growing attraction to art, he detected there a disorder to which he himself was not entirely immune: a displacement of religion by the culture of gentility.

Eliot's earliest poems quietly register the American tendency to associate culture with what is foreign: Hamlet, Michelangelo, Chopin, a Dresden clock, "*cauchemar!*" Genteel taste prefers its art not only ornamentally dead – Eliot disdains it as "bric-à-brac" – but also imported from offshore. (Both preferences make it reasonable for a young American artist to leave a society doubly prejudiced against what he produces.) Another import, ethnic violence between Greeks and Poles, locates "Portrait of a Lady" in an American city. Coming at the problem another way, Boston's Anglophile climate exposes the hostess to a charge of historical forgetfulness. In a cunningly accusative detail, she serves the "tea" which in 1773 had occasioned an act of revolutionary theater. Colonial habits proving hard to break, these nuances imply that cultural independence, and social peace, lag far behind political sovereignty.

Eliot's own keen taste for English and European culture, moreover, may well have sharpened his youthful criticism of those who seemed to worship it. "Portrait of a Lady" satirizes her aesthetic culture as weak-mindedness, verging on blasphemy.

> "So intimate, this Chopin, that I think his soul
> Should be resurrected only among friends
> Some two or three, who will not touch the bloom
> That is rubbed and questioned in the concert room."

Eliot relishes how her loose talk – "soul" and "resurrected" – mixes up sacred language with aesthetic reverie. Besides echoing Paul's due process objection in Acts 24:21, her speech unknowingly quotes the famous scripture, Matthew 18:20: "For where two or three are gathered together in my name, there am I in the midst of them." With the touching, rubbing, and questioning of an Arnoldian touchstone, her swoon edges toward unseemliness as she compares Chopin's "intimate" little études with the presence of the Holy Spirit. But if the visitor senses her confusion, she also sees that he is false. (With fine authorial self-mockery, inside his brain he hears a "dull tom-tom:" more fascinating rhythms follow.) When her probings fluster his pose of composure, each has found a truth in the other's Achilles' heel.

Eliot summarized cultural gentility by saying that "the society of Boston was and is quite uncivilized but refined beyond the point of civilisation."[8] Although not all of them found it there, nearly every American poet and writer of his generation left for Europe in search of living art. Even as Eliot settled in London, however, his poetry drew life from another, different America, one at odds with both religious and genteel piety.

Coming of age during a flowering of American popular culture, Eliot put something of its dynamism into his poems. His early verse often echoed American music. The first draft of *The Waste Land* originally opened with a slangy vignette of a pack of young men helling around Boston, accompanied by four contemporary songs. One, the 1909 "The Cubanola Glide," is considered a prime example of ragtime, the new century's first hit musical style. All were cut, but a fifth song, another rag, survived.

Eliot might have preserved it to recall ragtime's Missouri origins. His family home lay only a short walk from the Chestnut Valley "sporting district," where inside the saloons and whorehouses along Chestnut and Market Streets St. Louis became the world's ragtime capital during the ten years before 1906. A St. Louis publisher issued the first rag written by a black composer, Tom Turpin's "Harlem Rag," in 1897. In 1900, John Stark, the major ragtime music publisher, moved from Sedalia to St. Louis, where Scott Joplin produced his ragtime opera, "A Guest of Honor," in 1903. Turpin, an impresario who owned the Rosebud Bar (at 2220 Market Street, six or seven blocks from the Eliot home at 2635 Locust), mounted a

National Ragtime Contest for the 1904 St. Louis World's Fair. The most popular music of its day, ragtime filled the St. Louis air. It is not impossible that the strains of a rag could have floated on a breeze to Locust Street where they might drift through upstairs windows open on some "soft October night."

> O O O O that Shakespeherian Rag –
> It's so elegant
> So intelligent

These lines, however, quote "That Shakespearian Rag," written by Buck, Ruby, and Stamper for the 1912 Ziegfeld Follies. Hence Eliot probably heard its lyric, "That Shakespearian rag, Most intelligent, very elegant," in a Boston vaudeville house.

Although no derivation for "ragtime" has gained acceptance, one stems from how songs were written in the era before sheet music publication. Employed at fairs, honky tonks, and houses of ill repute, pianists gathered in back rooms after hours and spliced together strands of melody and patches of harmony into jointly composed "rags."[9] Eliot's lines may call *The Waste Land* a kind of rag, a rhythmical weaving of literary and musical scraps from many hands into a single composition.

It could be argued that Eliot's quotation, following closely on an image from "The Tempest," condemns popular art for spoiling a classic by the slightest contact. Dismayed by its vigor and success, some contemporary critics issued this sort of dire warning about ragtime from behind the barricade of traditional culture. Eliot's ragtime fragment, however, functions more elegantly, and intelligently, than this sour reading. "O O O O" the line begins, the wind moaning under the door but also bringing a song of convivial life to penetrate the bleak marital flat. The introductory "But" contrasts ragtime's lively, frisky charm to the strained, baleful couple, starved for a bit of fun. The four Os also start ragtime's marching left-hand rhythm, whose regularity Eliot quickly alters by adding a playful syllable to "Shakespeherian." The epenthesis underscores ragtime's most pronounced feature, syncopation. Is it too much to suppose that American popular music, whether from ragtime or Tin Pan Alley, helped to cultivate Eliot's ear for rhythm? Though impossible to define, Eliot wrote, what is essential about a country "is most effectually expressed through rhythm."[10]

Beware of false reverence about art, the lines also seem to say, rebuking genteel misapprehension by joining two remote art forms, ragtime and Shakespeare. Eliot may also have had in mind his efforts to renew poetic drama. In 1923, noting modern drama's lack of rhythm, Eliot declared that each generation of playwrights had to find "a more plausible reason for beating a drum. Shakespeare and Racine – or rather the developments which led up to them – each found his own reason. The reasons may be divided into tragedy and comedy. We still have similar reasons, but we have lost the drum."[11]

Sweeney Agonistes tried to realize this idea. Eliot's most bizarre use of American popular culture precedes another vaudeville song in "Fragment of an Agon," where a stage direction calls for "Swarts as Tambo. Snow as Bones." Named for the tambourine and bones they played as they joked, danced, and sang during the opening act of a minstrel show, these two "endmen" in blackface flanked a semi-circle of seated musical performers. Their metaphysical rhythm section accompanies Eliot's parody of a 1902 rag, Johnson, Cole, and Johnson's "Under the Bamboo Tree." As it recognizes how black American and African cultures had come into vogue in London in the 1920s, Eliot's lyric also recalls the sounds of his youth. Somehow, somewhere, Eliot got rhythm:

> Tell me in what part of the wood
> Do you want to flirt with me?
> Under the breadfruit, banyan, palmleaf
> Or under the bamboo tree?

Strong and syncopated, these lines sway with the rhythms of black American speech, most likely learned from southern accents Eliot heard in St. Louis. To Henry, Stephen, and Charlie Jones, for instance, three generations of a black family who helped run the Eliot homes and the Mary Institute next door, Eliot no doubt listened as carefully as he did to the cadences spoken in Boston drawing rooms. "A man who devises new rhythms is a man who extends and refines our sensibility," Eliot wrote, "and that is not merely a matter of 'technique.'"[12]

"Fragment of an Agon" thus merges black American culture with two examples of the many Gothic effects appearing throughout Eliot's work. Tambo and Bones in *Sweeney Agonistes* – a pretty macabre piece, what with that gallon of lysol in the bath – links the skull, skeletons, and bones of Gothic convention with its mirthless, cruel, or hysterical laughter: "Hoo ha ha."

To distinguish for a moment between tactical and artistic goals, Eliot may have treated Mr. Bones to an encore in *Sweeney Agonistes* because everybody missed his debut in *The Waste Land*. Minstrel performers honored a superstition that the show would suffer unless they made up their mouths perfectly with moistened burnt cork. The makeup whitened the teeth, thickened the lips, and widened the mouth to evoke humor or, so construed, horror.[13] As the endman clicked his instrument – originally made of real bone – and cracked his jokes, Eliot heard less a comic turn than a Gothic omen:

> But at my back in a cold blast I hear
> The rattle of the bones, and chuckle spread from ear to ear.

Like the "Shakespeherian rag," the minstrel image follows the word "but," signaling a shift in mood. Instead of a sweet melody of good times, however, this laughter strikes Marvell's note of menace, a "cold blast" of warning, a shock. Again Eliot unites two traditions that superficially might seem quite remote.

As is well known, Eliot's verse incorporated American landscapes, particularly the New England coastline's fog, granite islands, birds, and pine woods. There he returned in memory to his summer sailing voyages, "between one June and another September," basing "Marina," for instance, on Casco Bay, Maine.[14] St. Louis figures less prominently until Eliot joins his two boyhood locales in *The Dry Salvages*. American history, to be sure, echoes elsewhere in Eliot's poems. "Old men ought to be explorers" remembers the colonial claiming, naming, and surveying of uncharted territory. The Spanish de Soto came first to the Mississippi Valley, followed by the French Marquette, Jolliet, and La Salle in the seventeenth century. In 1764, on high ground above the river, Pierre de Laclède founded St. Louis as a trading post for trappers: "Money in furs." The Americans soon followed, Lewis and Clark embarking up the Missouri from St. Louis in 1804, and Zebulon Pike leaving the city the next year to seek the headwaters of the Mississippi.

The last expeditions set out at the behest of President Jefferson, who wanted to know what bargain he had struck by acquiring the Louisiana Territory in 1803. Until that sale, the 1783 Treaty of Paris had declared the Mississippi River – "at first recognised as a frontier" – the new country's western boundary. Jefferson's purchase brought the whole Mississippi basin under one jurisdiction. Within a few years, as steamboats began to ply the river, it became "useful, untrustworthy, as a conveyor of commerce," the dangerous yet vital axis of trade between New Orleans and the upper midwest.

The "Mississippi system" transformed St. Louis into a great inland port, a supply and transshipment point for a vast zone extending from New Orleans to Pittsburgh and Montana. (Eliot's father began his career overseeing freight on the waterfront.) Celebrating the river's romance and demonic trickery, Twain's *Life on the Mississippi* also told how the Civil War and the railroads ended the steamboat era. When bridges crossed the Mississippi at Rock Island, Burlington, Quincy, and Dubuque, St. Louis found itself stranded without rail contact. Belatedly the city engaged James Buchanan

Eads to grapple with the river's fifteen-hundred-foot width; powerful scouring currents and winter ice jams; wide swings in volume between low water and flood stage; and a sixty-foot change in the depth of bedrock. Eads spanned the "problem confronting the builder of bridges" by three upright ribbed arches of cast steel, each stretching more than 500 feet between piers sunk over 100 feet through water and sand to rest on sloping bedrock. When it opened July 4, 1874, the bridge was the largest ever built. Thus it entered St. Louis lore, an engineering and aesthetic masterpiece.[15]

In 1930 Eliot wrote that "the big river" made "a deep impression on me; and it was a great treat to be taken down to the Eads Bridge in flood time."[16] Although a city dweller, Eliot had not forgotten the "brown god." About ten miles north of St. Louis, the Mississippi must receive the silt-laden Missouri. As Twain relates, Parkman called the Missouri "that savage river," which "descending from its mad career through a vast unknown of barbarism, poured its turbid floods into the bosom of its gentle sister."[17] Longer than the Mississippi itself, draining loose prairie soils from a vast contributary area extending into Canada, and prone to violent seasonal variations in its flow, the Missouri muddies the greater river's clearer water, changing its color from blue to brown.

The river in The Dry Salvages changes as it moves through time and space, a channel for commerce but also a stream of consciousness. Shifting from public to personal history, the first verse paragraph ends with images from Eliot's St. Louis childhood. A large Ailanthus altissima, the Chinese "tree of heaven," "rank" both for its rapid growth and for giving off a foetid odor, stood near his house in a yard where Eliot could play.[18] The aromatic "grapes on the autumn table" were an American cultivar, the Concord, known for its pungent, "foxy" fragrance and named for the Massachusetts village (with literary and Revolutionary War associations) where it was discovered.[19] Connoting the seasons as well as the cadence of music and poetry, the river's rhythm appeared in secure, domestic places – nursery, dooryard, and dining room or parlor.

Although "patient to some degree," its "rages" also transform the river into a "destroyer," bearing victims before it. Rhythms occur in time, yet

> Time the destroyer is time the preserver,
> Like the river with its cargo of dead negroes, cows and chicken coops

"Cargo" shares "r," "g," and "o" sounds with "Negro," and begins an alliterative series with "cows" and "coops." These dead join a crew of Eliot's drowned corpses: the last lines in "Prufrock" present the image first, but "worried bodies of drowned men" drift through "Mr. Apollinax," followed by Bleistein and Phlebas.

As if the image were not chilling enough, it also has a historical dimension, Gothicism transmuted into realism while remaining hellish, grotesque, unbelievable. Besides denying people the fruits of their labor, slavery sanctioned their sale at an owner's whim. Among the worst fates a slave could suffer was to be "sold down the river," shipped to a sugar-cane plantation on the lower Mississippi where work was hardest and conditions the most difficult.[20]

Because Eliot seldom commented specifically on his poetry, the self-interpretation in his remarkable essay on *Adventures of Huckleberry Finn* gives it the utmost significance. There he repeats this image, slightly generalized, from *The Dry Salvages*, as if to telegraph its importance. Emphasizing the river's treachery even when flowing normally, Eliot remembered that "at another season, it may obliterate the low Illinois shore to a horizon of water, while in its bed it runs with a speed such that no man or beast can survive in it. At such times, it carries down human bodies, cattle and houses."[21]

Family lore had passed down a story of the greatest flood, in 1844. Then Rev. Eliot had stepped from a second story window at the St. Louis levee onto the upper deck of a ferry boat, which sailed east for ten miles before it could discharge passengers on the first high ground in Illinois.[22] The great river flooded several times during Eliot's childhood, with high waters in 1892, again in 1897, and most notably in 1903. On June 3 in that year, the *St. Louis Post-Dispatch* reported fifteen houses "borne under the Eads bridge on the rising flood" during the morning. On the same day, the paper reported from Kansas City that although waters had begun to recede, "possibly ten bodies have been seen floating since Sunday," with eight persons known to have drowned.[23] Such reports and his repetition of the image in his Twain essay suggest that Eliot heard about, or may even have witnessed, the image or something like it. As he stated in his *Huckleberry Finn* essay, a writer understands an environment first by spending childhood in it, by "living in it at a period of life in which one experiences much more than one is aware of."

Not only was Eliot's boyhood divided between two quite different American places, but his background also acquainted him with American society's cultural and racial complexity. During the 1920s, for instance, he showed a "delighted and highly critical immersion in records of 'The Two Black Crows,' especially of a record involving 'All aboard for St. Louis.'" A companion in the 1940s reported how Eliot, in unguarded moments, sang "music hall songs of his youth, or Negro spirituals" such as "Swing Low, Sweet Chariot."[24] Disenchanted with high-minded New England culture, he may have used popular culture, especially its Afro-American forms, as antidotes to liberal Protestantism and lifeless gentility. That argument, however, goes only so far, because New England Unitarianism and black American history touch at a crucial point.

Among their other contributions to the American core culture, many Unitarians played leading roles in the anti-slavery movement. This motive must partly explain why, following his friend James Freeman Clarke (who had taken a Unitarian pulpit in Louisville the previous year), Rev. William G. Eliot left Boston for Missouri in 1834. He never joined the militant Boston party of Garrison, Higginson, or Samuel J. May. He had to defend his Unionism and "gradual emancipation" against the radicals' criticism. But nobody in St. Louis doubted where he stood. During the Civil War Rev. Eliot was known as "the city's only open abolitionist for many years."[25] There for three decades he had worked to end slavery.

Rev. Eliot's last book, *The Story of Archer Alexander From Slavery to Freedom*, was written "for the benefit of my grandchildren, that they may know something of what slavery was, and of the negro character under its influence." Its chapter, "Slavery in the Border States," describes slave sales and trades, deceitful denials of freedom, and outbreaks of whippings and mob violence. These grim episodes, Rev. Eliot points out, took place not on some benighted deep South plantation but in St. Louis. Each of Stowe's fictional atrocities, he added, had an actual parallel, known to or seen by him, in St. Louis before the Civil War.

The book tells how Alexander escaped and became the last slave prosecuted under Missouri's fugitive slave law, and how Rev. Eliot removed the legal cloud thus cast upon the twice-arrested Alexander's freedom. The book's occasional paternalism does not discredit Rev. Eliot's willingness to help Alexander personally and to wage patiently the greater struggle against slavery: proof that he lived by his values of giving, sympathizing, and self-control. Besides its vivid scenes and the author's use of irony to express his moral anger, what distinguishes the book remains the sense that of all Rev. Eliot's many accomplishments, this one meant the most. That factor may suggest why, when T. S. Eliot's mother closed up her St. Louis home in 1920, he asked her to send *Archer Alexander* to him.[26]

Charlotte Eliot's 1904 biography of Rev. Eliot devoted nearly half its length to her father-in-law's views on gradual emancipation, his efforts on behalf of the Union and abolitionist causes, and to his activities during Reconstruction. Henry Ware Eliot, Sr.'s unpublished 1910 memoir gives a third clue to how the family recalled the struggle. Revisiting the St. Louis he remembered just before the Civil War, the author describes each household, the breadwinner's profession, the church the family attended, and says something about their dwelling. More than once he bluntly notes that a family owned slaves. No moral tantrums are thrown. Requiring no condemnation from a memoirist writing for his own children, the fact of slave ownership speaks for itself, silently but plainly opening up a moral chasm between a slaveholding neighbor and the righteous Eliots.

Thus did the memory of the anti-slavery movement, long after it had ended, persist in the family consciousness. Growing up in this circumstance likely caused T. S. Eliot to pay attention to black people and to what they and their culture had to offer. However distant socially – and Eliot felt near enough to consider his boyhood accent a drawl like that of black people, a fascinating admission – some part of Afro-American experience was not remote, but shared.[27] His poems borrowed a measure of the humor, rhythm, and musical expression of Afro-American culture, while also acknowledging its peculiar burden of morality and history – distinct from, yet related to, Eliot's own.

Eliot's use of American materials reflects a feeling that his experience was significant, and should be written down. That feeling he shared with his father, mother, and grandfather. Some things you cannot forget. Condemning what he saw as a "vile traffic," Rev. Eliot had witnessed gangs of slaves led shackled through St. Louis streets in chains "on the way to the steamboat for the South."[28] Such incidents – and their phrasing as well – lie behind Eliot's Dantesque figure of corpses borne as cargo on the flood. They also give Eliot's words an inherited moral leverage he might formerly have wished to evade but which *Four Quartets* deliberately exerts.

> But the torment of others remains an experience
> Unqualified, unworn by subsequent attrition.
> People change, and smile: but the agony abides.

Although admitting that "anything may happen," in 1940 Eliot doubted whether "Civilisation" was destined to move west to the United States after the Second World War. "One thing that Civilisation has never done yet, is to pass from a parent to a colonial society." By 1953, however, Eliot no longer drew sharp distinctions between the parent and the colony or between the old world and the new. In St. Louis, speaking at the university his grandfather founded a century earlier, Eliot called attention to a new chapter in literary history. Regarding the United Kingdom and United States, he said, "I believe that we are now justified in speaking of what has never, I think, been found before, two literatures in the same language."[29] That this discovery might conceivably contain a measure of self-justification seems as true as that Eliot's peculiar life entitled him to propose it. His idea ratified what he had assumed as a young man and proved as a mature one: that American and British literature had not drifted so far apart that someone from one society could not enter the literary culture of the other.

American writers use a medium removed from its circumstances and tradition, a source of tension Eliot's life confronted more expressly than that of any other figure. If language and nationality diverge, changing citizenship may try to bring them into alignment. But citizenship is not quite the same thing as nationality; no mere change of legal status can instantly reshape the residue of acquired culture. Defining culture – what is it? how do we get it? what good is it? – raised another key issue, with many personal dimensions, which Eliot's life decisions forced him to explore. Perhaps he was surprised, upon securing his literary position, to find his American past seeping into his poetry. Sometimes he suppressed it: there evidently exists a manuscript of *Ash-Wednesday* titled, "Next Boat for Natchez, Cairo, and St. Louis." Yet in his last poems American images came flooding back, and *Four Quartets* reunites all the locales of his life, St. Louis, New England, London, England.

The Dry Salvages stakes Eliot's claim as an American writer. His *Huckleberry Finn* essay argued that the second way a writer understood an environment was "by having had to struggle for a livelihood in that environment – a livelihood bearing no direct relation to any intention of writing about it, of *using* it as literary material." Eliot's implied contrast emerges forcefully. Twain grew up by the great river and then fought to make a living on it, adult experience elaborating childhood ones within a single environment. After a boyhood divided between Missouri and Massachusetts, as an anonymous banker and well-known poet and an American in London, Eliot led a double and a quadruple life. Speaking of the "sources" of his poetry, Eliot acknowledged that "in its emotional springs, it comes from America."[30] His attribution by no means refers to American literature, several of whose major authors Eliot seems not to have read until adulthood, if then. His family, its past, and its moral atmosphere; people in the household; memories of the landscape; the dominant cultural forms, those of popular entertainment; the accents and rhythms of speech; and United States history: these "emotional springs" made Eliot and his poems products of America.

NOTES

1 See Eliot's 1928 letter in Sir Herbert Read, "T. S. E. – A Memoir," Allen Tate (ed.) *T. S. Eliot: The Man and His Work* (London: Chatto & Windus, 1967), p. 15, and Eliot's "Preface," Edgar Ansel Mowrer, *This American World* (London: Faber & Gwyer, 1928), pp. xii–xiv. On Eliot's family origins, see William A. Deiss, "William Greenleaf Eliot: The Formative Years (1811–1834)"

in Earl K. Holt III, *William Greenleaf Eliot: Conservative Radical* (St. Louis: First Unitarian Church of St. Louis, 1985), p. 3; and Henry Eliot Scott, *The Family of William Greenleaf Eliot, 1811–1887, and Abby Adams Eliot, 1817–1908* (San Francisco: n.p., 1988), 5th edn., pp. v, 1, 1–A, 5, and 25–33.

2 William G. Eliot, *Discourses on the Doctrines of Christianity* (Boston: American Unitarian Association, 1881), p. 97.

3 William G. Eliot, *Early Religious Education Considered as the Divinely Appointed Way to the Regenerate Life* (Boston: Crosby, Nichols, & Co., 1855), pp. 6–9.

4 On inspiration, see Eliot's "A Note on Ezra Pound," *To-Day* 4 (September 1918): 4, and "The Mysticism of Blake," *Nation & Athenaeum* 41 (September 17, 1927): 779.

5 Holt, *William Greenleaf Eliot*, p. 92.

6 Give: W. Eliot, *Early Religious Education*, p. 13; sympathize: "Christ and Liberty," a sermon quoted in Charlotte C. Eliot, *William Greenleaf Eliot: Minister, Educator, Philanthropist* (Boston: Houghton, Mifflin, 1904), p. 338; control: W. Eliot, *Earl Religious Education*, pp. 15–16.

7 Samuel Eliot Morison, *Three Centuries of Harvard: 1636–1939* (Cambridge MA: Harvard University Press, 1946), p. 422.

8 "Henry James:: The Hawthorne Aspect," *Little Review* 5 (August 1918): 49; on Eliot and American gentility, see Eric Sigg, *The American T. S. Eliot: A Study of the Early Writings* (New York: Cambridge University Press, 1989), ch. 4.

9 Rudi Blesh and Harriet Janis, *They All Played Ragtime* (New York: Oak Publications, 1971), p. 17. On ragtime, see Terry Waldo, *This Is Ragtime* (New York: Hawthorn Books, 1976), and Edward Berlin, *Ragtime: A Musical and Cultural History* (Los Angeles: University of California Press, 1980).

10 "A Commentary," *Criterion* 14 (July 1935): 611.

11 "The Beating of a Drum," *Nation & Athenaeum* 34 (October 6, 1923): 12.

12 "Isolated Superiority," *Dial* 84 (January 1928): 5. On the Jones family, see Eliot's "Address," *From Mary to You: Centennial, 1859–1959* (St. Louis: Mary Institute, 1959), p. 134, and *Letters* I, p. 199.

13 Carl Wittke, *Tambo and Bones: A History of the American Minstrel Stage* (Westport, CT: Greenwood Press, 1968), pp. 140–41, and p. 233, on Charles Backus, whose made-up mouth stretched "from ear to ear"; see generally, Robert Toll, *Blacking Up: The Minstrel Show in Nineteenth-Century America* (New York: Oxford University Press, 1974).

14 Lyndall Gordon, *Eliot's New Life* (New York: Farrar Straus Giroux, 1988), p. 13.

15 Howard Miller, *The Eads Bridge* (Columbia: University of Missouri Press, 1979), pp. 79–87 and 107; C. M. Woodward, *A History of the St. Louis Bridge* (St Louis: G. I. Jones Co., 1881.)

16 M. W. Childs quotes Eliot, "From a Distinguished Former St. Louisan," *St. Louis Post-Dispatch*, October 15, 1930, p. 3B.

17 Mark Twain, *Life on the Mississippi* (New York: Penguin, 1984), p. 47.

18 Eliot, "Address," *From Mary to You*, p. 134. The tree trunk, Eliot, and a playmate appear in *Letters* I, plate 8B, with *Ailanthus* foliage visible in the background.

19 In *Letters* I, p. 199, Eliot identifies the Concord grape. It ripens with a "foxy" aroma attributable to methyl anthranilate, whose concentration, consistent with Eliot's memory, peaks in late October. (A. J. Winkler *et al.*, *General Viticulture* (Berkeley: University of California Press, 1974), pp. 20, 167, 171–72.) Ephraim Bull, who introduced the Concord grape in 1853, lived near Hawthorne and Emerson, whose *Journals* extravagantly ranked Bull with Columbus, Newton, and Shakespeare.

20 Mitford M. Mathews (ed.) *A Dictionary of Americanisms on Historical Principles* (Chicago: University of Chicago Press, 1951), vol. II, p. 1403.

21 "Introduction," *Adventures of Huckleberry Finn* (London: Cresset Press, 1950), pp. xii–xiii.

22 H. W. Eliot, Sr., "Brief Autobiography" (William Greenleaf Eliot Papers, Washington University Libraries, n.d.), p. 3.

23 See also *St. Louis Post-Dispatch*, March 19, 1897, front page headline, "Fifty Negroes Drowned," and accompanying story on flooding down river from St. Louis, below Cairo.

24 I. A. Richards, "On TSE," Tate (ed.), *T. S. Eliot*, p. 6; Gordon, *Eliot's New Life*, pp. 198, 214.

25 James Neal Primm, *Lion of the Valley: St. Louis, Missouri* (Boulder, CO: Pruett Publishing Co., 1981), p. 265; see also Douglas C. Stange, *Patterns of Antislavery Among American Unitarians, 1831–1860* (Cranbury, NJ: Associated University Presses, 1977), pp. 223–25.

26 *Letters* I, p. 399.

27 Eliot's "drawl" in Read, "T. S. E. – A Memoir," Tate (ed.) *T. S. Eliot*, p. 15.

28 C. Eliot, *William Greenleaf Eliot*, p. 131. William G. Eliot, *The Story of Archer Alexander From Slavery to Freedom* (Westport, CT: Negro University Press, 1970), p. 100.

29 "On Going West," *New English Weekly* 16 (February 15, 1940): 251. "American Literature and the American Language," *To Criticize the Critic* (London: Faber, 1978), p. 51.

30 Interview with T. S. Eliot, George Plimpton (ed.) *Writers at Work* (New York: Penguin, 1977), 2nd series, p. 110.

3

RICHARD SHUSTERMAN

Eliot as philosopher

I

T. S. Eliot began his career by training as a professional philosopher rather than as poet or critic. He ambitiously pursued this academic study at such major philosophical centers as Harvard, the Sorbonne, Marburg, and Oxford, between 1908 and 1915; completed a Harvard doctoral thesis on the philosophy of F. H. Bradley in 1916; and even published between 1916 and 1918 a number of professional articles and reviews of philosophy. Most studies of Eliot recognize that his early absorption in philosophy was very important for his development as poet and critic, though opinions sometimes differ as to which ways and through which thinkers the philosophical influence was most powerfully and beneficially expressed. Bergson's notions of *durée*, memory, and intuition have been recognized in the flow of consciousness of Eliot's early poems; and Royce, Bradley, and Russell have been cogently invoked to explain such Eliotic notions as tradition, poetic impersonality, the objective correlative, analytic precision, and critical objectivity.

Typically, however, these studies of Eliot as philosopher confine themselves to Eliot as "young philosopher," the aspiring, well-trained novice who soon abandoned philosophy to pursue a literary career. Philosophy in these studies remains a past, residual influence of youth rather than a continuously active interest and vital concern of Eliot's entire career. This essay will instead insist on showing how Eliot pursued philosophical questions throughout his career, though he ceased to do so through professional philosophical channels. Instead, Eliot insightfully attacked these questions in his criticism, social theory, and poetry. In doing so, he helped by both argument and example to highlight and challenge the narrowness of professional, academic philosophy, so that philosophy could become closer to what is today in the academy often called "theory," a genre where non-professional philosophers like Walter Benjamin can be studied for their philosophical import and where Eliot himself deserves a better place.

Through continued pursuit of philosophy, Eliot himself underwent a significant philosophical development which reflects the major developmental current in twentieth-century Anglo-American philosophy. This movement begins with the early scientific realism and positivistic objectivism that was inspired by the revolt against the Hegelian idealist tradition represented by Bradley, but then turns to a growing awareness of the hermeneutic, historicist, and pragmatic character of human understanding. In showing this development, my essay will also differ from most accounts of Eliot's philosophy by devoting less time to tracing the past influences of Eliot's student days and more to examining the relations between Eliot's thought and more recent philosophy, not only that of Eliot's contemporaries but of our own. But we cannot understand Eliot's development without noting his philosophical beginnings and the early influence of Bradley.

II

After completing his undergraduate work at Harvard where he majored in philosophy and literature, Eliot spent the year of 1910–11 in Paris studying the work of Bergson. He returned to Harvard for his doctoral studies (1911–14) where he was employed as a teaching assistant in the philosophy department and served for a time as President of the University's Philosophical Society. His courses at Harvard covered a wide range of philosophical topics from symbolic logic to Indian metaphysics (in which for some time he took an intense interest). Ultimately he settled on the philosophy of F. H. Bradley as the topic of his doctoral research, which was supervised by the renowned Harvard idealist Josiah Royce, whose work Eliot also closely studied. Though Royce was an idealist like Bradley and had a distinctively Christian and traditionalist dimension to his thought, he had also acquired a strong pragmatist orientation by the time Eliot encountered him. Acknowledging his specific debt to Peirce, Royce called his new philosophy "absolute pragmatism"; and Royce's pragmatism (together with the powerful Harvard presence of William James) may well have nourished the pragmatist dimension of Eliot's thesis and the pervasive pragmatist tendency of his thought, which will be subsequently examined.

Having completed his course requirements and with the aid of a travel scholarship, Eliot pursued his philosophical research, first briefly at Marburg (July 1914) and then for three terms at Merton College, Oxford (1914–15), where he studied Aristotle with Bradley's closest disciple, H. Joachim. Eliot's thesis on Bradley, originally titled "Experience and the Objects of Knowledge in the Philosophy of F. H. Bradley" was completed and sent to Harvard by April 1916, most of it having been written during

Eliot's stay at Oxford. The thesis was enthusiastically received by the Harvard faculty, Royce describing it as "the work of an expert"; and only Eliot's failure to return for his oral defense (wartime conditions made it difficult and risky to cross the Atlantic) prevented him from being awarded his doctorate in philosophy. None the less, between 1916 and 1918 he continued to do academic philosophy, publishing two articles (on Leibniz and Bradley) in *The Monist* and numerous reviews of philosophical books in the *International Journal of Ethics* and the *New Statesman*. At the same time Eliot began to publish essays in literary criticism, the best of which were gathered into his first book, *The Sacred Wood* (1920), which established him as an important critic before he had achieved equal fame as a poet.

Since Eliot's critical career so closely follows his intense study of Bradley and since he himself recognized an influence of Bradley in his own prose style and poetry, many have insisted that Bradley's philosophy is the key to understanding Eliot's practice and theory of criticism. While Eliot himself confessed that he did not even understand it when it was later published in 1964 (*KE*, p. 10), Ann Bolgan (who rescued the thesis from the oblivion to which Eliot had consigned it) and Lewis Freed both affirm that the philosophy of Eliot's criticism both early and late is thoroughly Bradleyan in character.[1] Certainly, interesting connections can be drawn between Bradley and Eliot's criticism, apart from their shared style of urbane skeptical critique. Perhaps the most important is Bradley's Hegelian holism, an organicism where the meaning of any thing is never autonomously given but always a function of its place and interrelations with other things in a wider whole. This is surely congenial to Eliot's theory of tradition, where the meaning of a poet or a work of art depends on its relations with all the other elements in the tradition. The theory of tradition is also supported by the pragmatic idealism of Eliot's Bradleyan thesis which argues that the existence of our common world relies on our sharing a stable consensus about what we mean and think, a stability which tradition both provides and depends on. Our world is only "one world because there is only one world intended" (*KE*, p. 144), and this cooperative consensus is motivated by our shared pragmatic aim of coping with experience. The existence of any common object "depends upon our recognition of [its] community of meaning ... and this community of meaning is ultimately practical" (*KE*, p. 161). Thus, in Eliot's thesis, the enduring consensus of tradition is essential not merely for literature but for all thought and indeed reality.

But Eliot's early criticism also differs radically from the Bradleyan philosophy of his thesis. Bradley's whole philosophy was essentially motivated by a radical repudiation of empiricist thought. This involved both denying the existence of a plurality of facts and rejecting the method of analysis.[2]

Facts were condemned as mere abstractions, while analysis was decried as a mutilating alteration of reality, which is essentially one indivisible whole. Such an attitude is alien to Eliot's early criticism with its insistent advocacy of precisely these two notions – facts and analysis – and with its empiricist outlook, where "all knowledge is . . . in perception," and critical intelligence is "the analysis of sensation to the point of principle and definition" (SW[1928], pp. 10, 11). Throughout *The Sacred Wood* and other criticism of that period Eliot insists that "the critical attitude is to attempt to analyze" and that the critic needs "a sense of fact" since his presentation of "facts . . . is a service of value" (SW [1928], pp. 60, 5, 37, 14, 96, 124).

With its Bradleyan rejection of fact, Eliot's thesis affirms that all truth is "only an interpretation," and hence there is necessary value in the "sort of interpretation . . . [done by] the historian, the literary critic, and the metaphysician" (KE, pp. 164–65). But Eliot's early criticism contradicts this by boldly claiming that "the work of art cannot be interpreted; there is nothing to interpret"; and that the critic's "chief task" "is the presentation of relevant historical facts which the reader is not assumed to know" (SW [1928], p. 96). Now "'interpretation' . . . is only legitimate when it is not interpretation at all, but merely putting the reader in possession of facts." The critic should not only be "dealing with his facts" but should try to have the nebulous feelings and meanings of poetry "clarified and reduced to a state of fact" (SE [1951], pp. 31–32).

With this striking reversal of the valencies of fact and interpretation, there is a similar reversal of the valencies of the private, the subjective, and the internal versus the public, objective, and external. While Eliot's thesis awkwardly combines the rejection of any substantial "distinction between inner and outer," subjective and objective (KE, pp. 20–21, 31, 138–39), together with a firm assertion that "all significant truths are private truths," which "as they become public . . . cease to become truth" (KE, p. 165), his early criticism contrastingly insists on strongly distinguishing objectivity, shared public truth, and "Outside Authority," from the private subjectivity of "the Inner Voice," elevating the former and violently repudiating the latter (SE [1951], pp. 26–33).

What caused this radical change from Eliot's doctoral philosophy to that which informs his early criticism? While one cause may simply be the change from academic epistemology to practical criticism, a more powerful explanation is the influence of Bertrand Russell and his philosophy of logical, analytic empiricism, particularly as expounded between 1914 and 1924, when it came to dominate English philosophy under the label of "logical atomism." But before moving on to analytic philosophy, we should mention one feature of Eliot's Bradleyan philosophy which is helpful for understanding his early poetry, even that written before his Bradleyan thesis.

The thesis contains an entire chapter on the problem of solipsism, a problem raised by the fact that in any human experience of the world, the world is always experienced from an individual perspective or (in Bradley's term) "finite centre." An individual's mental life consists in a changing series of such finite centres, and there is no guarantee that his centres will harmonize with others or even with themselves. There is thus no guarantee that one's experience or self will be understood by others (or even by one's subsequent self). Communication of the inner life is always a courageous act of faith across a gulf of privacy and difference; and "the life of a soul does not consist in the contemplation of one consistent world but in the painful task of unifying (to a greater or less extent) jarring and incompatible ones, and passing, when possible, from two or more discordant viewpoints to a higher which shall somehow include and transmute them" (*KE*, pp. 147–48). We see here the terrifying problem of personal communication already poetically expressed in early works like "Prufrock" and "Portrait of a Lady," and "the painful task of unifying . . , jarring and incompatible perspectives" clearly points forward to the fragmentation and synthesizing efforts of *The Waste Land*.

III

Russell's philosophy was not an immediate influence on Eliot. Impressed by Russell's personality and reputation, he attended Russell's course on Symbolic Logic given at Harvard in 1914. But he neither warmed to nor distinguished himself in this subject and doubted whether it had "anything to do with reality."[3] This attitude quickly changed once Eliot arrived in England, where Russell was clearly recognized as leading the new wave of philosophy; and already after his first term in Oxford, Eliot was deeply absorbed in Russell's classic *Principia Mathematica*. In the next few years Eliot was closely exposed to Russell's subsequent views, and not only from reading. For in 1915, shortly after his marriage and the consequent break with his family in America, Eliot and Russell's friendship was renewed with tremendous intensity, when Eliot and his bride moved into Russell's London flat, and for quite a long time Russell played an important (and equivocal) role in the couple's unhappy marriage.

Russell's analytic philosophy, through its aims, methods, and spirit, served Eliot's early criticism as a paradigm of rigorous critical thinking. In essays dating from 1917 to 1920, he frequently praises Russell's philosophy as "clear and beautifully formed thought" and "a victory . . . of science" which liberated English philosophy from German influence. He even presents Russell's philosophy (and style) as superior to Bradley's; it is not a skeptical "perfection of destruction" but the constructive work "of a man of science . . . who has invented a new method."[4] Of course, Eliot never accepted Russell's liberal atheist ethics and *Weltanschauung*. What guided his early criticism was Russell's technical philosophy – its logical method, its strategies of linguistic analysis, its scientific empiricism and emphasis on facts.

Russell held that philosophy is essentially and primarily "logical analysis," even if some "logical synthesis" may be achieved on the basis of analytical work.[5] Eliot's early criticism emulates this stress on analysis as the critic's most basic and important activity (*SE* [1951], p. 32; *SW* [1928], pp. 5, 21, 31, 36): in short, "the critical attitude is to attempt to analyse" (*SW* [1928], p. 60). Russell employed two different types of analysis. Reductive analysis aimed at getting to the metaphysically basic by reducing certain alleged entities to non-existence, for example, by showing them to be merely logical constructions or logical fictions (as in analysing material objects into sense-data or analysing "the average man" into a quotient of real men). But there was also analysis which aimed simply at elucidating concepts and propositions into a more precise and less misleading form (as in Russell's theory of descriptions). Eliot used both these forms of analysis. His critique that *"vers libre* does not exist" is based on an incisive reductive analysis which shows it to be an empty "battle cry" or logical fiction (*TCC*, 183–86). His account of rhetoric in "Rhetoric and Poetic Drama" provides a fine example of clarificational analysis, taking a confused concept and showing, through analysis of its application to certain works, how "a precise meaning can be found for it" (*SW* [1928], p. 79).

Russell's emphasis on analysis is based on the idea that our philosophical confusions are often generated by linguistic errors, often due to vagueness and speculative abstraction. Eliot similarly condemns "the abstract style in criticism" as a "verbal disease" which breeds confusion, and he significantly chides Hegel and his followers (always a prime target of analytic philosophy) for having "taken for granted that words have definite meanings" and corrupted them into "indefinite emotions" (*SW* [1928], pp. 2, 8, 9). Eliot moreover adopts several aspects of Russell's philosophy of language, for example, its ideal of precision and the direct, sturdy link between word and object in proper and healthy language. Throughout *The Sacred Wood* Eliot emphasizes the superiority of the precise, clear, and definite, while deploring the vague, general, and indefinite, not only in literary criticism but in literature itself (*SW* 1928: pp. 9, 43, 67, 78, 126). This early criticism does not employ an organicist account of meaning (where a word gets its meaning from its relation to other words), but rests on a Russellian referential theory of language where words get their meaning from the objects they refer to and where the primary objects were sensations or "sense-data." Thus, Swinburne's verse is criticized because "the meaning is merely the hallucination of meaning," since "the object has ceased to exist"; while Donne's is praised because "sensation became word and word was sensation" (*SW* [1928], pp. 129, 149).

Concern with the objects of sense involves another feature of Russell's philosophy which informed Eliot's early criticism – a rigorous empiricism which insists that sense perception is the foundational source for language and knowledge, that science is superior to philosophical reasoning for getting at the truth, and that empirical facts should be preferred to speculation and interpretation. In *The Sacred Wood* poets were praised or condemned according to their powers of digesting and expressing sensation; since "not only all knowledge, but all feeling, is in perception" (*SW* [1928], pp. 10, 129, 131) and "all thought and language is based ultimately upon a few simple physical movements."[6] Russell argued that since "science has a much greater likelihood of being true . . . than any philosophy," it is "wise to build our philosophy on science" (*RLA*, p. 160), and Eliot's early criticism shows a similar distrust of most philosophy and an admiring faith in science. In "The Perfect Critic" he uses "philosophic" as a pejorative term for the vague, abstract verbalism of speculative philosophy, "to cover the unscientific ingredients of philosophy," and he contrastingly praises "the scientific" and the scientific philosopher. Aristotle is portrayed as the perfect critic because he has "the scientific mind – a mind which . . . might better be called the intelligent mind. For there is no other intelligence than this" (*SW* [1928], pp. 8, 13).

Science's superiority to philosophical speculation rests, for both Russell and Eliot, on empiricism's privileging of hard facts over interpretation. As the philosopher must build on the facts of empirical science (*RLA*, pp. 141, 160–61), so "a critic must have a very highly developed sense of fact," since the goal is to reduce the vague "narcotic fancies" about literature to the "sphere of fact, of knowledge, of control" (*SE* [1951], pp. 31–32). Therefore, "any book, any essay, any note . . . which produces a fact even of the lowest order about any work of art is a better piece of work than nine-tenths of the most pretentious critical journalism, in journals or in books" (*SE* [1951], p. 33). Not only must the critic collect facts, he must shun interpretation, which "is only legitimate when it is not interpretation at all, but merely putting the reader in possession of facts which he would otherwise have missed," for example, "a selection of the simpler kind of facts about a work – its conditions, its setting, its genesis." Like Russell, Eliot admits that facts may be dull and boring; "but *fact* cannot corrupt," while interpretations are "the real corrupters" supplying "opinion or fancy" rather than truth (*SE* [1951], pp. 32–33).

Russell's philosophical influence on Eliot was relatively short-lived, and by 1927 we find criticism of Russell's "scientific" philosophy for being "crude and raw and provincial" and for lack of "wisdom" (*SE* [1951], pp. 449, 454). But its scientific realism was crucial for Eliot's early objectivist critical theory, which remained his most influential, even after he had moved on to more subtle philosophical perspectives. Let us see how Eliot's struggle with the problems of objectivity eventually led him from scientific realism to a hermeneutic historicism which recognizes the inevitable role and value of the subjective.

IV

Eliot's early insistence on objectivity pertained to both poetry and criticism. Along with his famous theories of "the objective correlative" and "the Impersonal theory of poetry," he asserts that "critics are impersonal people . . . and avoid intimacies with authors."[7] In "The Perfect Critic," a critique of Coleridge's tendency "to take leave of the data of criticism" highlights the claim that good criticism is "the disinterested exercise of intelligence" which "looks solely and steadfastly at the object." Achieving the critical ideal of seeing "the object as it really is" requires "a pure contemplation from which all the accidents of personal emotion are removed" (*SW* [1928], pp. 11–15). This ideal of impersonal objectivity is pursued in "The Function of Criticism" (1923) where the critic is urged to "discipline his personal prejudices" and ignore "the inner voice," but rather confine himself to objective facts and common principles that are "outside the individual," so as to advance "the common pursuit of true judgement" – an objective "something outside ourselves, which may provisionally be called truth" (*SE* [1951], pp. 25–34).

But what is objectivity and how can it be achieved? There are two competing models of this notion: accurate correspondence to an independent external object versus consensus of judgment among a community of competent practitioners. Agreement does not guarantee objectivity in the first sense, just as accuracy does not entail consensus. The first notion aims to transcend all limited personal perspectives to reach a perfectly faithful God's-eye view of the object as it really is. Denying this possibility, the second sees objectivity or impersonality as conformity to perspectives that are widely shared, hence more than personal. Eliot's early struggle to maintain objectivism vacillates between these two notions in an attempt to forge a view of objectivity that would meet his needs as poet and critic and could stand up to philosophical scrutiny and skeptical questioning.

In "Tradition and the Individual Talent," which centers on the impersonal theory of poetry, Eliot begins by basing objectivity on a living tradition and the consensus it provides. But this had obvious weaknesses. First, such objectivism could degenerate into dogmatic conformist conservatism. On the other hand, since the consensus of tradition was never clearly articulated in shared principles, it seemed too vague and fragile a base for objectivity. Indeed, Eliot thought that tradition was already much debilitated, confused, and in need of shoring-up. Something powerful would have to be found outside the weakening circle of traditional consensuality to compel new consent and thus revitalize tradition. Here Eliot turned to scientific realism's model of objectivity as mirroring correspondence to independent objects. Thus we find his advocacy (in self-consciously scientific language) of the "depersonalization" of the poet into a "finely perfected medium" of "inert, neutral" perception which "has not a 'personality' to express"; even though this problematizes the poet's creativity (SE [1951], pp.17–21). And the same correspondence model also clearly inspires his critical ideal of a perfectly objective God's eye view purified of distorting personal limitations, "that stage of vision *amor intellectualis Dei*" where we "see the object as it really is" (SW [1928], pp. 14–15).

This notion of objectivity, however, is riddled with epistemological problems concerning the accessibility of its standard. How can we possibly separate the object as it really is from the ways we see it? Moreover, the way the "pure" object is typically pursued – by concentrating on mere sense-data or images and stripping experience of its conventional and personal interpretation – paradoxically ends by thrusting us back on our own impressions and inner world. For our interpreted sense-data, though undeniable, are also undeniably our own and not necessarily anyone else's. Finally, as Eliot notes after Russell, they are undeniable partly because, as immediate experience, they are neither true nor false (SW [1928], p. 5).[8]

Eliot thus returns in "The Function of Criticism" to a consensus model based on tradition and locating objectivity not in an impersonal object but in views and practices shared by subjects: "common inheritance," "common cause," and "common principles" for "cooperative activity" and "the common pursuit of true judgement." Such commonalities of tradition go beyond the private consciousness of any given person or narrow group and thus provide a notion of something objectively outside us, something which can compel more confidence than the "the Inner Voice" which Eliot virulently ridicules. But the problem again is how tradition's consensus can be recognized and preserved. Codifying it in explicit principles runs the risk of ossifying a living tradition into a dogmatic, conservative, conventionalism. But without such formulated criteria, how can we distinguish between objective verdicts issuing from our sense of traditional consensus and mistaken verdicts based on the abominated "inner voice" masquerading as tradition? In any case, the hotly contested nature of poetry and criticism and the decay of tradition in our "formless age" would not seem to allow for formulating a clear set of universally shared principles. Finally, if current consensus is not adequate for critical objectivity, is the goal of consensual objectivity worth the price of repressive coercion toward conformity?

Eliot could not find a satisfactory solution to these problems and eventually abandoned his early objectivism. In *The Use of Poetry and the Use of Criticism* (1933) it is rejected as impossible, since the appreciation of literature "cannot be isolated from one's other interests and passions . . . and must be limited as one's self is limited" (*UPUC* [London], p. 36). But more importantly, impersonal objectivity depletes our experience of poetry and the value it gives us, since these require that we engage the poem with our personality. Thus "a deliberate effort to put out of mind all [your] convictions and passionate beliefs about life" means "cheating yourself out of a great deal that poetry has to give to your development" (*UPUC* [London], pp. 97–98). Indeed, if you "adopt no attitude towards what the poet has to say, you will tend to evacuate it of all significance" (*UPUC* [London], p. 64). This commitment to the personal is reaffirmed in one of Eliot's last important critical essays, "The Frontiers of Criticism" (1958), where he asserts that the meaning of poetry is equivalent neither to authorial intention nor to some impersonal textual meaning, but is always to *some* degree a personal matter, potentially differing from reader to reader; that a poem's meaning "is what the poem means to different sensitive readers" and "a valid interpretation . . . must be at the same time an interpretation of my own feelings when I read it" (*PP* [London], pp. 113–14).

Eliot's turn from his early scientific objectivism to a recognition of the inevitability and value of personal, situated, understanding represents an evolution from foundationalist realism to hermeneutic historicism and pluralism, an evolution salient in contemporary philosophy. If objectivity in human inquiry cannot be conceived as the absolute God's-eye view of things, then its traditional claim to exclusive rightness dissolves, and a plurality of viewpoints becomes, at least in principle, acceptable. If consensual objectivity's value is in providing the unity and conformity necessary for effective cooperative action, surely this does not mean that difference cannot also be valuable, that total consensus in every aspect of life is the highest ideal. Eliot thus came to insist on a cultural ideal of "variety in unity" where "the variety is as essential as the unity" (*NTDC* [London],

p. 120; *PP* [London], p. 23), just as Anglo-American philosophers (for example Rorty, Putnam, Williams) urge the value of pluralism and continental theorists plead the virtues of alterity. For the mature Eliot (as for the Eliot of the thesis), difference of perspective is not only necessary given our different sociohistorical situations, but its productive tension can provide for richer understanding and wider experience.

This move toward pluralism and recognition of the subjective can also explain Eliot's second abrupt about-face on the question of interpretation. Radical objectivism aims to see the object as it really is in itself; while interpreting a poem always goes beyond the object-poem as it is presented, at the very least by supplying additional words which restructure and recontextualize the text and its experience, but also by introducing the plurality of interpretive perspectives. As Eliot's early objectivism involved denying interpretation's legitimacy in order to insist only on facts, so outgrowing this objectivism allowed him to reaffirm the central role of interpretation and the valuable personal aspects connected with it. The "impulse" to interpret is "fundamental," "imperative," and is and should be structured not only by the commonalities of traditional shared meanings but by our own particular situations and interests.[9] Interpretation aims neither at a God's-eye objectivism nor maximum consensus. Though it must be based on community of meaning, "a valid interpretation [of a poem] . . . must be at the same time an interpretation of my own feelings when I read it," and "a good deal of the value of an interpretation is – that it should be my own interpretation" (*PP* [London], p. 114). Consequently, as feelings and situations change and multiply over history, so do valid interpretations.

Moreover, as Eliot recognized with Wittgenstein, since language depends on social use, its meaning changes over history through the changing situations and applications which it must address (*TCC*, pp. 65–66). Indeed, even in the same historical epoch, an expression or assertion can change its meaning as we change our discursive practice or language-game; and Eliot recognized, again like Wittgenstein, the plurality of such games, even within the "single" domain of contemporary literary criticism: "Criticism seems to have separated into several diverse kinds" (*UPUC* [London], p. 27).[10]

V

Historicism points to the inexorable change of beliefs, aims, methods, vocabularies, and standards over the course of time. In recognizing the inevitability of change, it recognizes that of difference and the possibility that divergent views and practices may find rational justification in their respective, historically different communities. Three basic ideas impelled

Eliot toward a historicist pluralism regarding literary understanding. The first two are human finitude and situatedness as fundamental features which condition understanding, while the third concerns the mutability of man's situation over time and his perception of this mutability and temporality.

Situatedness expresses the idea that one is always and irremediably located in some part of the spatio-temporal, socio-historical world, and that one's perception and thinking are structured and motivated by one's situation. This idea is implicit in Wittgenstein's argument that all thinking and language presuppose for their intelligibility our living in a concrete social context, inhabiting a certain "form of life" expressed in a plurality of language games. Heidegger captures the idea of situatedness in his central notion of *Dasein* – "being-there" in the midst of the world and within a concrete historical situation; and it is similarly central to the hermeneutic philosophy of his student Gadamer. Eliot makes precisely the same point. "We are limited, by circumstances if not by capacities"; "limited by the limitations of particular men in particular places and at particular times" (*TCC*, p. 104; *UPUC* [London], p. 142). Thus in criticism, for example, "each generation, like each individual, brings to the contemplation of art its own categories of appreciation, makes its own demands upon art, and has its own uses for art" (*UPUC* [London], p. 109).

Finitude is a consequence of situatedness, and its meaning for historicist hermeneutics goes beyond the simple matter of mortality. Our perspectives are always those of "limited and transient human beings existing in space and time" (*ibid.*), limited by the horizons that our situation imposes; and there is no way for philosophical thinking to put itself outside time, space, and historical situation so as to achieve God's-eye objectivity. Indeed, as Eliot points out, our mortality makes it impossible for us to overcome the finitude of perspective by trying out all possible points of view, because our time for experiment is very limited and the world is anyway always changing; it is not as if "we were always the same generation upon earth" (*EAM*, p. 106). Finite and situated, "our vision is always partial and our judgement always prejudiced."[11]

The idea of understanding's finite situatedness is not simply a negative reminder of cognitive limitation and fallibility. It also conveys the point that being shaped by and serving the needs of a situation is not a bad thing for human understanding, since understanding's role is to promote the welfare of a creature whose needs in the world are overwhelmingly situational and pragmatic. As Gadamer and Eliot insist, prejudice and point of view provide not only the limits but the necessary direction and structure for understanding to take hold of what it grasps and appreciates.[12] Without the focussing limits of perspective and taste, genuine appreciation would be impossible: "A catholic taste . . . would be indistinguishable from no taste at all."[13]

As understanding is conditioned by one's finite situation, so that situation is conditioned and changed by time and history, which thus change our understanding. In *The Use of Poetry and the Use of Criticism*, Eliot illustrates how our understanding of poetry and criticism have undergone significant changes through history as a result of more general social changes, so that "our criticism from age to age will reflect the things that the age demands" (*UPUC* [London], p. 141). Gadamer later makes the same point when he argues that "every age has to understand a transmitted text in its own way, for 'the real meaning of a text' is not limited to what it meant to the author and whom he originally wrote for," but "is always partly determined also by the historical situation of the interpreter and hence by the totality of the objective course of history" (*TM*, p. 263).

For Eliot and Gadamer, the futility of trying to recover original authorial meaning is as much normative as it is epistemological. The main reason we understand (and *should* understand) past classics differently from the way their authors and contemporaries understood them is that we necessarily see them as *past* classics and seek to understand them not only because of but in terms of the role they played in a past history leading up to our present situation. As Eliot incisively puts it, "the difference between the present and the past is that the conscious present is an awareness of the past in a way and to an extent which the past's awareness of itself cannot show" (*SE* [1951], p. 16).

If literary interpretation should not aim at the recovery of a fixed authorial or textual meaning, but always involves understanding the text in terms of current contexts and thus issues in plurality, this does not mean that there cannot be great overlap and community of meaning among interpreters and that there are no general aims of interpretation. One aim stressed by Eliot is the achieving of a richly unified grasp of what is interpreted, whether this be "the whole design" of the work, "the work of one artist as a whole," or a unified picture of life and our experience as a whole. Through our appreciation of art we ultimately aim at achieving a "perception of order in reality" to satisfy our "need and craving for perfection and unity" and self-understanding.[14]

However, since understanding is always situation-dependent, and since the changing world is continuously imposing new situations and circumstances (including new works of art), we cannot rigidly hold to our past interpretations, assessments, and beliefs. Time's challenge to established dogma is one reason why Eliot insists that tradition itself must be constantly reinterpreted and revised to be preserved, that "tradition cannot mean standing still," since time and history never stand still (*ASG* [New York], p. 25). More generally, as we hear in the poetry of "East Coker," the shock of temporal change highlights the limits of all man's empirical knowledge:

> . . . There is, it seems to us,
> At best, only a limited value
> In the knowledge derived from experience.
> The knowledge imposes a pattern, and falsifies,
> For the pattern is new in every moment
> And every moment is a new and shocking
> Valuation of all we have been.

But limited value is not absence of value, and the fact that empirical knowledge's pattern is not immune to change does not render such knowledge worthless, even if it challenges the scientistic ideal which makes such knowledge supreme.

VI

Eliot's later philosophy thus abandoned the objectivist scientism of his early critical theory for a hermeneutic historicism which emphasizes the contextual limits and pragmatic functions of worldly human knowledge (as distinguished from the absolutes of faith). Pragmatism had been an important dimension of Eliot's doctoral thesis, which claimed that once we leave the metaphysical realm of the Absolute and concern ourselves with judging any theory about the experienced world, "all that we care about is how it works"; we must "put our theories to the pragmatic test" (*KE*, pp. 161, 169). Recognizing that "the theoretical point of view is the inevitable outgrowth of the practical," Eliot claimed "our theory will be found full of practical motives and practical consequences" (*KE*, pp. 137–38) – a claim which foreshadows his subsequent shrewd use of theory to advance his practical poetic goals (see Shusterman, *T. S. Eliot*, pp. 202–5).

By 1927, the year of his Anglican conversion, Eliot had concluded his flirtations with both Bradley and scientism, and could consign knowledge of the Absolute to religion; this left the field of secular human knowledge to pragmatism in a broad construing of the term. The kind of pragmatism Eliot most wanted to revive for modern life was not the philosophy of Peirce, James, and Dewey but the classical idea of practical wisdom, a form of knowledge which treats the contingent and changing, and which cannot be reduced to any articulated system, doctrine, or formula. This idea is elaborated by Aristotle in terms of the intellectual virtue of *phronesis*, which though based on natural intelligence or cleverness requires that this be developed by training and informed by moral virtue in order to achieve true wisdom. *Phronesis*, which treats of both means and ends, is essentially practical and deliberative, since it deals with choice and action under contingent conditions which do not admit of scientific proof or fixed methods. Here, to borrow Eliot's words, "there is no method except to be very intelligent" (*SW* [1928], p. 11). And the intelligence of *phronesis* extends beyond proper thought and action to include proper feelings as well, which can likewise be trained, and which are needed to ensure that proper action be done without incurring painful internal conflict.

The status of phronesis has largely been eclipsed and discredited in modern times by the alternative ideal of science, with its promise of immutable laws and precise predictions based on infallible foundations and standardized, universalizable methods. In order to realize "the wish that the classical conception of wisdom might be restored" (*EAM*, p. 117), Eliot attacked our "exaggerated devotion to science."[15] Recognizing that science is not free from ideology, he warned that "practitioners of both political and economic science in the very effort to be scientific . . . make assumptions which they are not only not entitled to make, but which they are not always conscious of making" (*EAM*, pp. 114–15). He moreover realized that not even the hard-nosed scientist could "get on for one moment without believing anything except the 'hows' of science."[16] For even the pursuit of science cannot exclusively rely on verified scientific knowledge and method; since theories need to be interpreted into real-world or laboratory conditions to be tested, and such interpretations require more than is given by the theory and by strict scientific method. Thus philosophers of science like Putnam and Polanyi contend that even exact science "typically depends on unformalized practical knowledge," on tacit socially acquired practices and sentiments, and that the scientist must "rely on his human wisdom."[17]

Less concerned with science itself than society as a whole, Eliot insists that "a really satisfactory working philosophy of social action . . . requires not merely science but wisdom"; and "wisdom, including political wisdom, can neither be abstracted to a science, nor reduced to a dodge" (*EAM*, pp. 116, 118). Eliot is greatly troubled by our sharp division of political and social theory from ethical thought and practice, a division (reinforced by our education system) where scientific, objective facts are rigidly separated from human values and emotions, the latter deemed to be utterly and irremediably subjective. "The modern world separates the intellect and the emotions. What can be reduced to a science . . . a limited and technical material, it respects; the rest may be a waste of uncontrolled behavior and immature emotion" (*EAM*, p. 117).

Eliot instead urges "the classical conception of wisdom" which is not merely instrumental reason but treats both means and ends, both action and feeling. It is a practical wisdom which involves the development of character and the education and discipline of the emotions. For without such ethical development, "a moral conversion" involving "the discipline and training of emotion," the knowledge of social truths and mastery of techniques of social engineering cannot achieve true social regeneration. Eliot thought that such emotional discipline was so difficult for the modern mind as to be "only obtainable through dogmatic religion" (*EAM*, p. 130; "Religion Without Humanism," p. 110). This in key part is Eliot's pragmatist justification for rejecting secular liberalism and maintaining a traditional religious perspective which offers a definite, time-tested version of the good life, and a solid, reinforcing community and social practice for its pursuit.

Eliot's philosophy thus leads smoothly into his theology, social criticism, and theory of tradition, topics of other chapters in this book. But we can understand neither his ethics nor his philosophy of mind without highlighting his firm belief in the social construction of thought and sensibility. Our taste for liberalist individualism and our dissociation of sensibility is not only the heritage of Cartesian epistemology based on individual mental consciousness, but the product of a society whose politico-economic and cultural institutions at once privilege and fragment the individual. Thus there is no real way of saving or understanding ourselves without understanding and improving society; nor any way of bettering the latter without improving ourselves. For Eliot,

> the problem of the unification of the world and the problem of the unification of the individual are, in the end one and the same problem; and the solution of one is the solution of the other. Analytical psychology . . . can do little except produce monsters; for it is attempting to produce unified individuals in a world without unity; the social, political, and economic sciences can do little, for they are attempting to produce the great society with an aggregation of human beings who are not units but merely bundles of incoherent impulses and beliefs.　　　　　　　　　　　　　("Religion Without Humanism", p. 112)

In his critique of bourgeois liberalism and its individualist ideology, Eliot converges with the radical philosophy of Adorno.[18] Here, as in his historicist pluralism, hermeneutics, and critique of positivist science, Eliot speaks to us as a philosophical contemporary.

NOTES

1 See Ann Bolgan, "The Philosophy of F. H. Bradley and the Mind and Art of T. S. Eliot: An Introduction," S. P. Rosenbaum (ed.) *English Literature and*

British Philosophy (Chicago: University of Chicago Press, 1971), and Lewis Freed, *The Critic as Philosopher* (LaSalle: Purdue University Press, 1979).

2 "Reality is one. It must be single, because plurality, taken as real, contradicts itself." "It is a very common and most ruinous superstition to suppose that analysis is no alteration." F. H. Bradley, *Appearance and Reality* (Oxford: Clarendon, 1930), p. 28; and *Principles of Logic* (Oxford: Clarendon, 1922), p. 95.

3 See Lyndall Gordon, *Eliot's Early Years* (Oxford: Oxford University Press, 1977), p. 49.

4 See *SW* (1928), pp. 9, 66, 75 and "Style and Thought," *The Nation*, March 23, 1918, pp. 768–70.

5 See Bertrand Russell, "The Philosophy of Logical Atomism" (1918) and "Logical Atomism" (1924), David Pears (ed.) *Russell's Logical Atomism* (London: Fontana, 1972), p. 162; henceforth abbreviated *RLA*.

6 T. S. Eliot, "Studies in Contemporary Criticism," *Egoist* 5 (1918): 114.

7 "Marivaux," *Art and Letters* 2 (1919): 80.

8 See Bertrand Russell, *The Problems of Philosophy* (1912: repr. Oxford: Oxford University Press, 1959), p. 65.

9 See Eliot's "Introduction" to G. Wilson Knight, *The Wheel of Fire* (1930; London: Methuen, 1962), pp. xiii, xvi–xvii, for Eliot's self-conscious declaration of the reversal of his "previous scepticism" about interpretation.

10 For a detailed account of Wittgenstein's philosophy of criticism and its relation to Eliot's, see Richard Shusterman, *T. S. Eliot and the Philosophy of Criticism* (London: Duckworth; New York: Columbia University Press, 1988), ch. 4.

11 T. S. Eliot, "Experiment in Criticism," *Bookman* 70 (1929): 225–33.

12 See Gadamer's arguments that "all understanding inevitably involves some prejudice," since such prejudices constitute the structure and initial directedness of our experience; in H.-G. Gadamer, *Truth and Method* (New York: Crossroad, 1982), pp. 239, 245–47 (henceforth abbreviated *TM*); and Eliot's remark that "if it be objected that this is a prejudice . . . I can only reply that one must criticize from some point of view" (*SE* [1951], p. 114).

13 T. S. Eliot, review of E. E. Kellett, *Fashion in Literature: A Study of Changing Taste, English Review* 53 (1931): 635.

14 T. S. Eliot's "Introduction" to G. Wilson Knight, *The Wheel of Fire* (1930, London: Methuen, 1962), pp. xvii, xix; *PP* [London], p. 87; "Poetry and Propaganda," *Bookman* 70 (1930): 598–99.

15 T. S. Eliot, "Religion Without Humanism," N. Foerster (ed.) *Humanism and America* (New York: Farrar and Rinehart, 1930), p. 112.

16 T. S. Eliot, "Literature, Science, Dogma," *Dial* 82 (1927): 242.

17 See Hilary Putnam, *Meaning and the Moral Sciences* (London: Routledge & Kegan Paul, 1979), pp. 72–73; and M. Polanyi, *Personal Knowledge* (London: Routledge & Kegan Paul, 1958).

18 This convergence is discussed in my "Reactionary Meets Radical Critique: Eliot and Contemporary Culture Criticism," L. Cowan (ed.) *T. S. Eliot: Man and Poet* (Orono, ME: National Poetry Foundation, 1990), pp. 367–93. See also my *Pragmatist Aesthetics: Living Beauty, Rethinking Art* (Oxford: Blackwell, 1992), ch. 6.

4

TIMOTHY MATERER

T. S. Eliot's critical program

In 1917 T. S. Eliot compared the literary critic to a bee building a hive. Even the most gifted thinker, he claimed, is unable to conceive more than a few original ideas:

> With these, or with one, say, hexagonal or octagonal idea, each sets to work and industriously and obliviously begins building cells; not rebelling against the square or the circle, but occasionally coming into collision with some other Bee which has rectangular or circular ideas.[1]

This conception of the cooperative nature of the literary enterprise is grounded in what Eliot called "the old *aporia* of Authority v. Individual Judgment" (*PP* [New York], p. 113).[2] Although he found the criterion for genuine art within the literary tradition, his innovative conception of that tradition also gave authority to the individual artist. He developed his traditionalism with such hive-building thoroughness that it seemed revolutionary rather than conventional. In describing such "new ideas," Eliot observed that an old idea may be "so perfectly assimilated as to be original."[3] His deep assimilation of the "old *aporia*" of tradition and the individual made it a virtually new concept.

Eliot's intellectual thoroughness and respect for the past made him the kind of "exhaustive critic" he described in *The Use of Poetry and the Use of Criticism* who dares to review the entire history of a literary tradition (*UPUC* [New York], p. 108). Eliot also belonged to a line of poet-critics which includes John Dryden, Samuel Johnson, and Matthew Arnold. In the formative years of his literary career, from 1917 until the early twenties, he played the role of the "exhaustive critic" with unfailing energy and assurance.

With the exception of his fellow expatriate Ezra Pound, no modern writer of English rivalled Eliot in his influence on the development of modern literature. Authors such as James Joyce, Wallace Stevens, or Ernest Hemingway had relatively little interest in literary criticism; and E. M.

Foster, Virginia Woolf, and D. H. Lawrence, despite their critical powers and insights into cultural issues, did not devote so much of their talent to it. Ezra Pound alone matched Eliot's ambition to influence literary opinion in England and America through both his art and his criticism. But Pound succumbed to the temptation, which merely troubled Eliot, of becoming a social and political pundit rather than a relatively detached cultural critic. In his early years as a poet-critic, Eliot explicitly compared himself to Henry James. He wrote to his mother (1919) with pardonable pride that a "small and select public" considered him "the best living critic, as well as the best living poet, in England . . . I really think that I have more *influence* on English letters than any other American has ever had, unless it be Henry James" (*Letters* I, p. 280).

Like James, Eliot saw his literary criticism as a way of improving the appreciation of his own art. By setting "the poets and the poem in a new order," he could make a place for his own revolutionary poems. This literary ambition developed rapidly in the years between 1914, when he went from Harvard University to Oxford for a year to work on a doctoral degree in philosophy, and the publication in 1920 of his first major volume of criticism, *The Sacred Wood*. Eliot was finishing his dissertation on F. H. Bradley out of a sense of obligation to his family, who were supporting his studies. However, as he wrote to a friend in 1915, for him philosophy really meant "literary criticism and conversation about life . . ." (*Letters* I, p. 81). His determination to follow a literary career dates from his meeting with Ezra Pound in 1914, which he said had changed his life because Pound recognized his poetic gift (*Letters* I, p. xvii). Although he continued to write his dissertation, he also began writing for literary journals, partly to help earn his living after his marriage in 1915. Thanks to Pound, his poems were appearing in magazines like *Poetry* (Chicago) and *BLAST* (London) in 1915; and he began reviewing philosophical books for the *International Journal of Ethics* and the *Monist* in 1916. After this modest start, he began writing serious literary journalism in the *Egoist* (becoming its assistant editor in 1917) and in the *Little Review*.

His *Egoist* reviews of contemporary poetry, appearing under the title of "Reflections on Contemporary Poetry" (1917), expressed ideas that he would develop in his mature criticism. His single most important essay, "Tradition and the Individual Talent," first appears in the *Egoist* in 1919. Despite the limited circulation of the *Egoist*, Eliot's essays became well known and earned him an invitation from John Middleton Murry to become assistant editor of a more prestigious journal, the *Athenaeum*. Wisely judging that the *Athenaeum* post might not be secure, Eliot kept the position he took at Lloyd's Bank in 1917 but wrote frequently for the

journal and was warmly encouraged by Murry, who hoped that their "collaboration will not be interrupted until we have restored criticism" (*Letters* I,
p. 286, n. 1). Eliot's famous article on "Hamlet and his Problems" appeared
in the *Athenaeum* in 1919, and he began to theorize about the art of criticism itself in "The Perfect Critic" of 1920, which became the opening essay
of *The Sacred Wood*. In September of 1919 he was asked to write for the
Times Literary Supplement and told his mother that the invitation was "the
highest honour possible in the critical world of literature" (*Letters* I, p. 337).
In the same letter, he informed her of his plans to establish his critical eminence with new books of both poetry and criticism.

By 1919 Eliot had published only two small volumes of verse with *avant-
garde* presses, *Prufrock and Other Observations* (1917) and *Poems* (1919). In
1920 he considerably strengthened this record with a new volume of *Poems*
(1920) from Knopf and *The Sacred Wood* from Methuen. This latter book
bears the mark of his experience of literary journalism as well as his writing
of his doctoral dissertation on F. H. Bradley. He wrote to a literary patron
that he wanted his book of criticism to be "a single distinct blow." The
blow was directed against the contemporary lack of standards of good
writing for both verse and critical prose represented by that "huge journal-
istic organism the 'critical' or Review press" (*Letters* I, p. 355).

In *The Sacred Wood*, Eliot studies some of the canonical works of English
literature and tries to isolate the qualities that inform their greatness. On the
basis of this analysis, Eliot then tries to generalize principles that will help
the critic evaluate both classic and contemporary literature. In addition to
the principles he derived from certain works, however, Eliot brought to his
criticism premises he conceived while studying F. H. Bradley. Indeed, his
"two or three new ideas" come from this period of philosophical thought.
The dissertation's analysis of solipsism, of the way language enriches reality
as it allows us to grasp it, and of how Time conditions our perceptions of
the world also reveals the recurring concerns of his poetry.

His work on the dissertation influenced Eliot's criticism by developing in
him a habit of skeptical inquiry into ideas and by teaching him Bradley's
"scrupulous respect for words" (*SE* [1950], p. 404). Words such as "sensation," "feeling," "emotion," and "fact," which are essential to Eliot's analysis of how we perceive reality, are scrupulously and subtly employed in the
dissertation. Eliot rejects the naive realism that says the world is simply
there before us, insisting that our ideas and feelings condition even our most
direct sensations of the world. Similarly, a "fact" is not something that is
simply there before our consciousness. Eliot argued that each fact had a
pre-arranged place in a system which gives it its status as a fact (*KE*, p. 60).
In a late poem, Eliot wrote that "We had the experience but missed the

meaning . . ." (*DS* ii). This famous line expresses Eliot's sense that no experience is "real" nor any "fact" valid unless it fits into a pattern or system of relations that gives it meaning – even though this meaning can never be final since the pattern is always changing and the system always developing. Rather than leading him into skepticism, this view convinces Eliot of the need for an informed consensus before we conclude that we know something (*KE*, pp. 163–64). He concludes in his dissertation that "lived truths are partial and fragmentary" and that therefore any interpretation must be taken up and "reinterpreted by every thinking mind and by every civilization" (*KE*, p. 164). This conviction leads directly to the key topic in *The Sacred Wood*, the role of tradition in interpreting and evaluating art.

The Sacred Wood contains many reinterpretations of the English literary tradition, especially in the book's second half. But the heart of the work appears in the first half, which contains the more theoretical essays. "Tradition and the Individual Talent" is the classic statement of Eliot's critical theory. As an experimental writer who had at first found it difficult even to publish his verse much less earn critical or popular favor, Eliot was aware that "traditional" ways of interpreting poetry only hindered his generation of writers. He therefore looked for a way that artists could be judged by the standards of the past" but "not amputated" by them (*SE* [1950], p. 5). He found the answer in his highly personal conception of tradition.

In its conventional sense, "tradition" is a "handing down" and might connote an unhealthy respect for past generations. For Eliot, however, tradition is not simply received or "inherited" but "obtain[ed] by great labour." This conception of tradition implies a sense of history which is

> a perception, not only of the pastness of the past, but of its presence; the historical sense compels a man to write not merely with his own generation in his bones, but with a feeling that the whole of the literature of Europe from Homer and within it the whole of the literature of his own country has a simultaneous existence and composes a simultaneous order. (*SE* [1950], p. 5)

The intense conviction of this passage is also reflected in Eliot's claim of affinity with the Elizabethan and Jacobean poets, and with Nineteenth-Century French poets, rather than with poets of the Victorian or Georgian periods. He knew that he could not be understood or valued unless he were placed in a context free of provincial ties to his own time and language. For Eliot, this relating of the present and past is a principle not only of historical but also of aesthetic criticism. He insists that we should be constantly evaluating past writers as well as current ones. The "fitting in" of a work of art is "a test of its value" (*SE* [1950], pp. 4–5). Eliot applies the theory of interpretation formulated in his dissertation to the evaluation of literature. When a revolutionary work of art takes its place within the "existing monuments" of literature:

> the *whole* existing order must be, if ever so slightly, altered; and so the relations, proportions, values of each work of art toward the whole are readjusted; and this is conformity between the old and the new.
>
> (*SE* [1950], p. 5)

Like "facts," individual works of art are not static but dynamic entities that are constantly changing their relationships and so must be constantly reinterpreted.

Eliot hoped such a criterion of judgment would bring order to the undisciplined journalism of his day so that, for example, a comparison of a poet to Donne rather than to last season's successful poet would expose the new poet's triviality, or the criticism of a poet for not practicing a Wordsworthian or Tennysonian expressiveness would be seen for the provinciality it was. Eliot calls this doctrine of tradition "part of my programme for the *métier* of poetry" (*SE* [1950], p. 6). A second part of what he calls his "Impersonal theory of poetry" is posited in part two of the essay when he compares the poet's mind to the platinum which is the catalyst of a chemical reaction. The platinum is the agent of change but nevertheless remains "inert, neutral, and unchanged" (*SE* [1950], p. 7). For Eliot, the greater the artist, the more completely separate in him would be "the man who suffers and the mind which creates" (p. 7).

The emotion of art should be in the poem rather than the poet. Eliot demonstrates this principle in the essays on specific writers in the second half of *The Sacred Wood*. The most famous essay in this section of the work, if only because it introduces the term "objective correlative," is "Hamlet and His Problems." In attempting to readjust the relative ranking of Shakespeare's plays (of which he preferred the later ones), Eliot argues that Hamlet is a "failure" because in it Shakespeare does not objectify the "inexpressibly horrible" emotion which he is evidently striving to express. The passions expressed in the play, such as Hamlet's disgust with his mother, are not grounded in its character or action. The play therefore fails because

> The only way of expressing emotion in the form of art is by finding an "objective correlative"; in other words, a set of objects, a situation, a chain of events which shall be the formula of that *particular* emotion; such that when the external facts, which must terminate in sensory experience, are given, the emotion is immediately evoked.   (*SE* [1950], pp. 124–25)

In itself, this rather arrogant dictum cannot express an artistic criterion. Since no one can say exactly what emotion Shakespeare, or any other poet, was trying to express, one can hardly criticize him for not expressing it. But it does successfully emphasize that the emotion must be in the poem and not dependent upon any speculation about what the poet was feeling. More significantly, its claim that the emotion must be expressed through "sensory experience" is a principle that underlies some of Eliot's most perceptive criticism. A test of authenticity is not only how well a poet "fits in" to the tradition, but also how vividly a poetic emotion seems to arise out of physical sensations or images linked to these sensations. Despite *Hamlet*'s "failure," Shakespeare is a master in a literary age when "the intellect was immediately at the tips of the senses" (*SW* [1928], p. 129).

As we read in *Knowledge and Experience*, experience comes to us most directly through sensations, which then become associated with feelings and are subsequently worked up into complex emotions. Poetry should affect the reader as directly as a physical sensation.[4] Eliot expressed this view of poetry best in "The Metaphysical Poets," which he first published in the *Times Literary Supplement* in 1921. The essay substantiates his view of tradition by revealing how Eliot himself, as the author of genuinely traditional works, could make us see that John Donne and the Metaphysical poets were more in the "direct current of English poetry" than critical authorities such as Samuel Johnson had thought. In poets such as Donne, Herbert and Marvell, and in playwrights such as Chapman and Webster, Eliot finds a "direct sensuous apprehension of thought, or a recreation of thought into feeling . . ." (*SE* [1950], p. 246). Unlike writers such as Tennyson and Browning, who "do not feel their thought as immediately as the odour of a rose," the Metaphysicals are intent on "trying to find the verbal equivalent for states of mind and feeling" (*SE* [1950], pp. 247 48). In a surprising juxtaposition, Eliot compares Donne and Chapman to Jules Laforgue and Tristan Corbière. "Transmuting ideas into sensations," these poets looked "into the cerebral cortex, the nervous system, and the digestive tracts" (*SE* [1950], p. 250) as well as the heart or soul.

Eliot's attempt to value the Metaphysicals over the Victorians, to raise the status of the Jacobean playwrights, and to praise Dante at the expense of Blake (as he does in the last two essays of *The Sacred Wood*), raises the question of why for Eliot poets of an entire age tend to be superior to those of another. In "The Metaphysical Poets," he claims that the Metaphysicals were fortunate to live in an age before "a dissociation of sensibility set in, from which we have never recovered . . ." (*SE* [1950], p. 247). The phrase "dissociation of sensibility," which Eliot felt had a "truly embarrassing success" as a literary term (*PP* [New York], p. 117), should be examined in the context of Eliot's developing sense of the relation of poetry to social and political conditions.

The 1928 edition of *The Sacred Wood* reveals Eliot's increasing interest in the social conditions necessary for great art. The preface contains his well-known and misleading statement that "Poetry is a superior amusement." He admitted that the statement was not a "true definition" of poetry but that he was using it "because if you call it anything else you are likely to call it something still more false." What then to call it? Eliot's problem was that, just as certainly as poetry is meant to give pleasure, it also has "something to do with morals, and with religion, and even with politics perhaps, though we cannot say what" (*SW* [1928], p. x). Eliot had "passed on to another problem not touched upon in this book: that of the relation of poetry to the spiritual and social life of its time and of other times" (viii).

His claim that he had not touched on the problem is greatly exaggerated. For example, he praised Shakespeare's era in the "Philip Massinger" essay as a "period when the intellect was immediately at the tips of the senses" (*SW* [1928], p. 129) and implied that it was morally superior to later ages. In the "period of Milton," to which Massinger's works belong, Eliot deplored the "decay of the senses" and the playwright's failure to be "guided by direct communications through the nerves" (p. 136). This failure is in part a failure of "intellectual courage" (p. 142) and in part of living in an age of "dissociation of sensibility," when life is no longer felt to be a moral struggle and morality itself becomes abstract. Although he does not mention any specific social conditions in the seventeenth century, Eliot apparently considered the Puritan revolution and the beheading of Charles I, who was both King and head of the Church, drastic symptoms of the decay of ortho-dox authority.

The concluding essays of *The Sacred Wood*, "Blake" and "Dante," also relate the morality of an age to the vitality of its poetry. Like Massinger and later poets, Blake suffers from living in a "formless age" (p. 64) which lacks any framework of traditional ideas (*SW* [1928], p. 158). Blake's age, moreover, is still further on from the seventeenth century "dissociation," which Massinger's age was only beginning to undergo. The Romantic period was so formless that Blake was forced to erect his own framework for his poetry. Unfortunately, creating his own philosophy distracted Blake from the "problems of the poet" (p. 158), which involve expressing rather than inventing ideas and emotions. Still further into the "dissociation," Tennyson is a yet worse case of a poet "almost wholly encrusted with parasitic opinion, almost wholly merged into his environment" (p. 154). Less censorious of Blake than of Massinger or Tennyson, Eliot speculates that the fault may not be with Blake himself, but with a culture that failed to provide what a poet of his visionary kind needed (p. 158).

What the poet needed is clear in the Dante essay. Dante was fortunate to live in an age when philosophy and theology, religion and actual belief, and public and private morality were not dissociated. He benefited from "a mythology and a theology which had undergone a more complete absorption into life . . ." (*SW* [1928], p. 163). In contrast, Milton suffered a division between the philosopher, or theologian, and the poet (*PP* [New York], p. 163). Dante could concentrate on the poet's proper task, "to *realize* ideas": ". . . Poetry can be penetrated by a philosophic idea, it can deal with this idea when it has reached the point of immediate acceptance, when it has become almost a physical modification" (pp. 162–63).

This formulation brings us back to Eliot's second criterion for authentic poetry (the first being its vital relation to tradition): poetry should affect us as a direct sensation. In a later essay on Dante (1929), he praises Dante as virtually a master of the "objective correlative" because he makes his readers experience the reality of Hell "by the projection of sensory images" (*SE* [1950], p. 212), and "apprehend sensuously the various states and stages of blessedness" (p. 226). However, his unique concentration on this poetic task of realization (greater even than Shakespeare's, who lived in a relatively "formless age") would have been impossible without the Christian framework. Dante was uniquely successful in expressing a philosophy as something he directly and passionately perceived (*SW* [1928], pp. 170–71).

Next to "tradition," no term is more crucial to Eliot's work than "criterion." By 1928 he was concerned with the difficulty that a tradition could be valid and available only if the culture that transmitted it was a healthy one. But the problem of a tradition's dependence on culture and society appeared too complex for any one literary or cultural figure to address. Moreover, Eliot's notion of tradition itself assumed a developing consensus of aesthetic judgment by many critics and readers. If a culture is too shallow or disunified for a consensus to arise, people who care about culture need to band together to encourage its development. Thus Eliot in 1922, despite ill health and marital and financial problems, helped to found a journal which he edited for seventeen years, *The Criterion*. As he recalled in 1949, his two goals for the journal were to bring together the best writers in England with the best on the international scene, and to establish relations with similar publications in Europe (*Nouvelle Revue Française, Neue Rundschau*, for example) which had a similar goal of "the circulating of ideas while they are still fresh" (*NTDC* [New York], p. 119). This job Eliot did superbly, soliciting articles from international writers such as Herman Hesse, Ezra Pound, and Benedetto Croce. He published essays not only on figures he admired, such as Dostoevsky and Paul Valéry, but also on figures he did not, such as an excellent and favorable appraisal of Freud by Jacques Rivière. After a year of publication, Eliot stated the goals of his journal in "The Function of Criticism" (*Criterion*, October 1923).

Eliot begins this essay by quoting his definition of tradition from "Tradition and the Individual Talent" and applying what it says of the artist to the critic. Eliot explains that in his earlier essay he conceived of literary works as "systems in relation to which, and only in relation to which, individual works of literary art, and the works of individual artists, have their significance." This conception of literature implies that there is something beyond the artist which commands the artists's allegiance (*SE* [1950], pp. 12–13). He conceives of *The Criterion* as an organ of a community of writers who might counteract the excessive individualism and lack of standards in the literary world. Contemporary criticism is characterized as "a Sunday park of contending and contentious orators, who have not even arrived at the articulation of their differences." Instead of the "common pursuit of true judgment," the critic pursues "his opposition to other critics, or else to some trifling oddities of his own with which he contrives to season the opinions which men already hold" (*SE* [1950], p. 14). A criterion that would distinguish the genuine from the meretricious in criticism might eliminate the confusion. In literature, Eliot considered the artist's relation to tradition and the ability to convey direct sensation as marks of true art. In criticism, he similarly looks to how a critic fits into a developing consensus or community of opinion and (corresponding to the "direct sensation" criterion for poetry) whether the critic conveys a sense of "fact" (*SE* [1950], p. 21). Unlike an opinion, a fact cannot "corrupt taste." The critic who deals in fact, and in conveying fresh ideas as the *Criterion* writers do, opens up "the possibility of co-operative activity, with the further possibility of arriving at something outside of ourselves, which may provisionally be called truth" (p. 22).

Here and throughout these essays, Eliot is still meditating on a central problem, the "*aporia* of Authority v. Individual Judgment." The trend within these meditations, however, is clearly toward the "Authority" side of this dialectic. In "The Function of Criticism," his new insight into his earlier view of tradition is that the problem was "generally a problem of order." It is necessary to find something "outside ourselves" to anchor our judgments, to provide a center without which consensus is impossible. "The Function of Criticism" introduces into the discussion the terms Classicism, which connotes order and rationality, and Romanticism, which connotes individualism and emotionalism. The Romantic-Classic debate occupied the *Criterion* writers for many years.[5] Eliot's "Commentary" in the April 1924 *Criterion* affirms that a new classical age would be reached when "the dogma, or ideology, of the critics is so modified by contact with creative writing, and when the creative writers are so permeated by the new dogma, that a state of equilibrium is reached."[6] Eliot found signs of such a development in writers such as Georges Sorel, Charles Maurras, Julien Benda, T. E. Hulme, Irving Babbitt, and Jacques Maritain. This list of authors, as well as the term "new dogma," shows that Eliot was now looking for a criterion of judgment and a principle of order outside a strictly literary tradition.

Eliot addressed his new concern with the relation of literature to fields such as religion and politics in a *Criterion* essay in January 1926, "The Idea of a Literary Review." The essay dismisses "pure literature" as a "chimera of sensation." Even a literary journal should include material relating to general ideas in history, archaeology, anthropology, and the physical sciences.[7] In 1926, his *Criterion* "Commentary" notes that the dispossessed artist, who finds the age's formlessness hampering his work, has been "driven to examining the elements in the situation – political, social, philosophical or religious – which frustrate his art."[8]

This steadily increasing concern with the political, social, and religious issues of his age was driving Eliot himself toward a commitment that no merely literary tradition could inspire. Under the prodding of his former teacher Paul Elmer More in 1927, Eliot decided to "come out into the open" about the religious beliefs that were guiding his development (*TCC*, p. 15). Thus in the preface to his brief volume *For Lancelot Andrewes* (1928), subtitled "Essays on Style and Order," he declared his orientation as "classicist in literature, royalist in politics, and anglo-catholic in religion" (p. ix). All three stands affirmed his belief in traditional order, but the key one of course referred to his 1927 conversion to the Christian faith, which indeed gave him a principle of order "outside the self."

The literary implications of Eliot's conversion are clearly seen in the lectures he gave in America in 1933, *After Strange Gods: A Primer of Modern Heresy*. In his first lecture, he returns, as he did in the 1926 "Function of Criticism," to his seminal essay, "Tradition and the Individual Talent." He remarks that the problem addressed in "Tradition" no longer seems as simple as it did then nor does it now appear a "purely literary one" (*ASG* [New York], p. 15). To Eliot in 1926, tradition involves a variety of customs – including everything from greeting a stranger to participating in a religious rite – which are dependent on a stable society and a unified religious background (*ASG* [New York], pp. 18, 20).

He now believes that "Tradition by itself is not enough; it must be perpetually criticised and brought up to date under the supervision of what I call orthodoxy . . ." (p. 67). In *After Strange Gods*, as well as *The Idea of a Christian Society* (1940) and *Notes Towards the Definition of Culture* (1949), a unified religious background means Christianity alone, since Eliot believes that for western civilization the only alternative to a Christian society or culture is a pagan one. At times, as in his "Dante" essay of 1929 or "Poetry and Drama" of 1951, his religious beliefs admirably focus his attention on a literary problem. But in works like *After Strange Gods*, "Religion and Literature" (1935), and "What is a Classic?" (1944), it narrows his judgment and sympathy. The terms "Tradition and the Individual," or "Classic and Romantic," are drastically narrowed when they are transformed, in *After Strange Gods*, into "Orthodoxy and Heresy." His concern with criteria is similarly limited when he writes that the "number of people in possession of any criteria for discriminating between good and evil is very small" (p. 66) and that Christian orthodoxy must provide an "external test of the validity of a writer's work" (p. 68).

When T. S. Eliot was an experimental poet, rebelling against literary convention, his respect for tradition generated a creative dialectic in his work. The balance between the individual and external authority was always shifting in unexpected ways as he developed his sense of tradition. As he leaned more and more to the authority side of this dichotomy, this creative tension was lost. Eliot himself recognized the change. In 1965 he admitted that his earlier essays had an urgency and a "warmth of appeal" that the later, relatively detached essays lacked (*TCC*, p. 16).

In compensation, Eliot's post-conversion essays often express the maturity and judiciousness of a master of criticism. But the "role of the moralist" that he adopted in *After Strange Gods* stays with him for the rest of his career; and at times he gives the impression, to adapt Wilde's quip on Henry James's fiction, that he writes criticism as if it were a "painful duty." After the tasks of the "exhaustive critic" were substantially completed in the late twenties, his excitement at discovering his "two or three original ideas" seems to have waned. Before it did, Eliot's conception of art as direct sensation, of the impersonality of the artist, and of tradition as an endlessly reinterpreted consensus, had transformed modern literary criticism.

NOTES

1 T. S. Eliot, "Reflections on Contemporary Poetry," *The Egoist* 4.10 (November 1917): 151.
2 When he wrote in 1961 of "my recurrent theme of Classicism versus Romanticism" (*TCC*, p. 17), he referred to a similar dichotomy.
3 Eliot, "Reflections," p. 151.
4 For a discussion of how Eliot uses "direct sensation" as a literary criterion, see Richard Shusterman, *T. S. Eliot and the Philosophy of Criticism* (New York: Columbia University Press, 1988), ch. 2. Shusterman's book is an excellent discussion of Eliot's entire career as a critic.

5 For an account of this debate and of Eliot's editing of the *Criterion*, see John D. Margolis, *T. S. Eliot's Intellectual Development: 1922–1939* (Chicago: University of Chicago Press, 1972).

6 T. S. Eliot, "A Commentary," *The Criterion* 2.3 (April 1924): 232.

7 T. S. Eliot, "The Idea of a Literary Review," *The New Criterion* 4.1 (January 1926): 4. In this essay, he wrote that a review should have no "programme" but simply reveal a "tendency" (p. 3).

8 T. S. Eliot, "A Commentary," *The Criterion* 4.3 (June 1926): 420.

5

PETER DALE SCOTT

The social critic and his discontents

INTRODUCTION: ELIOT AND CULTURAL POLITICS

Few of those who admire Eliot have done so for his social and political criticism. Usually this prose has been used to elucidate difficult poems, or ignored altogether, or seen as gratuitously problematic, and a hindrance to the survival of Eliot's reputation. But for those who continue to be struck by the unity and importance of Eliot's art, the social criticism cannot be so marginalized. The result is not just a problem but a perplexity, and at times a scandal.

Great visionary poets have usually had visionary politics as well, and have frequently devoted their prose to immediate causes which in retrospect seem not only reactionary but futile. One thinks of Dante's hopes to resurrect a Roman Empire, or Milton's last-ditch defense of the Commonwealth. We think today of their social criticism on a higher level: as efforts to redefine their relationship, and that of their age, to the cultural authorities of the past. In their oppositional use of canonical texts against the entrenched rulers of their own age, they form a single tradition, as much progressive as reactionary. We may perhaps think of them, in their largely successful claims upon the minds of the future, as practitioners of cultural politics.[1]

The tradition of cultural politics in England may be traced back to Milton's efforts to defeat on the battlefield of poetry, with the assistance of Scripture, the Stuarts who had bested his cause on another level. With *Four Quartets* and *The Idea of a Christian Society*, Eliot hoped to make the same type of appeal to the future that Milton had made with *Paradise Lost* and *De Doctrina Christiana*. Some day he may be remembered less for what he had to say about royalism, dogma, and free-thinking Jews, than for his critique of complacent liberalism, corporate exploitation, and secular visions of progress.

For Eliot's talent was to think critically, not synthetically. His two mature volumes of social criticism (the *Idea of a Christian Society* [1939], and *Notes*

Towards the Definition of Culture [1948]) failed, not only to resolve the social and cultural problems they presented, but even to serve as epitomes of Eliot's political thinking. Instead the best of his political writing is to be found in his critical essays and the Commentaries he wrote for the *Criterion* and the *New English Weekly*. Those who have read through Eliot's social criticism may agree that his life-long project was to strengthen liberal democracy, and protect it against lapsing from an open milieu of self-criticism into a closed milieu of self-gratulation. But it is difficult to summarize this contribution, since it consists of a mental activity rather than concrete instrumentalities.

In Eliot, as in Yeats and Pound, we see the cultural alienation definitive of modernism, which drove all three poets to *emigré* obsession with the cultural defectiveness of their homelands. Rather than simply participate in the prevailing liberal discourse of their age, all three developed oppositional critical perspectives which looked for spiritual insights from elsewhere, above all from eastern as well as western tradition. Of the three Eliot was (a) the best educated and most philosophically trained mind, (b) the most aware of his own talent's relation to tradition, and (c) significantly, the most sensitive and insecure.

These factors combined to make him the most articulate of the modernist social critics, and also the most determined to supply, not only a *critique* of liberalism, but also a positive intellectual alternative. Like Coleridge, Arnold, and Ruskin before him, his critical activity made him speak for ultimate values of our culture, to affirm what is permanent, to be that kind of writer whose dialogue is with the dead more than the living. Because of what Eliot called the "doubleness" of the human condition, engaged with both the temporal and with something else, his "idea" of society is more like an incitement, a Platonic, even Utopian paradigm, laid up (like Plato's Republic) in heaven for those who have the eyes to see it.

Thus, despite practical disagreements as to the value of monarchy or republics, Eliot's use of culture in defense of the permanently valuable is an agenda assimilable to those of Milton, Wordsworth, and Coleridge; and the problems with this agenda are not his alone. It may be that no author nor reader can quite reconcile in prose the competing social claims of the permanent and the progressive, of the irrational and the rational. And yet this cultural task, first seriously attempted in English by Coleridge, continues to be urgent; and Eliot's failed efforts in particular, for want of a better alternative, still influence and perplex cultural critics of the left and the right alike.

In general Eliot has worked, by a series of Gourmontian discriminations, to enlarge and empower this realm of sociocultural critique. At his best he has written not just about culture but for it, and to an audience not narrowly circumscribed by any prejudice. Today left and right can share in Eliot's disaffection with the nineteenth century as an age of bustle and "revolutions which improved nothing, an age of progressive degradation" (*SE* [1951], p. 427). When Eliot revived a passage from Baudelaire that resonates with the aspirations of Dante's Comedy and Virgil's Fourth Eclogue (*La vraie civilisation n'est pas dans le gaz, ni dans la vapeur, ni dans les tables tournantes. Elle est dans la diminution des traces du péché originel*; *SE* [1951], p. 430), Eliot in effect redrew the cultural roadmap of Baudelaire's century. Since then the cultural radical Herbert Marcuse has used the same passage as "the definition of progress beyond the rule of the performance principle."[2] It is of secondary importance that Eliot's eye was caught by the word "sin" and not the word "diminution," even though this bias led to perverse loyalties (especially to the writings of Charles Maurras, and Maurras's English imitator T. E. Hulme) which his mature style never quite escaped.

Eliot's remapping of the past helped authorize his famous question, still unanswered, in response to England's capitulation at Munich in 1938: "Was our society . . . assembled round anything more permanent than a congeries of banks, insurance companies, and industries, and had it any beliefs more essential than a belief in compound interest and the maintenance of dividends?" One need not be an Anglo-Catholic to share this cultural anxiety, which as Eliot noted was not a simple criticism of a government, but a doubt about the validity of a civilization (*ICS*, [1939], p. 64, *C&C*, p. 51). Skepticism on this profound cultural level requires credentials if it is to influence the future; Eliot had them.

There is nothing paradoxical or controversial in Eliot's simultaneous defense of liberalism as an attitude, and his critique of it as an ideology. Skepticism and criticism, desirable in themselves, are in Eliot's view not stable elements of a society, but "transitional" products of religious deliquescence, which lead, if not counterbalanced by an affirmative faith, to their opposite, totalitarianism. This conservative version of the Frankfort School's "dialectic of Enlightenment" helps explain why Eliot's thinking proved so compatible with Karl Mannheim's. But Eliot's personal affirmation of a Christian orthodoxy may prove less influential than his critiques, not only of liberalism, but of the alternatives put forth by others to it.

ELIOT'S INCLUSIVE AND EXCLUSIONARY PARADIGMS

To summarize Eliot's social thought is not easy, and his own polemical efforts to do so are singularly unhelpful. Eliot refines a tradition of cultural self-consciousness, peculiar to England, that derives from Coleridge, Arnold, and (in the realm of economics) Ruskin (all authors, like Eliot, whose legacy is greater than their readability). The chief importance of this tradition has been (as Mill observed of Coleridge) to reaffirm those permanent traditional, individual, and spiritual values which are threatened by materialist instrumental change and its Benthamite advocates. In this tradition Eliot was the first (at least since the self-taught Coleridge and Carlyle) to ground this cultural outlook in philosophical training, above all in the generative overviews of German idealism, chiefly Kant and Schiller, as mediated by the English philosopher F. H. Bradley.[3] Thus, though he owes much to the oppositional criticism of Arnold, Eliot continuously undermines Arnold's complacencies about religion, culture and "best self, or right reason" in the light of a more skeptical and pessimistic Bradleyan analysis. What Eliot particularly reproves is Arnold's "inconsistency," as opposed to "the unity of Bradley's thought" (*SE* [1951], pp. 452–53).

In an assessment of American humanism published in 1930, Eliot expressed his belief that the problem of the unification of the world and the problem of the unification of the individual were one and the same problem, the solution of one being the solution of the other:

> Analytical psychology . . . can do little except produce monsters; for it is attempting to produce unified individuals in a world without unity; the social, political, and economic sciences can do little, for they are attempting to produce the great society with an aggregation of human beings who are not units but merely bundles of incoherent impulses and beliefs.[4]

This little-known but thoughtful epitome of Eliot's deeply integrative vision, at once psychological and social, can provoke assent even from those alienated by his more sectarian views.

Great poets strive after integrative visions of totality. Eliot's vision of a unified world led him to oppose the liberal break-up of the medieval curriculum, with its displacement of theology and ethics by new "social sciences" less worthy of belief.[5] But Eliot's efforts to reintroduce ethics into social thought seem less controversial today than his efforts to visualize a social unity that achieves its cultural coherence by exclusion.

ELIOT, L'ACTION FRANÇAISE, AND FASCISM

Eliot's exclusionary "tradition" owed much to the "integral nationalism" of Charles Maurras and l'Action Française. At first Eliot's *Criterion* looked *outward* from English to European tradition and beyond it, to Hesse, Dostoievski, and Sanskrit.[6] By 1926 it had begun to sound, as *The New*

Criterion, increasingly polemical and sectarian. Eliot, committing the *Criterion* to "the idea of a common culture of western Europe," evoked the precedent of Maurras's *L'Avenir de l'intelligence*, and published an article by Henri Massis, "The Defence of the West," which explicitly attacked Hesse's "Asiaticism," his vision of spiritual renewal from Oriental chaos.[7] Eliot carefully dissociated himself from this statement of "the problem as it appears to a Frenchman"; and he pointedly balanced it with essays on Dostoievski, Hindu music, and Babbitt's derivations "from the humanistic Confucius in China and from the religious Buddha in India and the religious Jesus in Judea."[8] Nevertheless, by expanding his horizons to authorize the Maurrassian xenophobia of Massis – for example, the remark in "The Defence of the West" that "the Russian people have made almost no contribution to general civilisation" – Eliot had indicated his shift towards the factitious and restrictive Europeanism of *After Strange Gods*.

This restrictiveness had begun, in a veiled way, in "The Function of Criticism" (1924), with its sanitized echo of Maurras's (and his epigone Hulme's) oppositional "Classicism," their attack on romanticism as an internal enemy. People, he claimed, must give allegiance to something outside themselves. In politics they must profess allegiance to principles, or a form of government, or a monarch, and in religion to a church (*SE* [1951], pp. 25–27, 30). Eliot also praised the "Classicism" of Hulme's *Speculations*, which he called the forerunner of a new, reactionary and revolutionary, anti-democratic attitude of mind.[9]

Eliot read Maurras's seminal work, *L'Avenir de l'intelligence* (1904) in 1911, and he never wholly outgrew it. Maurras argued that the trappings of French Republican democracy had been a facade, behind which industrial and financial interests had vanquished the older landed and aristocratic classes; the spiritual authority of the church, meanwhile, had been destroyed. In all this the writers of the intelligentsia had been the losers. No longer writing for a critical and cultured audience, they were reduced to dependence (like Zola) on the whims of the masses, or else of those capitalists who hired them to write journalism for the newspapers. Maurras argued that the obscure struggles between political parties did nothing to alter the real location of power; only a nation united behind a monarchy could restore the balance of power between landed and bourgeois interests. And only in this equilibrium could the future independence of the intelligentsia be guaranteed.

In practice Eliot's efforts for a culturally integrated Europe brought the *Criterion* into alliance with critics of Maurras, such as the *Nouvelle Revue Française* of André Gide, Julien Benda, and Jacques Rivière, and in Germany the humanist and classicist scholar Ernst Robert Curtius.[10] Yet Eliot in 1927 wished to shock English complacency with a more alien stimulus that that of Rivière or Curtius, believing as he did that if anything, in a generation's time, would preserve us from a sentimental Anglo-Fascisim, it would be a system of ideas deriving from a study of Maurras.[11] Even so, Eliot's affinities within l'Action Française were less with the "integral nationalism" of Maurras than with Henri Massis's and Jacques Maritain's vision of a united, federal, Catholic Europe.

Eliot's problematic bias towards the lost cause best explains his quixotic defense of l'Action Française in 1928, after the controversial Papal condemnations of it in 1926–27. Seen in the context of his comments over forty years, Eliot's views of both Maurras and l'Action Française seem more conventional than critics have made them out to be. In 1919 Eliot criticized Maurras's "intemperate and fanatical spirit," and for this reason he conceded the criticism, made by Julien Benda in *Belphégor*, "that M. Maurras is a 'romantic'."[12] Like the Roman Church, Eliot also regretted Maurras's Comtian disposition "to regard politics as a 'science' independent of morals."[13]

Although Eliot has been accused of a "flirtation with fascism," in this respect he can be distinguished from less fastidious writers: Yeats, Pound, Lawrence, and Wyndham Lewis. Eliot never warmed to a movement that was (in his eyes) so demotic, chauvinist, anti-intellectual, intolerant, and ultimately pagan (see Kojecký, *T. S. Eliot's Social Criticism*, especially pp. 11–12, 90–102). Eliot reproved both fascism and communism for being too conventional: revolts against capitalism that merely accelerated its present slide into materialism.[14] Like all ambitions for an earthly paradise, Eliot argued, they had "low ideals and great expectations." A classical or catholic perspective, in contrast, should have absolute ideals and moderate expectations (*EAM*, p. 122). This political *doubleness*, or beholding of secular expectations from an outside, spiritual perspective (more Buddhist or Platonic perhaps than Christian), is central to Eliot's critique of liberalism as well. But there is no doubt that this reduces fascism and communism to the status of inadequate alternatives to an inadequate *status quo*, Eliot's fundamental objection to fascist doctrine being that it is pagan (*ICS* [1939], p. 20; *C&C*, p. 15).

AFTER STRANGE GODS: ANTI-SEMITISM AND INTOLERANCE

Ultimately what is reprehensible in Eliot's treatment of Maurras was his failure to address, let alone condemn, Maurras's virulent anti-Semitism. For Maurras's integral nationalism, and with it Pierre Lasserre's polarizing distinction between romanticism and classicism, had been born out of the anti-Semitic reaction against the *metèque* Dreyfus and his allies (Weber, *Action Française*, pp. 178–79, 198–201). The effective Maurrassian legacy was not the Catholicism which led in 1927 to a papal interdict, nor the royalism which led to a break in 1937 with the monarchist pretender: it was the anti-Semitic anti-Republicanism which led to the Vichy régime and its anti-Semitic legislation (Weber, *Action Française*, pp. 442–48). But there is no acknowledgment of this in Eliot's praise of Maurras, in 1953, for his monarchism, his sense of hierarchy, and the style of his "magistral pages" (Kojecký, *T. S. Eliot's Social Criticism*, p. 68). Eliot's clipped elegance ignored Maurras's invective against enemies like Léon Blum and his cabinet, invective larded with reference to "crooks, pederasts, traitors, prostitutes," which led to his conviction for incitement to murder (Weber, *Action Française*, pp. 374–75, 462–63, etc.).

Today Eliot's critics, such as Christopher Ricks, are coming to see how much more important than Eliot's royalism and alleged fascism are the issues raised by his conscious avowal and exploitation of prejudice. In his middle years Eliot acknowledged a certain acceptance of prejudice and dogma to define what a culture included and excluded, even as he professed to be even-handed about this. The world needed narrowness and fanaticism as well as breadth and tolerance (*SE* [1951], p. 488; cf. *NTDC* [New York, 1949], p. 81). For art was bound in a special way to prejudice, the public predisposition to respond predictably to the artist's stimuli.[15] His need to exploit, as well as confront, this disposition explains his willingness to be "untolerated, intolerant, and intolerable."[16]

Ricks is brilliant in situating Eliot's anti-Semitism; but there is the risk of getting lost among his Empsonian discriminations. One welcomes his response, "This is shameful," to *The Criterion*'s dismissal of an early exposé of Nazi anti-Semitic persecutions as "an attempt to rouse moral indignation by means of sensationalism."[17] Here Eliot, like the culture he had adopted, was participating in processes of rationalization and denial, for which we may better seek psychological than logical explanations. But one cannot in this space resolve the issues raised by Eliot's intolerances. The reader is best advised to read both A. D. Moody's dispassionate examination of Eliot's "alleged anti-Semitism," and Cynthia Ozick's disillusioned argument that "it is now our unsparing obligation to disclaim the reactionary Eliot."[18]

The clearest instance of Eliot's anti-Semitism, and one for which there is no parallel elsewhere in his social criticism, is his notorious effort, in *After Strange Gods*, to visualize a positive alternative to our society, "worm-eaten with Liberalism:"

You are hardly likely to develop tradition except where the bulk of the population is relatively so well off where it is that it has no incentive or pressure to move about. The population should be homogeneous; where two or more cultures exist in the same place they are likely either to be fiercely self-conscious or both to become adulterate. What is still more important is unity of religious background; and reasons of race and religion combine to make any large numbers of free-thinking Jews undesirable. There must be a proper balance between urban and rural, industrial and agricultural development. And a spirit of excessive tolerance is to be deprecated.

(*ASG* [London], pp. 19–20)

Not the least controversial aspect of this remark was its timing. Delivered in spring 1933 at the University of Virginia, it was published in February 1934, while Hitler's boycott of Jewish shops had already been proclaimed in April 1933. The Maurrassian and exclusionary fear of racial contamination that Eliot reveals in this passage also underlay his view of tradition as something almost effaced by the influx of "foreign populations" (*ASG* [London], p. 15). His Virginian audience, he claimed, had a better chance to re-establish a native culture than would, for example, a New York industrialized and invaded by foreign races (*ASG* [London], p. 16). The ironies of this spurious nativism seem to have escaped this migrant scion of migrants.[19]

The subtitle of *After Strange Gods, A Primer of Modern Heresy*, can be seen as Eliot's response to Pound's Cavalcanti essay of 1931–32, where Pound, as if to needle Eliot, had praised Cavalcanti's "natural" freedom of thought, and attacked Dante's "theocentric" willingness "to take on any sort of holy and orthodox furniture."[20] Eliot in turn criticized Pound for preferring Cavalcanti *because* "Guido was very likely a heretic" (*ASG* [London], p. 42). Eliot's cure for heresy was the supervision of what he called orthodoxy, not through clerical censorship, but from the influence of "the Church itself, in which orthodoxy resides" (*ASG* [London], p. 32). Despite this appeal to Catholic language, Eliot, as much as Dante or Milton, trusted in his own reading of texts rather than another's. In the next few years Eliot would find himself asserting his private "orthodoxy" against the communal wisdom of the English established church.[21]

The problems of *After Strange Gods* were not just theological but affective: deriving from not just Eliot's heterodoxy but, in a time of personal and collective crisis, his lack of charity. In lines partly quoted by Eliot (*SE* [1951], p. 259), Dante challenged, in *Purgatorio* 16, the doctrine of Original Sin which for a while was Eliot's obsession; and by placing Joachim of Flora among the doctors of the Fifth Heaven he hinted at the future Earthly Paradise Eliot so dogmatically renounced. But Eliot does not mention Dante's central inspiration: the spiritual potential of human beauty and love.

After Strange Gods, the most pathological of Eliot's prose works, is also in some ways the most revealing. If Eliot could say of Babbitt that he seemed "to tear himself from his own context," and was in that act a product of "Protestant theology in its last agonies" (*SE* [1951], p. 475), the same assuredly was true of Eliot himself, in the act of appealing to a disembodied "orthodoxy" which no one else believed in. It is this very Miltonic alienation that makes Eliot a writer for us and for the future. But in his social books, we see Eliot's futile efforts to disguise this, his extreme individualism, even from himself.

After the war and the revelations about the Holocaust, Eliot regretted "the tone and content," of *After Strange Gods*, and refused to allow it to be reprinted.[22] At the same time, he never chose to recant his remarks about free-thinking Jews unambiguously in public. For the problem lay not in the sentence about Jews, but in his construction of a positive Christian society built about religious unity, and threatened by the invasions of foreign races. This he never recanted, returning in his major books about politics and culture to the same recipe for unity and permanence: a positive culture with a positive set of values, in which dissentients remained marginal (*ICS* [London], p. 46; *C&C*, p. 36).

After the small-mindedness of *After Strange Gods*, it is remarkable that Eliot could have so swiftly written *The Use of Poetry and the Use of Criticism*, perhaps his most balanced book-length prose, and perhaps also his most sustained and successful example of cultural politics. In it the inclusive paradigm prevails, as when he wrote that cultural interaction was a condition of vitality in literature (*UPUC* [London], p. 152). Eliot was talking here about the interaction between poetry and prose, but we can extend the argument to cover his insightful dictum about Wordsworth's social interest inspiring his novelty of form in verse (*UPUC* [London], p. 74). He interprets the stylistic innovations of Wordsworth's *Lyrical Ballads* as an act, not of self-expression, but of cultural reintegration and renewal, a healing of the "splitting up of personality" which he sees in the history of English poetry (*UPUC* [London], pp. 84–85).

The critic Michael North has noted how this goal of cultural reintegration is one shared by his *semblable* Georg Lukács, and how one can only work for this goal "through modernism, through what Habermas calls 'the subversive force of modern thought itself'."[23] He points to Eliot's praise of Joyce's mythical method as a destructive step toward the "order and form" that is "so earnestly desired." He might as well have cited Eliot's grudging advancement of Shelley's "kinetic or revolutionary theory of poetry": Shelley's argument that beneficial change occurs in periods where "there is an accumulation of the power of communicating and receiving intense and impassioned conceptions" (*UPUC* [London], pp. 94–95; cf. 75). Here is illustrated the strength of Eliot's cultural critique, just as his efforts to espouse royalism illustrate its weakness.

THE FAILURE OF ELIOT'S OPPOSITIONAL ROYALISM

In 1927, when Eliot proclaimed himself to be classicist, anglo-catholic, and royalist, he intended these terms to be provocatively oppositional in a French manner. The problem was that the English monarchy and established church were not just, as in France, symbols of a past order overthrown; they were now external trappings for those powers "with which we must all reckon, the Chancellor of the Exchequer and the Bank of England" (*SE* [1951], p. 382). Eliot's response at first was to challenge the English Revolution of 1688 as Maurras had the French Revolution of 1789; but this attempt falsified his search for a catholic *via media*.

We see this in his instructive efforts to make of the Stuart apologists Bramhall and Bolingbroke something they were not, proponents of a communitarian as opposed to personal royal power. Eliot's essay of 1927 on Archbishop John Bramhall, Primate of Ireland under Charles II, offered Bramhall's political thinking as "a perfect example of the pursuit of the *via media* . . . of all ways the most difficult to follow":

> Bramhall affirmed the divine right of kings: Hobbes rejected this noble faith, and asserted in effect the divine right of power, however come by . . . To Bramhall the king himself was a kind of symbol, and his assertion of divine right was a way of laying upon the king a double responsibility. It meant that the king had not merely a civil but a religious obligation toward his people . . . Bramhall . . . obviously leaves a wide expedient margin for resistance or justified rebellion.　　　　　　　　　　　　　　　　　　　(*SE* [1951], p. 360)

Unfortunately Bramhall's notion of divine right left no such margin at all, as Bolingbroke had recognized. Eliot's nostalgia for a *via media* was in fact Hookerite rather than Jacobean, and he soon modified his views accordingly. By 1931, after a brief espousal of Bolingbroke, Eliot had come to focus on the Church, rather than the Monarchy, as the anchor of principled tradition: "Unless Toryism maintains a definite and uncompromising theory of Church and State, Toryism is merely a fasces of expedients."[24]

This shift reflected Eliot's increasing participation in the Chandos Group of so-called Christian sociologists. In a book, *Coal*, they had seen in the economic crisis a need for spiritual discipline and Church intervention against the materialism of the prevailing political establishment.[25] Reviewing the book in 1927, Eliot had commented: "If the Church is to do what they want, it must have more power, and if it is to be strengthened, then the Kingship must be strengthened."[26] By 1934, inverting the relationship, Eliot wrote that the royalist "can admit only one higher authority than the Throne, which is the Church." He added that "devotion to the Throne (as distinct from personal devotion to a popular King) may act as a check and balance upon devotion to the party, the party leader, or the State."[27] Here Eliot moves away from Bramhall's divine right of a king, and towards the check and balance of a throne, as became even clearer after the Abdication Crisis of 1936. In that crisis Eliot sided with the Church, and his friends in the Chandos Group, against the King and his Social Credit supporters, some of them also Eliot's friends. After thus supporting the Church against the monarch, Eliot fell tactfully silent about either Bramhall's divine right or Bolingbroke's Patriot King.[28]

Thus it is no accident that the *Idea of a Christian Society*, his effort at a positive political ideal, should be silent on the subject of King and Kingship. Already in 1930 he was writing that the Jacobean-Caroline period was on all sides "an age of lost causes . . . and impossible loyalties"; both Milton and King Charles the "Martyr" expressed modes of life ennobled by the experience of failure.[29] The following lines from *Little Gidding* celebrate the reconciliation in defeat of Charles and Milton (the latter much more Eliot's cultural precursor):

> We have taken from the defeated
> What they had to leave us – a symbol:
> A symbol perfected in death.

Thus to contemplate Kingship is not to engineer change but to establish perspective on the present: as he wrote, not faith in life but faith in death is what matters.

THE RETURN TO A *VIA MEDIA*: IDEALIZING SOCIETY, DEFINING CULTURE

Many factors combined, in the later 1930s, to force Eliot towards political moderation as others became more extreme. He now faced the clear enemy of fascism itself. Above all, Eliot had finally found a community and readership where political ideas could be shared and moderated, not merely flung out as provocations. His service on the church discussion forum, "The Moot," helped to temper his social criticism, to make it more considered and even charitable.

The discussions in the Moot produced Eliot's two major books of social criticism (*Idea of a Christian Society* and *Notes Towards the Definition of*

Culture). These are valuable less as paradigms (or notes towards them) than as processes (influenced by F. H. Bradley) of mental exploration. In Roger Kojecký's book we have a summary of the Moot debates which gave rise to them, and which continued from 1938 to 1947. There Eliot was in extended and intimate dialogue with thinkers like the Roman Catholic Christopher Dawson (whose "totalitarian Christian order" Eliot found lacking in local distinctions), the Christian pacifist John Middleton Murry, and the *émigré* German sociologist Karl Mannheim. Mannheim's ideas of utopia, intelligentsia, and élites provide a generative sub-text to Eliot's two books, but Eliot and the Moot also convinced Mannheim, a free-thinking Jew, that "Christianity could play an important role in shaping the communal consensus necessary for the survival of democratic society."[30]

It is important in these books to distinguish between what we might call their diagnostic and their prescriptive cultural judgments. The latter continue, as in *After Strange Gods*, to be exclusionary: they still aim (though more tactfully than in *After Strange Gods*) at a unified society and culture where "the great majority of the sheep belong to one fold" (*ICS* [1939], p. 46; *C&C*, p. 37). But *The Idea of a Christian Society* is memorable not for its prescriptions but for its critique: of "mass society organised for profit" (*ICS* [1939], p. 39; *C&C*, p. 32), with the consequences of unregulated industrialism, "the exploitation of the earth," and "a wrong attitude toward nature":

> a good deal of our material progress is a progress for which succeeding generations may have to pay dearly . . . For a long enough time we have believed in nothing but the values arising in a mechanised, commercialised, urbanised way of life: it would be as well for us to face the permanent conditions upon which God allows us to live upon this planet. And without sentimentalising the life of the savage, we might practise the humility to observe, in some of the societies upon which we look down as primitive or backward, the operation of a social-religious-artistic complex which we should emulate upon a higher plane. (*ICS* [1939], pp. 61–62; *C&C*, pp. 48–49)

The worth of this passage lies less in its single insights and sentences, than in its mental process of integration towards a coherent overview. (I remember the almost shocked derision when, in a political science symposium of the early fifties, I endorsed Eliot's notion that we could learn from the cultural coherence and ecological balance of small-scale societies. That notion, still unfashionable then, is so no longer, thanks partly to Eliot and later poets.)

The humility and self-doubt of the *Idea* is consistent with the tone of reconciliation, and the subordination of the historical to the permanent, in *Little Gidding*, published one year later. Eliot's Quartets, which A. D. Moody has persuasively called Eliot's "true political testament," are also his most fully Christian poetry. It is thus significant that they acknowledge, as much as or even more than *The Waste Land*, the Eurasian commonality behind our culture, from *Burnt Norton*'s vision of the lotos to *The Dry Salvages*' meditations on the *Bhagavad Gita*. Eliot has at last glimpsed the possibility of a cultural perspective that would allow him to be doctrinal (and even take issue with the humanism of Sir Thomas Elyot) without being exclusionary.

One can imagine his having reached the same high reconciliation in his social criticism, but his last prose books seem to fall just short of doing so. In the *Idea* he wrote that no one could now defend the idea of a National Church (a Maurrassian term), without balancing it with the idea of the Universal Church, "keeping in mind that truth is one and that theology has no frontiers" (*ICS* [1939], p. 53; *C&C*, p. 43). But whatever the implications of that last clause, Eliot had apparently renounced them in the *Notes*:

> A world culture which was simply a *uniform* culture would be no culture at all. We should have a humanity de-humanised. But on the other hand, we cannot resign the idea of a world-culture altogether . . . We are therefore pressed to maintain the ideal of a world culture, while admitting that it is something we cannot *imagine*. We can only conceive it, as the logical term of relations between cultures. (*NTDC* [New York], p. 62; *C&C*, p. 136)

This seems strangely inverted. As a poet, Eliot had already helped imagine "the ideal of a world culture"; it was as a critic that he failed to conceptualize it.

Notes Towards the Definition of Culture is unfortunately the record of that failure: in some ways a more generative book than *The Idea of a Christian Society*, it is also less satisfying. The distinction Eliot tried to clarify was the intractable one between culture in the anthropological sense, an empirical fact transcending conscious direction or amendment, and the more normative high culture, not distinct from the first but growing out of it, which he wished to promote. These two senses of culture became three, when he recognized the importance of an intermediate level, both normal and artificial (i.e. educated) in which high culture was embedded. That such recognitions of continuity make definition difficult cannot be regarded as Eliot's fault or failure. But the book swiftly became much more controversial.

At its heart is an extended dialogue with Karl Mannheim's argument that what they both see as a cultural crisis in liberal-democratic society (*NTDC* [New York], p. 37; *C&C*, p. 111) can be eased by the progressive replacement of hereditary classes by achievement-selected élites. Eliot argues that this solution does not adequately address the problem of "the *transmission of culture*" (*NTDC* [New York], p. 39; *C&C*, p. 113), since the family remained the most important channel of such transmission (*NTDC* [New York], p. 42; *C&C*, p. 116). A larger issue is the failure of separately recruited and trained élites to guarantee a unified culture that is more than the sum of several activities: that is a *"way of life"* (*NTDC* [New York], p. 40; *C&C*, p. 114). In his 1944 essay "On the Place and Function of the Clerisy," he followed Coleridge in attributing this role to an élite *clerisy*, defined as "at the top, those individuals who originate the dominant ideas, and alter the sensibility, of their time" (including, therefore, some painters, musicians, and writers).[31] Though not the exclusive transmitters of culture, such authors, writing for a small public, are a necessary ingredient: "the clerisy writing for the clerisy." In the *Notes* all reference to such a democratic clerisy has been eliminated. Instead, producers of culture are distinguished from *"the* élite, the major part of which was drawn from the dominant class of the time" (*NTDC* [New York], p. 40; *C&C*, p. 114), whose function it is, "in relation to the producers, to transmit the culture which they have inherited" (*NTDC* [New York], p. 41; *C&C*, p. 115). It is a pity that, in the one book explicitly addressed to the problem of culture, we should find so little of Eliot's cultural *critique*.

It is possible that Eliot's destructive explorations of fascism, and of the similarities between capitalism and communism, may have helped spare England the hard-edged intellectual antagonisms of the continent. His work for European dialogue as an editor, introducing England to other Europe-minded thinkers like Jacques Rivière, Max Scheler, Paul Valéry, Henri Massis, Jacques Maritain, and E. R. Curtius, helped prepare for the post-war European mentality of academic Comparative Literature and the Congress for Cultural Freedom. Herein lies Eliot's achievement and also his limitation: his chief influence was on the academic and cultural establishments he once mistrusted.

But Eliot's political modesty and self-restraint should be counted among his positive achievements. His quest for sanity, and his partial achievement of it, should not be slighted in a century so bent on nightmares. Today the search to integrate eastern and western perspectives is an on-going project to which Eliot's art and social criticism still contribute, when we focus on the lotos and the heart of light, not just on the local embodiment of a parochial established Christianity. At a still higher level of abstraction, cultural thinking now seeks like Eliot to reconcile the values of small-scale and developed cultures, and to achieve the right balance between nature and the city. His perceptions, and above all his unifying perspectives, will be especially meaningful to the increasing world of those who are, like himself, border-crossing migrants.

However we read him, for better or for worse, Eliot has clearly taken his place among those authors whose cultural politics have sought to subordinate secular aberrations to a vision of more enduring values.

NOTES

1 "Cultural politics," as I here define it (the oppositional use of canonical texts against entrenched temporal authority) should be understood as the effort to subordinate temporal politics to the *desiderata* of culture. This must be contrasted with the exactly opposite phenomenon: subordinating the literary canon to review and political correction by the prevailing standards of temporal politics. The distinction may sometimes be difficult to maintain in practice; but it was important to Eliot (when he was not confused by his own temporal prejudices). It could even be said that the attempt to clarify and give weight to this distinction underlay Eliot's major social and cultural criticism.

2 Herbert Marcuse, *Eros and Civilization* (Boston: Beacon, 1955), p. 153. Cf. Virgil's Fourth Eclogue: *sceleris vestigia nostri . . . solvent.*

3 Eliot confirmed to me orally in 1956 that he had read or been exposed to Schiller, possibly in the volume *Idee und Gestalt* by Ernst Cassirer (Berlin: G. Cassirer, 1924).

4 T. S. Eliot, "Religion Without Humanism," Norman Foerster (ed.) *Humanism and America* (New York: 1930), p. 112. Cf. *EAM*, p. 123.

5 *EAM*, p. 117. Eliot once retorted that "Economics *is* a science, in the humane sense; but it will never take its due place until it recognizes the superior 'scientific' authority of Ethics" ("A Commentary," *Criterion* 10.39 (January 1931): 310–11).

6 *Criterion*, 1.4 (July 1923): 421. Meanwhile, to intensify *The Waste Land*'s allusion to the turmoil in Eastern Europe, Eliot added a footnoted quotation from Hesse's *Blick ins Chaos* (*A Glance at Chaos*, 1920), a book he found so "serious" he approached Hesse about excerpting it in the first issue of *The Criterion* (*Letters* I, 509–10). Hesse's book, a series of Nietzschean meditations on Dostoievski, saw in the minds of heroes like Prince Myshkin an "acceptance of chaos" and "return to the incoherent, to the unconscious, to the formless, to the animal and far beyond the animal to the beginning of all things." Dostoievski's "Asiatic ideal" or "a return to the mother, to the sources," was viewed affirmatively by Hesse, as a return from culture to nature that "will lead like every earthly death to a new birth" (Hermann Hesse, *Blick ins Chaos* [Bern: Seldwylda, 1920], pp. 92, 71, 79; quoted in Eugene Stelzig, *Hermann Hesse's Fictions of the Self* [Princeton, NJ: Princeton University Press, 1988], pp. 152–53).

7 *Criterion* 4.2 (April 1926): 224–43; 4.3 (June 1926): 476–93.

8 *Criterion* 4.2 (April 1926): 222; 4.3 (June 1926): 552, 538, 501.

9 "A Commentary," *Criterion* 2.7 (April 1924): 231.

10 Ernst Robert Curtius, "Restoration of the Reason," *Criterion* 6.5 (November 1927): 397.

11 T. S. Eliot, "The *Action Française*, Maurras, and Mr. Ward," *Criterion* 7.3 (March 1928): 196–97.

12 *Athenaeum*, 4657 (August 1, 1919): 681; *T.L.S.*, 980 (October 28, 1920): 703; reprinted in *Letters* I, p. 416.

13 "The Literature of Fascism," *Criterion* 8.31 (December 1928): 290.

14 "Mr. Barnes and Mr. Rowse," *Criterion* 8.33 (July 1929): 683, 690.

15 *The Athenaeum*, May 14, 1920; cf. *SW* (1928), p. 64; Ricks, *T. S. Eliot*, p. 36.

16 *Listener*, April 6, 1932; quoted in Ricks, *T. S. Eliot*, p. 52. Cf. *EAM*, p. 129: "I think that the virtue of tolerance is greatly overestimated, and I have no objection to being called a bigot myself."

17 Ricks, *T. S. Eliot*, p. 51; *Criterion* 15 (1936): 759–60. The authorship of the *Criterion*'s note is uncertain, but Eliot must be held responsible for its publication.

18 Moody, *Thomas Stearns Eliot*, pp. 354–56 [1980 edn., pp. 370–72]; Cynthia Ozick, "T. S. Eliot at 101," *New Yorker*, November 20, 1989, p. 154.

19 Jews had of course arrived in Europe before the Christians, and in America before the Eliots.

20 Pound, *Literary Essays*, T. S. Eliot (ed.) (London: Faber and Faber, 1954), pp. 158–59; discussion in P. D. Scott, "Pound in 'The Waste Land'; Eliot in *The Cantos*," *Paideuma* (Winter 1990): 99–114.

21 In 1943 Eliot attacked his Church's proposal for a union of South Indian churches as a "mass movement of licentious oecumenicity." By objecting to one church's refusal to believe in the damnation of unbaptized infants, Eliot aligned himself with a splinter group of Old Believers as isolated in their defiant heterodoxy as Milton had been. See *Reunion by Destruction* (London: Council for the Defence of Church Principles on the proposed Church of South India, 1953), p. 19; Kojecký, *T. S. Eliot's Social Criticism*, p. 209.

22 For Eliot's apologies as to "tone," see Ricks, *T. S. Eliot*, p. 47; Moody, *Thomas Stearns Eliot*, pp. 335/371. The record is so defective as to compound the problem. As Moody has shown, he tinkered with a footnote in *Notes Towards the Definition of Culture* to approve (in the 1962 edition) of "close culture-contact between devout and practising Christians and between devout and practising Jews" (*NTDC* [New York], pp. 69–70; quoted in Moody, *Thomas Stearns Eliot*, p. 355/371). This grudging *pentimiento* never made it into the American edition (*C&C*, p. 144).

23 Michael North, "Eliot, Lukács, and the Politics of Modernism," Ronald Bush (ed.) *T. S. Eliot: The Modernist in History* (Cambridge: Cambridge University Press, 1991), p. 175.

24 "A Commentary," *Criterion* 11.42 (October 1931): 68–69.

25 Alan Porter, V. A. Demant, *et al.*, *Coal: a Challenge to the National Conscience* (London, 1927); Kojecký, *T. S. Eliot's Social Criticism*, pp. 79–80.

26 T. S. Eliot, "Political Theorists," *Criterion* 6.1 (July 1927): 73.

27 "A Commentary," *Criterion* 13.53 (July 1934): 629.

28 "Mr. Reckitt, Mr. Tomlin, and the Crisis," *New English Weekly*, February 25, 1937, p. 392. In this essay, Bolingbroke, once praised by Eliot, was now dismissed as an "eighteenth century writer whose notions about the Kingship were not complicated by religious orthodoxy."

29 "The Minor Metaphysicals: From Cowley to Dryden," *The Listener* 3, 66 (April 16, 1930): 641.

30 Colin Loader, *The Intellectual Development of Karl Mannheim* (Cambridge: Cambridge University Press, 1985), p. 158.
31 T. S. Eliot, *The Idea of a Christian Society and Other Writings* (London: Faber and Faber, 1982), pp. 159–67 (p. 162); reprinted also in Kojecký, *T. S. Eliot's Social Criticism*, pp. 240–48 (p. 243).

WORKS CITED

Kojecký, Roger. *T. S. Eliot's Social Criticism*. London: Faber and Faber, 1971.
Moody, A. D. *Thomas Stearns Eliot: Poet*. Cambridge: Cambridge University Press, 1979, 1980.
Ricks, Christopher. *T. S. Eliot and Prejudice*. London: Faber, 1988.
Weber, Eugen. *Action Française: Royalism and Reaction in Twentieth-Century France*. Stanford: Stanford University Press, 1962.

6

CLEO McNELLY KEARNS

Religion, literature, and society in the work of T. S. Eliot

By the time in which T. S. Eliot wrote, religion, literature and society in western culture had already, he knew, shared a long and ambivalent history. Often, literature had been a medium of critical support for such Judeo-Christian religious doctrines as creation, covenant, exile, incarnation and redemption, and a source of relative stability for various moral and social orders based on their premises. This "easy and natural" association between religion, literature and society, Eliot argued, had happened when society was moderately healthy and its various discourses in some relation with one another, though necessarily not always perfectly harmonious. Just as often, however, or so it seemed, literature had been either a monolithic reflection or a mode of subversion of society and religion, as each discourse set up its own creative and prophetic energies over and against the others, vying for a totalizing hegemony on its own terms (*SE* [1950], p. 390; *NTDC* [New York], pp. 67–69).

Eliot felt keenly the value of the rare moments of "easy and natural" association between literature, religion, and society (though he noted that "many of the most remarkable achievements of culture" had been made "in conditions of disunity" [*NTDC* [New York], p. 71]); and he spoke with eloquence of their combination of underlying order and deliberate if controlled cultivation of differences in point of view. As Eliot recognized, the maintenance of these differences made for cultural strength; just as their collapse into one totalizing discourse made for one-dimensionality, and their proliferation into a congeries of special interests for disintegration. He also felt, however, the difficulty of realizing the ideal of a harmonious but multivalent culture, especially in the midst of the "immense panorama of futility and anarchy" which was, for him, contemporary history.[1] The more dissolute ages of the West, including his own, were, he found, marked either by "chimerical attempts" to make art, religion, morals, culture and society synonymous, or by the isolation of each discourse to the point where it could have no bearing whatever on the others. "The alliances," Eliot insisted, "were as detrimental all round as the separations" (*SE* [1950], p. 393).

When he dealt with these and similar issues, Eliot wrote consciously as a representative, partisan, poet and critic of the West, and later, after his conversion in 1927, as a practicing Christian. He also wrote, however, with a sense of the similar problems affecting other religious and cultural traditions as well. As he said in "The Function of Criticism," he thought of the literature of the world, of its subset the literature of Europe, and of its further subset the literature of England, "not as a collection of the writings of individuals, but as . . . systems in relation to which, and only in relation to which, individual works of literary art, and the works of individual artists, have their significance" (*SE* [1950], pp. 12–13). These systems were, he saw, interdependent, and all were increasingly under threat, not only from wars, unregulated market forces and the "crudities of industrialism" (*SE* [1950], p. 383), but perhaps even more from dissolution and anarchy. When he dealt with issues of religion, literature and society, then, it was with a full awareness of their gravity and extent, which entailed the fate of peoples and nations as well as that of individual souls.

Because of this awareness of the fragility of cultures, Eliot felt the obligations not only of poets, who must reclaim, regenerate and transform these cultures, but of critics, who must evaluate, theorize, disseminate and transmit the results. In his paired essays, "Tradition and the Individual Talent" (1919) and "The Function of Criticism" (1923), Eliot laid down what he saw as the principles and operations of this task, and established the parallels as well as distinctions between the poet and critic they entailed. In general, he insisted that all writers must recognize something outside themselves to which they owed "allegiance" and "devotion," something in the light of which sacrifices of idiosyncracy, personality, and ideology might with justification be made. This "something outside" might be nebulous, at least for poets; it might indeed be no more than a vague sense of the exigencies of craft and the need for adequacy to a certain compelling vision. For critics, however, the nature of these allegiances must be explicit, both in order to maintain the distinctions – no longer self-evident – of particular cultural and religious points of view and in order to enable further debate and adjudication of their claims (*SE* [1950], pp. 3–12).

Eliot did not scant or evade the issues of judgment at stake here, nor did he pretend, against a tide of evidence, that all the resulting extended points of view could be of equal merit. While he affirmed the necessity and value of a number of competing perspectives, he did not think that these could stay forever within limits carefully designed to avoid either contact or conflict with one another. For, in order to make the kinds of claim on "allegiance" or "devotion" necessary for the preservation of a unified sensibility, each point of view had to make some pretense, at least, to an extended field of application. In doing so it had necessarily to raise broader questions, including questions of belief. While the answers to such questions must, Eliot insisted, be proximate, the questions themselves must be ultimate, and an awareness of both necessities was essential to keeping the frontiers of criticism open, permeable and yet clearly defined (*KE*, pp. 163–64; *PP* [New York], pp. 113–34).

To give only one example of the kind of criticism Eliot had in mind, Walter Pater's doctrine of art for art's sake drew his attention because it was a doctrine of ethics as well as of aesthetics. Indeed, in its own domain alone it was remarkably weak, expressing either a truism (writers must be committed to their craft) or else a patent falsehood (readers must read only for aesthetic effect). The minute it became a statement about life, however, Pater's doctrine gained a cogency that at least lent it a certain dignity (*SE* [1950], pp. 388, 392). Eliot wished, of course, both to contest this doctrine and to demote its influence, just as he wished to do with that of the apparently opposed Matthew Arnold. He was enabled to do so, however, precisely because of the extended and generous terms of his predecessors' arguments; these at least brought ultimate questions into view. The opportunity to take up and differ from a preceding position in matters cultural and even cosmic made, in Eliot's view, for a living as opposed to a dead tradition. Without it, neither literature nor religion nor society could flourish, either on their own terms or with relevance for one another.

A sense of the necessity for tackling overwhelming questions even where the answers must be proximate informed not only Eliot's study of Arnold and Pater, but his treatment of many other poets and writers as well, including Donne, Herbert, Milton, Pascal, Blake, and Baudelaire. He dealt not only with the respective philosophies, psychologies and techniques manifested by these writers but with their relations of value to one another. Eliot assessed with acuity, for instance, the aesthetic genius of Donne, but he also contrasted him critically with Lancelot Andrewes in terms of their relative usefulness as resources on which cultures and individuals might build (*SE* [1950], p. 302). Hence, too, he remarked on the running contrast between such catholic and cosmopolitan Europeans as Dante and Lucretius, who could draw imaginatively on a wide range of fully formulated doctrinal and ethical traditions in their work, and such narrower and more parochial figures as Blake and Milton, great in their own ways, but cut off by religious divides and sectarian allegiances from the wider resources of thought and tradition by which they might have been nourished.[2]

In more general studies, Eliot tried to articulate his own theory of the distinct but related connections between literature, religion and society, and to develop a cultural criticism equal to its demands. In such essays, lectures and books as The Clark Lectures, *After Strange Gods*, "Thoughts After Lambeth," "Religion and Literature," and *Notes Towards the Definition of Culture*, Eliot struggled again and again with the difficult intersections between knowledge and experience, dogma and literature, orthodoxy and feeling, skepticism and belief, without ever achieving a solution completely satisfactory to himself, much less to his readership.[3] His style was suave, his terms precise, and his tone judicious and restrained, but these virtues did not always conceal either the difficulty of the problems he faced or his own constant wrestle with words and meanings.

In dealing with these problems, Eliot could often sound deceptively magisterial. "Literary criticism should be completed by criticism from a definite ethical and theological standpoint," he pronounced firmly in his essay "Religion and Literature" (*SE* [1950], p. 343), echoing remarks already made in "The Function of Criticism" (*SE* [1950], p. 9) and made again in *After Strange Gods*. In fact, however, when he tried to spell out how such "completions" might occur without violation of either literary integrity, ethical and political obligation, engaged belief or the actual experience of reading, his answers were often far more nuanced and tentative than might at first appear. Hence, if he insisted, contra the aesthetes, that the greatness of literature could not be measured "solely" by literary standards, he also insisted that whether it *was* literature could be measured "only" by such standards (*SE* [1950], p. 343). Eliot also wavered back and forth on the question of the degree to which a belief shared with a writer – or the opposite, a dissenting position – would or should dictate a reader's response to a work, trying to examine his own readings of say, Dante, or Herbert, or the *Bhagavad-Gita* with these questions in mind (*SE* [1950], p. 230). He found that each situation required its own solution, but that one must at least begin by making an effort to pull back from a text with which one was in accord, and a corresponding but opposite effort to surrender to one with which one disagreed (*PP* [New York], p. 262).

Regardless of the changing state of his own personal beliefs, Eliot's basic framework for dealing with matters of religion, literature and society remained broadly sociological, anthropological and comparative (*NTDC* [New York], p. 69). Religion meant for him not just and not even primarily a system of beliefs but rather the sum total of the ritual, cultic, and related social practices of a given society, each of them in more or less functional relation to the others. Indeed, as Eliot put it in defining this and a number of related terms in his late work *Notes Towards the Definition of Culture*, "We may . . . ask whether what we call the culture, and what we call the religion, of a people are not different aspects of the same thing: the culture being, essentially, the incarnation (so to speak) of the religion of a people" (*NTDC* [New York], p. 27). This sociological definition, indebted among other things to his reading of Lévy-Bruhl, Frazer, Durkheim, and others, stood Eliot in good stead both as a poet and as a critic, opening his perspective to plural points of view, yet providing him with a strong stance from which to argue the integral and reciprocal roles of language, belief and culture. Belief, for Eliot, was a more specific and more limited term, related to religion as part to whole. It meant the more or less conscious and systematic set of views and doctrines held by individuals and shaped by their experiences in communities of interpretation, views and doctrines by which they supported, rationalized and reinforced their various faiths and commitments.

As he argued in his dissertation in philosophy, Eliot regarded all systems of belief as partial and subject to correction by other views; such systems, as he put it, are condemned to "go up like a rocket and come down like a stick" (*KE*, p. 168). Belief was accompanied for him, as Jeffrey Perl has argued, by a necessary skepticism, skepticism being "the habit of examining evidence and the capacity for delayed decision" (*NTDC* [New York], p. 28). The highest goal of the civilized being was, he once remarked, "to unite the profoundest scepticism with the deepest faith."[4] This habit he regarded as a sign of maturity, but in terms of cultural and of personal development, though taken to an extreme it could be self-defeating. "We need," he pointed out, "not only the strength to defer a decision but the strength to make one" (*NTDC* [New York], p. 28).

This skepticism, which extended to Judeo-Christian as well as distant, non-normative and/or esoteric traditions, prepared the way for Eliot's eventual conversion, conditioning on the one hand his rejection of mystical and esoteric paths to truths as a basis for belief, but also, on the other, his sense of the limitations of agnosticism as a way of dealing with the full range of human experience. Subject to moments of mystical illumination, Eliot was tutored enough in epistemology to find mysticism an inadequate basis for systematic beliefs; educated in democratic circles, he was cosmopolitan enough to grasp the possible value of religious and political hierarchy; and, endowed with a dark cast of mind, he was wise enough to see the necessity both for recognitions of futility and for affirmations of continued struggle against it.

The major principles of Eliot's thought were adumbrated in his postgraduate dissertation, a study of the late-idealist philosopher F. H. Bradley.[5] Bradley sought with considerable success and in a glittering, indeed coruscating style to deconstruct not only all claims for a correspondence theory of truth but even many for a coherence theory as well. In his own dissertation, Eliot demonstrated to his own satisfaction why this project was, by the simple extension of its own ineluctable logic, self-vitiating unless it terminated in some sort of an "act of faith." In undertaking this act, one passed, Eliot admitted, from a strictly philosophical to another type of discourse; one undertook a "pilgrimage," a "transmigration from one world to another" (*KE*, p. 162). Some such passage was, however, a necessity if one were to escape from the epistemological cul-de-sac into which Bradley's explorations had led.

Part of Eliot's critique of Bradley rested on his appreciation of a then recent trend in philosophy, the new realism of Bertrand Russell and G. E. Moore. Though he did not embrace its perspective unequivocally, the new realism offered Eliot the basis of a firm though qualified stress on the facticity of experience, and on the necessity of affirming or denying some moment of literal and experiential truth, however provisional, outside the perceiving mind. This moment, however, Eliot saw as changing the subsequent perceptions in such a way as to render impossible a return to a previous point of view for comparison and adjudication. "Facts" in the realist sense did not, Eliot argued, come out of the blue, but were themselves a construct and were correctly discerned only by intense cultivation of the mind. Once perceived, however, they altered the perspective forever, making a return to the state of belief before their perception inaccessible to objective comparison. While he did not use the term "fact" here in quite the uncritical sense it carried for others, neither did Eliot vaporize it into an ideal construct, mere symbol or projection of the believing mind. When it comes to some things, Eliot remarked in "The Function of Criticism," "if you find you have to imagine it as outside, then it is outside" (*SE* [1950], p.15).

The philosophical groundwork he laid down in *Knowledge and Experience* determined much of Eliot's approach not only to matters philosophical and to orthodox Judeo-Christian tradition, but to his thorough exploration of non-western and non-normative traditions and points of view as well. He had an extensive knowledge of eastern religions, especially Buddhism; several points of contact with the occult and with mysticism; and through his reading in anthropology a growing awareness of tribal cultures and the importance of their fast-vanishing legacies to world culture. Apparent to him, too, was the possibility of a kind of neo-paganism, a revival of the pagan gods that, like its Renaissance precursor, would be far deeper and more authentic than a mere donning of new fashions. Eliot saw that some such neo-pagan stance, especially when able to draw from anthropology and folklore on a much wider pantheon than the old Greek and Roman one, might offer considerable resources for a revitalized poetry, and he recognized the partial fulfillment of this possibility in such work as that of Pound, Yeats and to some extent even Lawrence, whose work he held in great respect as well as deep distrust (cf. *ASG, passim.*)

Buddhism attracted Eliot for its profound recognition of the pain inevitably associated with human desire, and its insistence that all merely personal self-identity is constructed upon lack, and has no essential subsistence except as a provisional, sometimes enabling, though often blinding illusion. This interest in Buddhism, especially intense during his years of graduate study and again about the time of writing *The Waste Land*, did not end with Eliot's formal conversion to Christianity in 1927, but persisted throughout his adult life and deeply colored his treatment of religious themes, dogmas and iconography in his plays and in *Four Quartets*. As late as *The Dry Salvages* Eliot was still musing on "what Krishna meant," and on the way in which "people smile and smile, but the agony abides" (*DS*, II). The use of the word *abide* in this line, so dark in its context, yet so deeply a part of Christian devotion and consolation (through the wide dissemination of the beloved hymn "Abide with Me") is characteristic of Eliot, for he often shadowed and sharpened Christian affirmations by means of this subtle and almost subliminal juxtaposition with a Buddhist negative way.

That Eliot did not "become" a Buddhist, a devotee of Robert Graves's pagan goddess, a Hindu or even (like Ezra Pound, Irving Babbitt, and I. A. Richards) a Confucian, was due to the pragmatism and sophistication with which, after his philosophical investigations, he tended to treat all such decisions. "After a year or two spent in the mazes of Patanjali's metaphysics," he remarked, speaking of one of the more major and more difficult Eastern texts, ". . . I came to the conclusion . . . that my only hope of penetrating to the heart of that mystery would lie in forgetting how to think and feel as an American or a European; which, for practical as well as sentimental reasons, I did not wish to do" (*ASG* [London], p. 34). The emphasis on the practical, cultural, and linguistic issues at stake in such matters of belief is typical of Eliot, as well as the suavity of tone with which he declined invitations which, had he accepted them, would have changed the direction of modern literature. Even after his decisions in these matters were essentially made, however, Eliot remained in some sense in touch with the possibilities he had forgone. *Four Quartets* for instance is in some respects a great poem of Buddhist wisdom, able to render extremely subtle concepts such as that of *sunyata* or divine emptiness in such memorable images as the lotos rising from the empty pool.

At a different and perhaps less intellectually engaged level, Eliot was also sensitive to occult and mystical resources for art though he treated these with the same philosophical caution evident in his dissertation. Susceptible himself to paranormal experiences and to accounts of them in such writers as Poe, Kipling and Yeats, Eliot could not help being attracted to a domain that might enrich his poetry and also account for much of his uncanny sense of the world, even while he was perfectly well able to debunk its cruder and more obscurantist manifestations. Madame Sosostris in *The Waste Land*, may have had a bad cold and an equivocal relation to her clients, but she could still produce a genuine frisson. Those who felt able to walk exclusively by their own internal lights Eliot attacked with a fiercely Buddhist astringency, noting that the proponents of The Inner Voice ride ten in a car to a football match, listening to "the Inner Voice," which breathes the eternal message of "vanity, fear and lust" (*SE* [1950], p., 16). Nevertheless, a genuine uncanniness and sense of esoteric illumination hovers over the "third who walks always beside you" in *The Waste Land*; and a later poem, *Little Gidding*, offers an unforgettable semi-esoteric encounter with a "compound ghost," part spiritual master, part deep self.

Eliot explored the writings of the famous mystics with more respect than those of the occultists, but with something of the same critical reserve. His undergraduate readings in William James's *Varieties of Religious Experience*, on which he took the careful notes that have provided so fascinating a record of his early interests, were supplemented throughout his life with studies of saints' lives and writings, devotional manuals and textbooks on meditation and contemplation, especially the work of St. John of the Cross.[6] Here again, the range of his reading was consistently cross-cultural; The Clark Lectures of 1926, for instance, make several allusions to the similarities and differences between western ways of illumination and those advanced by Patanjali, author of the Yoga-sutras. Eliot was later to mention both the studies of Abbé Brémond and those of the eccentric but interesting French practitioner of Zen, Hubert Benoit, as of particular interest (*PP* [New York], pp. 115–16; *UPUC* [London], pp. 137–40).

All of these readings and no doubt many experiences of his own lay behind the vivid renditions of mystical moments in Eliot's poetry, the moment in *The Waste Land* where "I could not / Speak" and "my eyes failed . . . / Looking into the heart of light, the silence" (I) or the climax of *Little Gidding* where "the fire and the rose are one" (V). Here again, however, Eliot saw a contradiction that made him unable to accept mysticism *tout court* as an adequate system of belief or even an ineluctable guide to life. As his university's prestigious philosopher Josiah Royce had long taught, the experience of mysticism cannot speak for itself; it requires interpretation and translation into more normative terms, and these must be evaluated upon rational criteria, bringing us, epistemologically speaking, back to square one. From inside the experience, a mystical intuition has one set of implications; from outside, another, and no one can remain on either side of this divide for long enough to establish an unassailable position. "We had the experience but missed the meaning," Eliot would later say in *Four Quartets*, "And approach to the meaning restores the experience / In a different form" (*DS*, II).

Eliot's awareness of tribal cultures, their religious sensibilities and their potential for art was also intense but critical, engaging him both at the intellectual and the emotional levels, but almost always with an awareness of countervailing points of view. Eliot's reading in anthropology provided him not simply with material for cross-cultural comparison but with the concrete details of cultic observances from which he constructed virtual worlds of belief and sensibility. If Eliot alluded powerfully to ritual sex, cannibalism, rain-making or the beat of a tribal drum in his poetry, he did so in part because his reading had led him to try out these forms of religious experience, metaphorically speaking, on his own pulse, not because he sought to "excite the membrane . . . with pungent sauces" or "multiply variety / In a wilderness of mirrors" ("Gerontion"). By undertaking a serious "suspension of belief" in the presuppositions of his own culture, and by regarding these other points of view as genuinely *possible*, Eliot was able to explore with authenticity and conviction worlds of otherness closed to many of his predecessors and contemporaries.

Although there were no doubt times when Eliot was tempted either to "go native" *à la* Conrad's Kurtz or to adopt a "scientific" or quasi-scientific attitude toward these worlds, he did not himself think that either approach was methodologically tenable for one in his position. As early as his graduate years, in a seminar on scientific method led by Josiah Royce, he had observed that the reasons for and functions of a fantasy or a religious myth, ritual, belief or practice were strictly speaking unknowable from a point of view either entirely outside or entirely within the experience. Arguing along the lines he had laid down in *Knowledge and Experience*, Eliot insisted that an insider's account of these phenomena would be blind in one way; an outsider's in another, and no certain third point of view could be established to adjudicate their claims. One could not know the real power of a rite unless one participated in it with full belief, and yet the immediacy of that participation and belief would alter the sensibility in ways from which there was no turning back, obviating both the question of prior origins and that of ultimate social function in the process.[7]

Because of his attraction to these mysteries coupled with his sense of the impossibility of penetrating them without a corresponding change in identity that would render their explanation in previous terms moot, Eliot's poetic explorations of anthropological material took often the form of caricature and parody, as well as of vivid rendition. To some extent, these literary modes helped Eliot handle and shape the horror, the "heart of darkness" he found at the core of all human social and moral experience. By the same token, however, it would not do to underestimate the pull on Eliot's imagination of other world-views unmediated either by scholarship, philosophical skepticism or modernist irony. He could capture like no one else, sometimes in a single phrase or cadence, a moment of alien cultic feeling, and capture it so vividly that it became the dark familiar of modes and moments closer to home. The "murmur of maternal lamentation" in *The Waste Land* (v), for instance, which was drawn from Eliot's reading about the fertility cult of Adonis, with its motifs of castration and female dereliction, resonates strongly against the poem's allusions to the sorrows of the women at the foot of the cross, creating a dissonant effect more reminiscent of Stravinsky than of a classical progression.

When it came to the resolution of such dissonances into tonic chords of full-scale affirmation or belief, Eliot was in his early years almost certainly an agnostic. His poetry and his reviewing of work in comparative religion and philosophy both give ample evidence of a profound resistance not only to occult, mystical, eastern, and tribal or neo-pagan points of view but to Christian faith as well. As Robert Crawford has pointed out, poems like "Mr. Eliot's Sunday Morning Service," "The Hippopotamus," "Whispers of Immortality" and even "Gerontion" express a radical distrust of modern religion, which seems to lack even the integrity and potency of its more sexually explicit and openly magical antecedents. In "Mr. Eliot's Sunday Morning Service," for instance, the feet of Christ are "pale," "thin," and "unoffending," which hardly allows them to compete for attention with the great hams of Sweeney, which bespeak a persistent, unreflecting violence and sexuality, having the virtue at least of unreflective being rather than Christian attenuation (Crawford, *Savage and the City*, 116–20). Likewise, one of the most powerful statements in the Christian scriptures, "In the beginning was the Word," is reduced by the poem's clever placement and control of tone to almost complete inanition, rather the ghost of revelation than an allusion to it.

In Eliot's more profound early poems, this resistance to Christianity gains force by modulating into a still skeptical but more deeply felt ambivalence. In such poems as "Gerontion," the incursions of Christ into the world, though powerful, are less healing than rending, a decadent but still disruptive form of ancient cannibalistic rituals in which body and blood are all too real, all too present. "Christ the tiger" comes in "depraved" May, "To be eaten, to be divided, to be drunk / Among whispers . . ." – "Us he devours," not we him. The close association and partial inversion of incarnation and eucharist in this poem is less syncretistic than disturbing, functioning not as a matrix for but as an obstacle to the affirmation of life and creativity which the original ritual was intended to instill. Though Eliot does not here entirely reduce a complex religion to a mere reflection or belated version of a primitive cult, he does by juxtaposition destabilize belief in either form of religious formation detached from awareness of its connections with the other.

Likewise in *The Waste Land* – which Eliot later denied was a statement of complete disillusion, though it was widely so read (*SE* [1950], p. 230) – the juxtaposition of modern and ancient, eastern and western, tribal and urban modes of incantation and sacrifice does not suggest the modulation of one into the other in an evolutionary scheme, but rather the transgressive and problematic nature of them all, as on every side, early and late, far and near, the limits of a humane rationality are left behind in the waste land of existential extremity. The poem does indeed hint at attempts to find affirmation and faith, if only by a kind of triangulation of cultural and individual moments of transcendence and revelation. The appearance of the ghostly "third who walks always beside you," half comforter, half projection of failing minds, is an example, for it lends itself easily to Christian typology through the Biblical story of the stranger on the road to Emmaus who turns out to be Christ. Yet the text of the poem itself by no means guarantees this interpretation; rather, it poses questions and suggests oblique and deferred answers, together with the recognition, more profound than either, that an ultimate resolution would change the terms of the whole debate.

A great deal of this ambivalence toward Christianity has its origins in Eliot's upbringing. His family were Unitarians, members of a Boston-based élite (though translated to St. Louis, where they felt they had a mission) with a long tradition of resistance to the more hierarchical and mystagogic forms of the religious life, as well as to the rebarbative dogmas and internecine quarrels of their Puritan and Calvinist forebears. Spiritual heirs of Emerson and Thoreau, these people had struggled hard for relief from the effects of such oppressive and divisive dogmas as original sin, hell and damnation, the nature and function of the trinity, and the literal truth of the incarnation. If they tended to substitute for theological precision a certain high-mindedness and for religious zeal a certain gentility, they did not do so without reason. Above all, Unitarians did not like the thought of bowing the knee, whether to Church or to State. "Do you kneel down in church and call yourself a miserable sinner?" wrote an Eliot aunt to a friend who had just become an Episcopalian. "Neither I nor my family will ever do that!" (cited Gordon, *Eliot's Early Years*, 126).

Eliot once remarked of his family's religion that he had been raised "outside the Christian Fold," where "The Son and the Holy Ghost were not believed in, certainly; but they were entitled to respect" (cited Crawford, *Savage and the City*, p. 73). In spite of its irenic intentions, this toothless form of religion, "full of high sentence, but a bit obtuse," did not appeal to him. Even the serious attempts of the philosopher Royce to reconstruct Christianity as a kind of useful communal myth struck him only as a method of "the last resuscitation of the dead."[8] Later, his temperamental aversion to liberal and revisionist religious views was strengthened by Harvard's anti-romantic Irving Babbitt, by the aesthetics of T. E. Hulme, and by the French intellectuals Charles Maurras, Julien Benda, and Paul Claudel, who placed a great value on the clarity and precise definition of classical theology even with respect to the deepest mysteries of faith. Eliot maintained the importance to him of these views even when he had later parted company with Babbitt, Maurras, and Benda on other grounds.

In spite of his recognition of the need for ritual, in spite of the opening his philosophical skepticism had left to belief, in spite of his admiration for the rigor and authority of classical theology, and even in spite of the affirmations to the brink of which the writing of *The Waste Land* had brought him, Eliot did not experience a quick, easy or automatic conversion to Christian faith. In his essay on Pascal, Eliot described the adult convert as proceeding largely by a process of rejection and elimination. He or she finds the world to be in a certain case, Eliot asserted, finds it inexplicable by any merely secular theory, and then finds in Christianity the most satisfactory account of reality, especially with regard to darkness of "the moral world within" (*SE* [1950], p. 360). We may take this rather programmatic version of the route to faith *cum grano salis*, especially from the lips of one who apparently astounded his family by falling to his knees before Michelangelo's *Pietà* (Gordon, *Eliot's Early Years*, p. 124). Nevertheless, there is no doubt that Eliot's Christianity was long meditated and perhaps even long deferred, and came in part as the result of having arrived at a very zero sum, in morals, in epistemology and in personal affairs as well.

The foundation of his final decision was then, for Eliot, less direct contact with the rock of ages than with a far more modern, more destabilized "ragged rock in the restless waters" (*DS*). He felt intensely the dark pre- and unconscious ironies of human existence and the necessity for dealing with them on terms adequate to their seriousness and extent. "Think," he had implored, well before his Christian days, "neither fear nor courage saves us. Unnatural vices / Are fathered by our heroism. Virtues / Are forced upon us by our impudent crimes" ("Gerontion"). Facing this reality entailed less metaphysical argument than sheer nerve, conditioned by a persistent sense of the ineluctable facticity of human sin and error, and coupled with a recognition of the necessity to "construct" something "upon which to rejoice" (*Ash-Wednesday*). Any such construct must, Eliot knew, have a dimension of relativity as well as of universality, though where one stopped and the other began was the work of many lifetimes and many historical formations to discern.

Sheer conviction of sin does not, however, make a Christian, or not alone; the reality of grace must be affirmed as well. This side of the equation was, perhaps, hardest for Eliot to achieve. There is no doubt that he came to believe wholeheartedly and without revisionism not only in hell and damnation, but in the more salvific doctrines, in what he called the "fact of incarnation" and the atonement and in what he took to be their corollary, the virgin birth (*SE* [1950], p. 361). He also believed with equally unqualified firmness in the other articles of the Anglican creed, especially – if *Four Quartets* be any indication – in the efficacy of prayer, the intercession of the Virgin and the communion of the saints (Ackroyd, *T. S. Eliot*, p. 163). These doctrines were for him precisely the kinds of truth "outside of [ourselves]" which, he proposed, every faith or committed point of view must at some point entail.

Eliot was able to embrace these doctrines, so temperamentally and intellectually foreign to him in many ways, in part through the operations on his sensibility of the poetry and art of the West. His response was not to religious or devotional works *per se* – a category he largely distrusted – but to the great classics of his own cultural tradition, classics ranging from Virgil to Valéry and from Shakespeare to Dante, regardless of their appearance of orthodoxy or lack thereof. His praises here are telling: of Baudelaire, for instance, for his understanding of the literal reality of the Satanic and its potential for revivifying that epicene Christianity of which he had complained in "Mr. Eliot's Sunday Morning Service" (*SE* [1950], p. 124), and of Pascal for his ability to make use of all through which he had passed, his worldliness, his philosophical training, his pain, leaving nothing behind in his leap of faith.

The most important factor in Eliot's conversion as well as his art, however, was without a doubt the poetry of Dante, of which the influence on him was overwhelming, "the experience," as he said, "both of a moment and of a lifetime" (*SE* [1950], p. 212). Dante's work influenced Eliot not only for aesthetic reasons – though these were weighty enough – but through its view of psychosexual maturation as well (*SE* [1950], p. 235). In The Clark Lectures, Eliot made clear how deeply he had always sought for "incarnation" in the linguistic and extra-linguistic senses alike, and how closely he identified this quest with Dante's poetic and religious achievement. Dante, Eliot argued, had been given the "gift of incarnation" to a high degree, both as the recipient of the blessings of Christian faith and as the donor in turn of an articulation of these as immediate as the odor of a rose. Dante also guided Eliot toward that understanding of the close relationship between sexual idealization, collapse of that idealization and the re-establishment of eros only as mediated by realities beyond death that so informed his later life and work.

The "gift of incarnation" in this Dantean sense did not come naturally to Eliot; it had to be cultivated and made his own by considerable effort. As Eliot once remarked: "Most people suppose that some people, because they enjoy the luxury of Christian sentiments and the excitement of Christian ritual, swallow or pretend to swallow incredible dogma. For some the process is exactly opposite. Rational assent may arrive late, intellectual conviction may come slowly, but they come inevitably without violence to honesty and nature. To put the sentiments in order is a later and an immensely difficult task: intellectual freedom is earlier and easier than complete spiritual freedom" (SE [1950], p. 438). The cultivation of that "complete spiritual freedom" entailed for Eliot not only continued intellectual inquiry, but, as Peter Ackroyd has rightly observed, the deliberate and conscious observance of the Christian sacraments (p. 161). Over time, this inquiry and observance did not further alienate but more deeply reconciled him to the natural order, to what he called, in "Animula," "the warm reality, the offered good." Through Christian theory and practice, Eliot eventually learned to temper his self-mortification with moderation, his detachment with compassion and engagement, and his aversion to the body with an acceptance, indeed an affirmation, of human sexuality and physicality.

The effect of his new faith on Eliot's social and political views and on the exercise of that critical faculty and function he took so seriously also took time to mature, and the process was not without its problems. Needing, as was consistent with his temperament and views, to take an oppositional stance toward the ideology of the moment among the literati, he began by announcing, somewhat provocatively, in 1928 that he was "classicist in literature, royalist in politics and anglo-catholic in religion" (For Lancelot Andrewes, p. 15). He went on to qualify this statement almost immediately in context, but the qualification was not heard, nor was it helped by further excesses, most notoriously a series of ill-considered lectures on "orthodoxy" and literature at the University of Virginia in 1933, subsequently published (it was a condition of their delivery) as After Strange Gods in 1934.

Like most calls for orthodoxy and purity, this one was directed at an aspect of himself Eliot sought most desperately to amputate or annul. When he regained his equilibrium after this period, and when history after Munich had brought home to him with a certain degree of shock the nature of his own previous blindness about current events and attitudes, he began to write a very different kind of criticism, evidenced among other things by such speculative works as *The Idea of a Christian Society* and *Notes Towards the Definition of Culture*. Behind these lay not only Eliot's conviction that a society based explicitly on Christian principles was the best defense against fascism, but his unyielding opposition to the untrammeled operations of modern finance capital and to the assumption in both domestic and foreign affairs of the necessity for and effectiveness of unprincipled *real-politik*. Eliot developed his views on these matters in colloquy with others of like mind, intellectuals and scholars gathered together in such more or less formal organizations as The Moot and the Chandos Group.[9] In contributing to these discussions, Eliot wrestled, and wrestled more honestly than many, with contradictions which still haunt societies historically based in the Judeo-Christian tradition, the contradiction between equality and hierarchy, for instance, or that between inherited and acquired virtues, collective as well as individual.

Perhaps Eliot's greatest contribution to these endeavors, and certainly the greatest witness that he had attained, by gradual degrees, something of the "complete spiritual freedom" of which he had once spoken lay less in his prose than in his poetry, where he experienced what was to him a rather unexpected blessing: that of the profound and unexpected renewal of his own inspiration. During the years of his maturity, Eliot's Christianity became the major source of his work, enabling such brilliant accomplishments as *Ash-Wednesday*, "Song for Simeon" and "Journey of the Magi," and such innovations as *Murder in the Cathedral* and *The Family Reunion*. Christianity also generated *Four Quartets*, perhaps Eliot's greatest poetic achievement, a sustained experiment in dialogic and meditative poetry that is at once the culmination of a certain tradition in the West and the potential point of departure for a new mode.

The specific religious challenge of these poems and plays, the challenge to affirm, as does *Little Gidding*, that "with the drawing of this Love and the voice of this Calling . . . all shall be well and / All manner of thing shall be well" (*LG*, v) is not, Eliot knew, one to be taken lightly, either by way of acceptance or by way of rejection. Nor can the issues of belief it raises be settled once and for all at any one time, either by an individual or a collectivity. As Eliot put it in *Knowledge and Experience*, "both God and Mammon are interpretations of the world and have to be reinterpreted," and because even "the finest tact" can give us "only an interpretation," therefore "every interpretation, along perhaps with some utterly contradictory interpretation, has to be taken up and reinterpreted by every thinking mind and by every civilization" (p. 164).

On the other hand, the question of "tact" is never entirely moot, at least when it comes to art. It matters, and matters greatly not only that the poet of these works had made up his mind on certain issues, but that the voices he summoned into being expressed the convictions of other and different minds too, and that he was able to give powerful articulation to skepticism as well as belief, to individuality as well as tradition, and to the points of view of many cultures and times as well as those of his own. Aesthetic achievement of this order requires primarily neither dissent nor endorsement but rather something of what Eliot himself, speaking of Dante, tentatively termed "poetic assent" (*SE* [1950], p. 288). This assent, Eliot argued, entails less a "suspension of disbelief" than a "suspension of belief" (*SE* [1950], p. 220), a mobile receptiveness and attention that moves beyond though it is not indifferent to matters of faith and doctrine. Such assent is possible, Eliot knew, only when prompted by art that is respectful of its audience, uncoercive in intent, and deeply in touch with the concrete realities of human existence. Eliot's art was of this order, and it is compelling not only for the ultimate questions it raises and the proximate answers it suggests, but for its power to intensify the very terms of their debate to a greater and more generous order of magnitude.

NOTES

1 "*Ulysses*, Order and Myth" (Kermode, *Selected Prose*, p. 177).
2 See "Dante" (*SE* [1950], pp. 199–240); "Milton I, II" (*PP* [New York], pp. 156–83); "Goethe as Sage" (*PP* [New York], pp. 240–65.
3 Eliot expressed his own dissatisfaction with his attempts at synthesis in a late pamphlet for the National Book League, *George Herbert* (London: Longman's, Green, 1962).
4 Eliot made this remark about skepticism and faith in *The Listener*, January 9, 1947 (Ackroyd, *T. S. Eliot*, p. 160). Ackroyd devotes several pages to Eliot's skepticism, but the fullest discussion is to be found in Perl, *Skepticism*.
5 Published under the title *Knowledge and Experience in the Philosophy of F. H. Bradley* (1964). It has recently been reissued by Columbia University Press (New York: 1989).
6 Eliot's notes on William James are in the collection of the Houghton Library, Harvard University; the Clark Lectures in the library of King's College, Cambridge.
7 Eliot's notes on his seminar with Royce are in the Houghton Library. Useful summaries may be found in Costello, *Josiah Royce's Seminar*, discussions in, among others, Gray and Crawford.
8 In an unpublished essay on Walter Lippman in the Houghton Library.
9 See Kojecký, *T. S. Eliot's Social Criticism* and Perl, *Skepticism* on The Moot and The Chandos Group, and Ackroyd, *T. S. Eliot*, p. 171; also Jewel Spears Brooker, "Substitutes for Religion in the Early Poetry of T. S. Eliot," *The Placing of T. S. Eliot*, p. 12, for Eliot's views of communism.

WORKS CITED

Ackroyd, Peter, *T. S. Eliot: A Life*. New York: Simon and Schuster, 1984.

Brooker, Jewel Spears (ed.). *The Placing of T. S. Eliot*. London: University of Missouri Press, 1991.

Costello, Harry. *Josiah Royce's Seminar, 1913–1914*, Grover Smith (ed.). New Brunswick, NJ: Rutgers University Press, 1963.

Crawford, Robert. *The Savage and the City in the Work of T. S. Eliot*, Oxford: Clarendon Press, 1987.

Gordon, Lyndall. *Eliot's Early Years*. Oxford: Oxford University Press, 1977.

Kermode, Frank (ed.). *Selected Prose of T. S. Eliot*. New York: Harcourt, Brace, Jovanovich, 1975.

Kojecký, Roger. *T. S. Eliot's Social Criticism*. New York: Farrar, Straus and Giroux, 1971.

Perl, Jeffrey. *Skepticism and Modern Enmity*. Baltimore: The Johns Hopkins University Press, 1989.

7

ALAN MARSHALL

"England and nowhere"

England was the scene of Eliot's encounter as a poet with the particularities of history and place. He went on to develop an idea of England of classical proportions. What follows is an attempt to understand both the encounter and the idea.

Eliot was in Marburg when Germany invaded Belgium on August 3, 1914. The British Government responded to the invasion with an ultimatum. The nation had become impatient for war with its belligerent, industrially confident rival. It was the impatience of an empire that had peaked and needed to reassert itself. German aggression was a challenge, something for an uncertain giant to measure itself against. From the beginning there was a self-conscious pride in the war as being of massive historical moment. Lloyd George described it as the "great conflict," and saw it as a chance for a nation, long used to empire, to wake up from the sloth of tropical prosperity, and recover its authority and right (Marwick, *The Deluge*, p. 89).

When war broke out Eliot packed his bags and headed for London. He was twenty-five years old and on study-leave from Harvard. He had already arranged to spend most of the year at Oxford, so the move was not a major inconvenience. It became more inconvenient when he realized how much he disliked Oxford which struck him as a quiet unprepossessing place to live, even before its numbers were depleted by the war.

As an American he was in a position of classic neutrality. Cut off from the action, and the citizen of a country which was determined to remain above it, he was perfectly placed to watch the Old World go mad – to watch it throw away life and limb in an unprecedented war of attrition. He remained an outsider for the duration of the war and would have been unaffected by the practical changes which it seemed to hurry forward. There was the extension of the electoral franchise to women over thirty and to all men over twenty-one (1918); there were ambitious new housing, education and national insurance programs (the first two shortlived); there was a new collectivist spirit in British politics, and in the coalition Government of 1915 the Labour Party got its first taste of power.

Perhaps because these changes did not affect him Eliot was among the first to recognize that any hope of less localized gains had been illusory; that there was no integrity in Europe or in Britain; and that in spite of the Treaty of Versailles the Empire was still dying – and would continue to die – with a niggling penny-pinching patience. As the historian Arthur Marwick observes, the survivors of the Western Front did not have much in common with Lloyd George's anachronistic coalition Government, which secured office in the 1918 election before one in four British servicemen was willing or able to vote. It was a triumph of public cynicism (Marwick, *The Deluge*, p. 304). The country was more divided than it knew. And when *The Waste Land* appeared in 1922, among the young and educated at least it struck a chord.

However the moment that one claims, as the influential critic I. A. Richards did, that the poem expressed the "plight of a whole generation" (Richards, *Principles*, p. 295), one runs up against the fact that Eliot rejected this kind of acclamation in the most withering terms. "When I wrote a poem called *The Waste Land* some of the more approving critics said that I had expressed the 'disillusionment of a generation,' which is nonsense. I may have expressed for them their own illusion of being disillusioned, but that did not form part of my intention" (*SE* [1951], p. 368). The writers of the twenties and thirties threatened to turn a poem which dealt, in an inevitably *private* way, with the disappearance of those common values which make a *public* language possible, into the very thing which Eliot felt no longer existed: a public language, common values. They identified with the poem too readily, and two brief quotations from "What the Thunder Said" can be used to illustrate the difficulty that the likes of Stephen Spender were failing to encounter (see, for example, Tate (ed.) *T. S. Eliot*, p. 48).

> Shall I at least set my lands in order?　　　　　　(*WL*, line 425)

What is at stake here is the social meaning of the term "order." The possessive adjective combines with the first person singular in a gesture that threatens to be isolated and exclusive. Compare the plural subject in the following:

> We who were living are now dying
> With a little patience.　　　　　　(*WL*, lines 329–30)

It is unlikely (though not impossible) that the *we* refers to Eliot: but in any case the uncertainty is indicative of the problem. Who does "we" refer to? What is its relationship to the "I" in line 425? To Eliot it was not through sentimental identification that one could get beyond the illusion of being disillusioned and find some genuine common ground – with oneself, with others, with the nation one was living in and the rest of Europe. For this reason the context of Eliot's disclaimer, as quoted from "Thoughts after Lambeth," is particularly important. It was 1931 and by now he was writing as a British citizen and a committed Christian, four years after a painstaking conversion to the Church of England. That one is speaking of the Anglican Church here, the national church, as opposed to any of the disestablished churches, such as the Quakers or the Methodists, is fundamental. Donald Davie is concise about this and a reading of "Thoughts after Lambeth" bears him out: "when it came to deciding what Christian sect he should join, it was of the utmost importance to him that he choose what should seem to be not a sect at all but a national norm, its normality shown in that it was backed by the secular and institutional forces of the nation-state" (Davie, *Eliot in His Time*, p. 186).

What I want to suggest is this: that Eliot's development as a writer from *The Waste Land* on is governed by his changing relationship to England – England understood as the *religious, secular, and institutional forces of the nation-state*. And his instinctive sense that he *hadn't* and *couldn't* have spoken for a "generation" had a critical part in that development. It led him on a career of circumspect salvation, in which he elicited what he saw as the essentials of empire from the absence of empire, by addressing the civic void in Christian terms.

England became the point of intersection between Eliot and history. Shortly after the war he wrote that a poet would not be able to continue beyond his twenty-fifth year if he was not sensitive to the pressure of history (*SE* [1951], p. 14). His own twenty-fifth year was the last one that he lived in America. But the value of England for Eliot, first as a point of historical intersection, then as a structural principle, tends to be underestimated by critics who, pointing to his American birthright, see him in the context of a native American tradition. One such critic is Lyndall Gordon.

Gordon's position is carefully understated, and it is founded on a remark Eliot made in an interview late in his life. "In its sources, in its emotional springs," Eliot said, his poetry came from America (*Paris Review*, p. 70). But Gordon doesn't quote the series of qualifications that led up to this statement (Gordon, *Eliot's Early Years*, p. 2). Eliot said that definitions were problematic; that his poetry would have been different if he'd been born in England, and different if he'd stayed in America; that it would not be what it was, and that it was a combination of things. Not only do these abstractions acknowledge the mysteries of origination and development, they underscore the symbolical gestures contained in the metaphorical consistence of "sources" and "emotional springs," in which there is more mythology than geography. They are a reminder that the speaker is the author of *Four Quartets*, a poem which is all about the difficulty of taking place or past for granted.

More intriguing than the citation of the interview, however, is the use Gordon makes of Ralph Waldo Emerson, deftly weaving allusions to him into her biography of Eliot wherever there might be supposed to be a parallel. The trouble with this is that, as Gordon allows, the contempt both men conceived for the barren theology of the Unitarian Church led them in opposite directions, and Eliot's whole career is in flagrant conflict with Emerson's theory of history, according to which the individual can find the meaning of history in America and in himself. It is misleading to quote Emerson (as Gordon does) on each man's spiritual right to personify history without quoting Eliot's irreverent rejoinder:

> (The lengthened shadow of a man
> Is history, said Emerson
> Who had not seen the silhouette
> Of Sweeney straddled in the sun.)

"Sweeney Erect" was published in 1920, and this is the most complicated image in the poem, nodding across the Atlantic to New England from a brothel or a boarding house, where the legendary English barber's naked "silhouette" is erected as an alternative to Emerson's "shadow," and "history" becomes a matter of perspective. It is, so to speak, a point of intersection. And implicit in it is the Jamesian idea, which Eliot only felt more acutely, that history is the record of the struggle to understand why, given the feeling of individuality, the shape of a person's life is not unique: there is always a precedent, another version, a mocking mirror image. This is what Isabel Archer discovers in Rome, in James's *The Portrait of a Lady*, and it is what Tiresias, the mind of Europe, prophesies in *The Waste Land* – who, blind androgyne that he (she) is, has nothing new to learn about the human animal.

Within a year of Eliot's arrival in England the personal, professional and vocational reasons for his remaining were very much in sympathy. The introduction to artistic London society helped to dissipate his need for the cultural insulation which, it probably seemed, was best acquired in America through an academic career – in Eliot's case as a professional philosopher. In September 1914 he met Ezra Pound, his livewire fellow countryman, who was full of admiration for the thoroughness with which Eliot had applied himself to the production of a new modern poetry and quickly arranged for the publication of "Prufrock." The following summer he married, interrupting a long period of diffidence and sexual frustration during which he had intermittently wandered around Paris and London as lonely and repelled as the Baudelaire of his essays. Pound's enthusiastic support was the beginning of the arduous process of gaining recognition as a man of letters, something which – as Pound explained to Eliot's father – an American had to do in London if he wanted to matter on the international stage (*Letters* I, p. 102). Eliot – who in 1917 took a job as a bank-clerk – compared becoming recognized to breaking open a safe (*Letters* I, p. 392). But by now he had calculated that he was *on the inside* – and, as he wrote to his mother in 1919, he had a considerable amount of say in determining who the inside was (*Letters* I, p. 280). It was a business for which Pound, who kept a finger in too many pies, was not cut out – he lacked the master plan which would appeal to England's sense of its heritage. Eliot found elbow room in the journals and had the energy to churn out a formidable number of reviews (twenty-five pieces in 1919 in *The Athenaeum* alone, and his first commission for *The Times Literary Supplement*); to these he brought the stir caused by his poems and an aspect of intimidating facelessness; and he was putting together a revolutionary body of opinion about the history of English poetry, which implied – when anybody stopped to consider where history was leading – a substantial part for himself in the continuation of it.

Before enlarging on any of these points I want to look at Eliot's England from another angle, in the hope of bringing out the difference between his early involuntary impressions of the place and the elaborate conception of it which emerged in later years.

No poet raises more consistently than Eliot and in more problematical terms the question of poetry's relationship to place. What becomes of England in Eliot's poetry? In what sense is it there? Where is he standing when he perceives it? From which direction is his voice coming? The problem is that one cannot simply map out a poet's relationship to place. A map of Eliot's England would prove nothing. What is needed is a way of testing out his experience of the true character of the place, which is something that will exist in at least three dimensions and cannot be conveyed on the easily reproducible surface of a map. What is called for is a geography that devolves on the senses – including, where possible, the sense of balance; for balance, which becomes so important in the poetry of Wordsworth – an interesting landscape-poet with whom to compare him – is a useful indicator of our involuntary relationship to space.

There are three distinct phases of England in Eliot's poetry. The first is best expressed in the verses which follow "Sweeney Erect" in *Poems – 1920*: "A Cooking Egg," which Eliot dated as 1917 (Moody, *Thomas Stearns Eliot*, p. 52). The poem is built around a series of images circumscribing the dusty cultural range of the English upper-middle class: its art, its money, its memorabilia, its flirtations with spiritualism, and its fear of encroachment. But eventually we notice the way in which the speaker foregrounds the "distance," the detachment, which along with the almost lifeless immobility of the object, the woman, engenders, in both senses, their narrowly satirical relationship. The gap between the speaker and Pipit is amplified by the frozen paraphernalia around her. By monitoring the behavior of the *speaker* we can see the whole poem as a study in attitude. And if we go so far as to say that "A Cooking Egg" contains within it an allegory of one stage of Eliot's relationship to England, then we can detect, in the pose of the speaker, a priggish pride in his own exquisite separateness – which is still essentially that of an unassimilated alien. Suddenly it is not so much a poem about England as about a foreigner's impressions of England; one who by striking a pose of rigid superiority is trying to assuage a nagging insecurity – an inertia of his own, a failure to be fully present.

On September 8, 1914, shortly after he arrived in London, Eliot wrote a letter which throws some light on the much more imaginative way in which place is conveyed in *The Waste Land*. It is a magnificent piece of sustained description, full of a witty impressionism which is rare in Eliot's business-like correspondence, and captures not just the lively innocence of the observer but the hectic combustible atmosphere of a country heading into war. Eliot was describing the quarter where he was staying, which was full of boarding houses, crowded with people of all nationalities but particularly French and Belgians, most of whom had fled from the European mainland. The hustle and bustle of the London that comes to mind is an effect of the adroitness with which Eliot *listens* – of the speed with which he cuts from one sound to another – to create a pattern of rapid transitions. "The noise hereabouts is like hell turned upside down" (*Letters* 1, p. 55). And what makes the writing so convincing is Eliot's ear for hell, which catches the necessary detail with sardonic nicety. He notes the languages, the conversation, the crying of babies, the playing of pianos, singers, street-musicians, and the simultaneous banging of the house gongs (at seven o'clock) signalling dinner or breakfast. He homes in beautifully with black-comic relish on any anomalous utterance: "what's to prevent him putting arsenic in our food?" – his ear quick to pick up sinister overtones, the suspicion of criminals, the small-scale nightmares of the bourgeoisie. Everybody it seems is making some sort of noise. The essence of the place and the reality of the people who inhabit the place are not primarily visual but auditory. The visual and the auditory meet in the lexical – in the two great newspaper headlines that Eliot records: "GREAT GERMAN DISASTER!," "LIST OF ENGLISH DEAD AND WOUNDED." Here not only the sound of the newspapers is imagined, but the shape of that sound, what that sound looks like. At the heart of Eliot's London in 1914 was a susceptibility to sound in all its manifestations.

The Waste Land can be read in similar terms – as a poem about a place that is made up of sound. The city that Eliot *sees* is a much less animated affair than the one that he listens to. The apostrophe to London which he omitted from the final version of the poem, when the city is seen by the "observing eye," probably fails for lack of individual detail (*WL Drafts*, p. 43). In Eliot's waste land most of the individual details about people and place are supplied by the ear, a phenomenon which coincides with the stress he later put on what he called the "auditory imagination" (*UPUC* [London], p. 118). London exists most frequently as a place that Eliot hears; as a place where one is accosted or visited by sound: the gloomy bell of St. Mary Woolnoth; the ingratiating French of Mr. Eugenides; Edmund Spenser singing to the Thames; the island noises of *The Tempest* –

> 'This music crept by me upon the waters,'
> And along the strand, up Queen Victoria Street.
> O City city I can sometimes hear
> Beside a public bar in Lower Thames Street,
> The pleasant whining of a mandoline
> And a clatter and a chatter from within
> Where fishmen lounge at noon.   (WL, lines 257–63)

The city is traced by the sound it makes, or by the sounds different parts of it make. Music gives directions and defines space (by . . . up . . . beside . . . from within). It creeps along, like the rat of line 187, on its way to the walls of Magnus Martyr, whose heart-of-light glimmer is seen but withheld (*WL*, lines 263–65). In "The Fire Sermon" some of Eliot's most elusive and evocative poetry seems to have been composed of his fascination with the mysterious properties of London names, rich in historical suggestion: Greenwich, the Isle of Dogs, Highbury, Richmond, Kew, and Moorgate.

The sensitivity of the ear also functions at a symbolical level. In a letter to Conrad Aiken anticipating his writings on Baudelaire, Eliot describes the tormenting sexual self-consciousness thrust upon him in the city. "One walks about the streets with one's desires, and one's refinement rises up like a wall whenever opportunity approaches" (*Letters* 1, p. 75). It is an image of highly sexed metropolitan isolation. The city is mapped and traced by desire – defined by the current of need that flows through it or is blocked by it. In *The Waste Land* desire is repeatedly figured in music – subdued and skulking, lewd and protesting, creeping along the Thames and winding through the streets.

The final phase of Eliot's England represents a radical departure from the England of *The Waste Land*. It is exemplified by *Four Quartets*, and three of the most important aspects of it can be adduced in terms of voice, land-scape, and abstraction.

Voice is the first and most obvious way in which the *Quartets* differs from *The Waste Land*. Whereas it would be difficult to enumerate just how many voices there are in *The Waste Land* or to set a limit to its ambiguity of tone, *Four Quartets* has a deliberately narrow vocal range. There are essentially two voices, sometimes sweetly merging, often drily separated: an abstract digressive voice, and a lyric voice; and despite the gradations between them we can say that the poem is founded quite emphatically on a rejection of *The Waste Land*'s style of aural empiricism.

In *The English Eliot* Steve Ellis has related the austere landscapes of *Four Quartets* to contemporary movements in art and architecture. He finds parallels in the work of a generation of British painters (of whom the best known is probably Paul Nash) experimenting with landscapes that avoided or else marginalized the human subject. What interests me here is related to this and again has to do with the eclipsing of the method of *The Waste Land*. Unlike the busy surfaces of that poem, with their incomplete super-ficial details which depend very much on what catches the poet's ear, the landscapes of *Four Quartets* are, as Ellis says, primarily visual. And they are observed with an elegant detachment in which nothing is left to chance. It is possible to illustrate what I mean by detachment by comparing them with Wordsworth's landscapes in the early books of *The Prelude*.

In Wordsworth's case it seems that the actual contours of the land get written into his work. At a quite fundamental level, before the poet has had time to name the place, the poetry testifies intimately to a violent experience of the shape and presence of the land. Movement is at the heart of it. *The Prelude* is not just a poem about the imagination: it is about the effect movement has upon the imagination. It is about movement's part in the poet's imagination. Wordsworth habitually describes himself moving—walking, running, rowing, skating, losing his balance. And movement presupposes place. As we saw in *The Waste Land*, a description of movement is a description of place:

> And oftentimes
> When we had given our bodies to the wind,
> And all the shadowy banks, on either side,
> Came sweeping through the darkness, spinning still
> The rapid line of motion; then at once
> Have I, reclining back upon my heels,
> Stopp'd short, yet still the solitary Cliffs
> Wheeled by me, even as if the earth had roll'd
> With visible motion her diurnal round.
> *(The Prelude*, book 1, 1805, lines 478–86)

Nothing could be further from the disembodied landscapes of *Four Quartets*. In Wordsworth the experience of place is inseparable from the experience of the body. The body is the seat or axis of movement. We know where the poet stops and stands – and we see how his body is caught up, or involved, in the motions of the planet.

But in *Four Quartets* the body is left out of the picture. If we look at the opening of *Little Gidding* we quickly see that it is a matter of indifference where Eliot *stands*. He is not a part of the place. He has no need to adapt himself to the contours of it. There is no question of his being caught off-balance and he looks at it with the detachment of a man looking at a photograph. And this is in keeping with the metaphysical disposition of the whole sequence, from *Burnt Norton* on. *Burnt Norton* begins with a passage that was never taken, a door that was never opened, a rose-garden in the mind. Place is becoming abstract. London is mentioned in the third section but nothing is said about it. The empty names of the suburbs are consigned to the "twittering world." There is none of the curious action, the erratic moving-around – like a rat, a criminal, or a popular jingle – that we find in *The Waste Land*.

Order is a recurrent term in Eliot's writing, and taking our bearings from his essay on Dante (1929), we can say that it signals movement away from a private language towards the ideal of a common one (*SE* [1951], p. 252). Eliot's critique of English poetry, from Shakespeare down, is based on the absence of what he believed had been brought to perfection by Dante: a common language. A common language is an *imperial* phenomenon, and expresses the *universality* of the idea which informs it. According to Eliot the European idea was Christianity, which matured in medieval Italy on the foundations of Virgilian Rome. And the disintegration of it was one of the reasons why, for example, a "great" poet such as Tennyson could never be the spokesman (the Virgil, the Dante) of his generation – except in the vaguest emotional sense (*SE* [1951], p. 334). There was no common mind, no order, no idea.

Eliot feared a similar fate for the poet of *The Waste Land*. Modernism had no answer to the problem of disintegration – like the Treaty of Versailles it was really an expression of it (*SE* [1951], p. 240). He argued in *The Criterion*, whose "Commentaries" were his way of addressing the public domain, that Modernism obscures the premises on which coherent thought depends (*Criterion* 8.31 [1928]: 188). In 1923 he had ventured to hope that myth might provide the missing order, the unifying principle, and these are the terms in which he praises Joyce (*Selected Prose*, p. 177). But with hindsight we can say that myth became the prototype of his subsequent Christianity, as Virgil *became* the prototype of Dante. Eliot's conversion to Anglicanism was private, that is it was discreet, but it was not merely personal; for it marked his accession to the European idea, a lost commonalty, "never and always" (*Little Gidding*). He put himself in the extraordinary position of speaking for a country which did not yet exist: *the idea of a Christian society*.

The unfulfilled Christian idea is the mature form, spiritually, of the lost imperial idea (*PP* [London], p. 130). Critics of Eliot's imperialism need to bear in mind that he was attached to the *idea*, as Frank Kermode has shown, and only incidentally to the historical realities of empire (Kermode, *The Classic, passim*). On the basis of a review Eliot wrote in 1918 of contemporary work in the field of eugenics, David Trotter asks whether the monologue in "A Game of Chess" dealing with the prolific childbearing of a lower-class couple betrays Edwardian upper-class "anxiety about the degeneration of the Imperial Race" (Trotter, "Modernism and Empire," p. 151). But the imperialism of *The Waste Land* is more disenchanted than that, and consists in searching out the absence of the imperial idea, not in concern for the imperial race. Along with most critics Trotter ignores the fact that Lil and Albert don't have the chance to speak directly, that their lives are submerged in gossip. Their experience is cut off from the language in which it is expressed, and what this wall of sound demonstrates is the non-existence of that social order which would make a common language possible. Like the quotation from the philosopher Bradley in the "Notes" the monologue exemplifies the degeneration of imperialism as such.

Eliot is consistent in his admiration for empire. But it remains an ideal. In 1928, in the same breath in which he compares the British Empire to the Roman Empire he is careful to evoke a more diplomatic destiny for his adopted nation: Britain is an island, geographically and historically, ecclesiastically and politically, and in the modern world her policy is to be a "bridge," a "middle way" (*Criterion* 7.3 [1928]: 194). But imperial ambition lingers warily in the absolute centrality of his definition; in this image of the universe tended by a nation.

As Eliot moved toward a comprehensive position on matters of Church and State, he developed his thinking on *community* in two extended pieces of social criticism, *The Idea of a Christian Society* (1939) and *Notes Towards the Definition of Culture* (1948). But the essentials of it were clearly stated in the choruses from *The Rock* (1934):

> There is no life that is not in community,
> And no community not lived in praise of GOD.

What Eliot seems to be saying here is that all communities are Christian *in tendency*. And this is very important when we consider the history of Eliot's drama, in which *The Rock* itself has a part. Nothing demonstrates more effectively what Eliot understands by community than the way in which his conception of the drama changes between 1923, the year of his obituary for the music-hall artist Marie Lloyd, and 1958, in which he wrote his last play *The Elder Statesman*; a change which is characterized by a deepening awareness of the theater as a public space. In 1926 Eliot's imminent commitment to the national church was quietly complemented by his skeptical interest in the possibility of a national theater. It is obvious that he took the idea seriously – but he hated the thought of what might be performed there, in the dubious interests of education and democracy. "A National Theatre is not a thing to educate anybody," he wrote, "it is something to which the public, in a very long time, must first be educated" (*Criterion* 4.3 [1926]: 418). The reader could be forgiven for thinking that in echoing his own famous words on tradition he was measuring himself, from a reasonably safe distance, against the enormity of the task (*SE* [1951], p. 14).

Perhaps the most prescient document in Eliot's struggle to define a public role for the drama is the obituary notice he wrote on the death of Marie Lloyd (*SE* [1951], pp. 456–59). Trying to understand how it was that she held her audience, and how, from being held, it in turn participated, Eliot uses the terms from the Upanishad as they are rendered in "What the Thunder Said": *give* ("no other comedian succeeded so well in giving expression to the life of that audience"); *sympathize*, and *control* ("Marie Lloyd's audiences were invariably sympathetic, and it was through this sympathy that she controlled them"). Here the therapeutic rite from the end of *The Waste Land* is transposed, unsystematically it seems and quite unconsciously, to an explicitly public theatrical domain.

With the exception of Eliot's first complete plays, *Murder in the Cathedral* (1935) and *The Family Reunion* (1939), which agonize too much over the fate of the individual, Eliot's theater is, at every level, from the language to the plot to the actors to the audience, a study in community – a series of exercises in the spirit of cooperation. "In the theatre, the problem of communication presents itself immediately," he wrote (*PP* [London], p. 79). And in the piece on Marie Lloyd he stressed the dramatic "collaboration" of the artist and audience (*SE* [1951], p. 458). This emphasis upon communication, which makes the poet responsible to his audience, qualifies the distinction Eliot seemed to make in "A Dialogue on Dramatic Poetry" between the High Mass and the drama – on the basis of the fact that people participate in the mass as they do not in the drama: for in the theater the audience also participates, has so to speak an unacted part, and the word "communication" adequately conveys the infinite possibilities of that (*SE* [1951], pp. 48–49). The difference Eliot was getting at comes down to belief (*ibid.*). Indeed Eliot's description of the effect of the drama, with its movement from Virgil to Dante, is enough to suggest a potentially religious occasion (*PP* [London], p. 87). Meanwhile the criticisms he made of his own drama consistently reflect a Christian standard of communal interplay. Just as the failure to complete the syncopated, modernist *Sweeney Agonistes*, first drafted in 1923 but not published for another three years (Moody, *Thomas Stearns Eliot*, p. 114), was a reflection of that play's communal indifference – an observation which is easily backed up by its volatile combination of solipsism, cannibalism, misogyny, anti-Semitism, and xenophobia generally.

It is a mark of Eliot's more sophisticated grasp of the meaning of community, and, accordingly, his more sophisticated grasp of theater – from which theater emerges as a model of community – that he learned, as his drama developed, to adjust the balance of attention away from the tortured individual, the ambivalent focus of the first plays, toward the community of characters. In the way that they grab our attention both Beckett and Harry can be seen to follow in the footsteps of the abortive Sweeney, whereas in the last plays our attention is invited to flow not over particular individuals, but over the ironic resolution of problems of human relationship. The most appropriate analogy for how these plays work is to be found in *Four Quartets*; in the image of a dancing consort of words. Like that poem the plays are, when successful, carefully choreographed satires of the superficial layers of reality. Consequently they are satires of place; hence their cavalier attitude to England's geography. I am thinking here of *The Confidential Clerk* and *The Elder Statesman*, and the part played by the home-counties in the absurdly elaborate off-stage action. The technique is anticipated by the sense of displacement in *The Cocktail Party* – as when Edward refers to the "*depths* of Essex" as if he meant the jungles of the Congo. The best defense of Eliot's country-house picture of English life is that he seemed to feel that there was only a thin partition between it and another reality.

By the time of the Second World War Eliot had accepted a Christian interpretation of history, and could speak with legitimate patriotism for a Christian version of the nation-state. In "A Note on War Poetry" (1942) he suggests that war, because it overrides the narrowly individual, gives us the chance to step outside ourselves, which is the first step on the road to Christian detachment. Even at his most patriotic, with the war raging about him, he was not prepared to stop at that kind of patriotism which is merely an extension of self-interest.

There are some lines in Eliot's final play, *The Elder Statesman*, which seem to bring together, as near as a sentence can, the various threads of Eliot's England:

> In England mistakes are anonymous
> Because the man who accepts responsibility
> Isn't the man who made the mistake.

These lines are central to a play which is all about deception, substitution and atonement. What they oscillate between is the idea of history as a series of accidents (Eliot's experience of World War I); and the idea of history as an accident made meaningful by Christianity (Eliot's experience of World War II): the image of history as a mistake – and the image of the mistake as Original Sin. If we think of the mistake as Original Sin, then an anonymous amoral society, an incoherent society, is transformed into a Christian *community*, responsible for its part in a mistake that pre-exists it.

For Eliot England was somewhere between these two. And the ambivalent tendency of the late poetry is to draw the real in the direction of the ideal; in the direction of the *abstract conception* ("A Note on War Poetry"). In the light of this it is not surprising that the proper noun England, whenever it occurs in *Little Gidding*, resists any attempt to prise a meaning from it. "There are other places," Eliot writes:

> But this is the nearest, in place and time
> Now and in England.

The meaning here is elusive. "Other places" introduces the hint we have seen of the arbitrariness of history, which is counterbalanced by the possible allusion to a spiritual afterlife. The line is echoed twice. The first echo occurs at the bottom of the next paragraph: "England and nowhere": with the pun on *now* (or even *here and now*). And the second echo, "History is now and England," effects the annihilation of history *through* history. Eliot chose an idea of history which abnegated itself: "Only through time time is conquered" (*BN*). It is a moment of supremely enigmatic deliverance.

WORKS CITED

Davie, Donald. "Anglican Eliot." *Eliot in His Time: Essays on the Occasion of the Fiftieth Anniversary of "The Waste Land"*. A. Walton Litz (ed.). Princeton: Princeton University Press, 1973: pp. 181–96.

Eliot, T. S. "The Art of Poetry 1: T. S. Eliot." *Paris Review* 21 (1959): 47–70.

(ed.). *The Criterion* (1922–39).

"Recent British Periodical Literature in Ethics." *International Journal of Ethics* 28 (1918): 270–77.

Selected Prose, Frank Kermode (ed.). London: Faber, 1975.

Ellis, Steve. *The English Eliot: Design, Language and Landscape in "Four Quartets."* London and New York: Routledge, 1991.

Gordon, Lyndall. *Eliot's Early Years.* Oxford: Oxford University Press, 1977.

Kermode, Frank. *The Classic.* London: Faber, 1975.

Marwick, Arthur. *The Deluge: British Society and the First World War.* 2nd edn. London: Macmillan, 1991.

Moody, A. D. *Thomas Stearns Eliot: Poet.* Paperback edn. Cambridge: Cambridge University Press, 1980; new edn. 1994.

Richards, I. A. *Principles of Literary Criticism.* 2nd edn. London: Routledge & Kegan Paul, 1926.

Tate, Allen (ed.). *T. S. Eliot: The Man and His Work.* Harmondsworth: Penguin, 1971.

Trotter, David. "Modernism and Empire: reading *The Waste Land*". *Critical Quarterly* 28. 1 & 2 (1986): 143–53.

8

J. C. C. MAYS

Early poems: from "Prufrock" to "Gerontion"

In the course of a late lecture, "The Frontiers of Criticism," Eliot recommended that readers of a poem should endeavor to grasp what the poem is aiming to be. Tentatively drawing on the language of philosophy, he suggested they should try to grasp its "entelechy" (*PP* [London], p. 110), a word which in Aristotle emphasizes purpose in contradistinction to cause. Eliot's recommendation offers a useful way to understand the relation of his early poems to those that follow, in terms of the end he thought they shared, and this end can be elucidated by means of a comparison with W. B. Yeats.

Take, for example, the well-known lines which close Yeats's "Among School Children," describing the image of the chestnut tree and the impossibility of knowing the dancer from the dance. What equivalent ecstatic moment is there in Eliot to set alongside these lines, when all is felt as unity? The images of the Chinese jar in its stillness in *Burnt Norton* and of the ceremonious dancers in *East Coker* come immediately to mind, but there are a dozen possibilities to choose from, across the whole span of Eliot's career, from *Four Quartets* back to *The Waste Land* and "Gerontion" and before. It is difficult to settle on any one of them, and the difficulty is indeed the first fact to emerge from the comparison.

There are also many similar passages in Yeats which extend the meaning of what he wrote in "Among School Children." For example, "Upon a Dying Lady" associates the dancing-place with a heavenly afterlife, the fourth stanza of "Byzantium" equates the dance with trance, and so on. But in Eliot the case is significantly different. Each of the possibilities is partial, haunting, suggestive. Altogether, they send the reader turning backward and forward, from one to another, and that is their nature; each set of lines needs another to complete its meaning, not just to add another dimension to a meaning which is already complete.

Eliot uses styles, quotes styles, "as a way of putting it." He represents things in ways which are beautiful and suggestive, but the representation does not pretend to embrace the whole of life, and what he says is no less memorable for its admitted incompleteness. Yeats, on the other hand, understands everything in terms of style; he creates a style in a poem and that is him; then nothing else. "Players and painted stage took all my love, / And not those things that they were emblems of." He gets his self and view of life onto paper, into an image, with a compelling air of completeness. His dancer turns with a movement beyond that of life, in her narrow luminous circle. "It was the dream itself enchanted me."

The comparison can be put another way. Both poets conceive the relation between life and art as tragic. Yeats's stance is characterized by pertinacity, audacity, integrity, intelligence, bravery, and because his poetry embodies such qualities it convinces us it is great. There is, however, nothing humble about it, and he cannot include in his poetry what would make it humble. Humility is Eliot's whole theme because it has to be: words never embrace meanings adequately, either because words are relatively inert or themselves too mobile. To the extent that distinctions are subtle, they are not suscept- ible of demonstration. Life discovers footholds in the interstices of art whose very suggestiveness rests on an exacerbated sense of insecurity.

The different relation between art and life in Yeats and Eliot highlights a central mood in Eliot: it is compounded of effort and inevitable failure, of pathos and insistence; it traverses an arc of feeling extending from the fore- suffering of Tiresias in *The Waste Land* to the exultant humility of *Little Gidding*. It sustained, in Eliot's lifetime, enormous, paradoxical authority.

This is the purpose his poetry aims to embody throughout, the entelechy he would have his readers grasp. It is what F. R. Leavis meant when he described Eliot's poetic technique as a "technique for sincerity" and his career as "a sustained, heroic and indefatigably resourceful quest for a pro found sincerity of the most difficult kind."[1] The quest is difficult because it shades into self-deceiving, as in Becket's last temptation in *Murder in the Cathedral*, to do the right thing for the wrong reason. Eliot describes it himself not as sincerity but, at the close of *Little Gidding*, as a condition of complete simplicity.

Another aspect of the comparison can be pressed to illuminate Eliot's technique. The question which closes "Among School Children" puts itself as unanswerable: "How can we know the dancer from the dance?" Yeats's authority rests on the presumption that themes and techniques in poetry – the what and the how – are identical. When the relation between them breaks down, poetry declines into either sentiment or melodrama: senti- ment, when we are aware that what is said is less than what was meant and cheques are drawn on emotional accounts which cannot be honored in terms of experience;[2] melodrama, when the reverse kind of breakdown takes place and what is said exceeds what was meant. Both kinds of breakdown derive from attempts to produce appropriate emotions on insufficient pretexts.

Eliot's starting-point takes breakdown for granted. It supposes that will cannot attain its object and that theme and technique cannot be reconciled in any fundamental way. Whereas Samuel Beckett felt the same breakdown as betrayal, Eliot responds without anger or violence and with sad acceptance. His strategy indeed exploits the disjunction between wanting and doing, and, by exploiting it consciously, pushes sentiment and melodrama into irony and the grotesque. He involves the self in the divorce between content and form, between what is intended and what can be said, and writes a parody of failure. Compare the opening of "The Lake Isle of Innisfree," which Yeats afterwards so particularly disliked, with the deliberate reversal of sentiment in the opening lines of "The Love Song of J. Alfred Prufrock." Where Yeats ends his poem still hearing "lake water lapping with low sounds by the shore" – that is, indulging a fancy that has all the force of an illusion – Prufrock describes his vision in terms of delusion – as a threatening world of dreams in which he drowns.

Eliot's two earliest volumes conform to the central and continuous tendency I have described. Themes and approaches which preoccupied him to the end of his career emerge already in "Prufrock," the opening poem of the first book. Prufrock divides into a *you* and an *I*, a public outward personality and a thinking, inert sensitive self; the dissociation is continually ascribed to a failure of nerve, an essential timidity. Prufrock does not dare to make his visit, just as the speaker in *The Waste Land* fails to address the hyacinth girl and the Hollow Men are transfixed by eyes they dared not meet in dreams. Eliot's heroes fail to confront their own selfhood from the beginning, whether this is conceived as a Dantesque heart of light or a Conradian heart of darkness.

The same timidity determines other characteristics of Eliot's verse such as the withdrawal of affirmative personality, the ironic tone, the use of quotation and allusion, the disjunctive structure. Rather than speak in his own person he created a poetry in which the reader supplies the voice, the connections, the argument; and because meanings come together in the echo-chambers of the reader's mind, meanings have a peculiar timbre, their own authority. The characteristic tone is of weary, ironic self-deprecation. Footfalls echo in the mind, their destination forgotten and irrelevant.

Eliot's claim to be a great poet rests upon this refusal of assertion. He is great to the extent that timidity is redefined as humility and the limits of poetry are ackowledged while he strives to break through them. And he is a great modern poet for the reason that he translated the sad accidents of his own life into poetry in a way that miraculously contained the exultation and despair of a generation. His achievement is a triumph of purpose over cause – of holding to what his poetry was aiming to be, like a thread through the labyrinth – though the coincidence which gave his writing its representative status reacted upon this purpose in a complicated way. His career has a retroactive shape which was not prospectively inevitable.

George Oppen described the alternative Eliot chose not to pursue by rewriting Prufrock's closing words: "till other voices wake / us or we drown."[3] His simple changes redirect attention onto the world outside the solitary, shipwrecked, solipsistic lyric self, a world from which rescue might have come but which was not available to Prufrock or to his creator. It can be argued that Eliot's need for security – social as well as spiritual – narrowed the choice on which his achievement rests. The choice brought him peace of mind and fame, but, in the years since his death, his example as witness has in general been more moving for readers than productive for other poets. The early poems are crucial to understanding both this curious fact and Eliot's present standing, and I shall return to the matter later.

"The Love Song of J. Alfred Prufrock" dominates the 1917 volume in which it appears. Its intellectual design is so clear, its emotional movement so satisfying, that it establishes a pattern readers expect other poems to conform to. Indeed it extends in this way beyond the volume itself: it strikes the tone of effort and the futility of effort which is central in Eliot's writing, and concentrates it with mesmeric force. Its features have been analyzed in a dozen textbooks and a thousand classrooms – the contradictory signals displayed by the elements of the title; the epigraph, pointing up the theme of paralysed self-consciousness; the counterpointed pronouns, *I, you,* and *we*; the movement of irregular and sometimes unrhymed lines; the undercurrent of threatening half-audible images, and the tendency of images, such as the fog imaged as a cat, to balloon away from their referents and assume an uncontrollable life of their own; the midway change of tense into the conditional, after Prufrock has decided not to pay his visit; the literary and other allusions. Though Pound argued that the Hamlet-Polonius passage should have been curtailed,[4] justly it seems to me, the final effect is extraordinarily persuasive.

Eliot coincidentally explained the effect of "Prufrock" in the course of his argument in "Tradition and the Individual Talent." The individual parts of any collection are affected by the supervention of a wholly novel element (*SE* [1951], p. 15): this poem is originary in the way it prompts succeeding poems to readjust their relations, proportions, values. Thus, it intersects with "La Figlia Che Piange" at the end of the volume, which becomes more obviously a redefinition of the theme of failure. With the balancing connection in mind, a reader of "Figlia" is particularly aware of how syntax runs through a sequence of grammatical changes, commands are overtaken by reverie, *I*'s and *he*'s and conditional tenses perform their ballet; of how the poem concludes in suspended inactivity, "a gesture and a pose" which would have been lost had they in fact been realized. "La Figlia Che Piange" had a very different origin from "Prufrock," its different scope and construction involve the reader differently, yet, in the orbit of the longer poem, it prolongs and attenuates the same motif.

"Portrait of a Lady" likewise. It follows directly on "Prufrock", as the same story told by two voices which merge, allowing more to a different but complementary point of view – that of a female version of Prufrock – who is similarly pathetic, inadequate, trapped by circumstance. Similar motifs recur: discussion of Chopin replaces talk of Michelangelo, the serving and drinking of tea, the mounting of the stairs. The poem is written as a counterpointed monologue, that is, the unnamed man's thoughts are thoroughly interpenetrated by the unnamed woman's, in rhymed and unrhymed lines whose length often falters; the movement is overall from frustrated hope towards unsatisfactory failure. It is in numbered sections, centred on successive visits through the seasons, but it moves through the same pattern of expectation, failure and suspended resolution as the poem which precedes it.

So also do "Preludes," "Rhapsody on a Windy Night" and "Morning at the Window," which follow in turn after "Prufrock" and "Portrait of a Lady." They reinforce and vary the note of boredom with different images of staleness. The first two "Preludes" rhyme an evening against a morning scene so as to collapse differences and hope of change; the second pair of "Preludes" rhymes dawn against dusk, and within each scene more drama is promised only to make it more evident that nothing will happen. "Rhapsody on a Windy Night" charts a progress through the night, towards a mounting stair, and then nothing. "Morning at the Window" is a reminder, as it cuts from image to response, that, as Hugh Kenner has observed,[5] these poems are not imagist exercises: Eliot's images are not presented as self-sufficient points of ecstatic rest. The images of cooking smells, dank housemaids and shuttered rooms imply an ache, a yearning after significance, and, while significance is withheld and to the extent that they are exactly perceived, they trouble and disturb. The image of "ancient women / Gathering fuel in vacant lots" at the close of the fourth "Prelude" is a good example of the way sentiment accumulates by means of repetition, from which the speaker then recoils.

"Gerontion," opening the 1920 volume, is wholly continuous in theme and mood, though it takes the same implications further. It is again a monologue spoken by a voice resembling Prufrock's, identified by the title as that of a little old man. The epigraph from *Measure for Measure* locates the limbo the voice comes from; the dry, barren, blocked situation the old man inhabits is invaded by promises of rejuvenation, which are grotesque and inadequate; memories of what might have been recreate an illusion whose temptations only underline failure. The speaker remains suspended among images: "Thoughts of a dry brain in a dry season."

There are deliberate echoes of "Prufrock." Prufrock's optative movement towards the woman of his quest through labyrinthine streets is picked up in Gerontion's movement through the labyrinth of history towards a protagonist who turns out surprisingly to be female and peculiarly sexual in the knowledge she promises:

> I would meet you upon this honestly . . .
> I have lost my sight, smell, hearing, taste and touch:
> How should I use them for your closer contact?

There is the same careful play with pronouns – *Us* and *I*, *We* and *you*; the same significant shift from *have* to *should*, the simple past accumulating a weight of obligation which is impossible to meet. Indeed, the whole transaction takes place only as a condition (*would*). Similar images conclude each poem, Prufrock's dandy vision of mermaids by the shore being matched by Gerontion's more isolated vision of a gull against the wind, remote and lost to man.

What "Gerontion" adds to "Prufrock" is the force of generality. It reduces the sense of personal depth and dimension of comedy and, at the same time, widens the range of reference. Gerontion is a less stable, less identifiable persona than any speaker in the previous volume. At the same time, what he speaks has more menace because it echoes more hollowly. This can be explained in different ways: Ronald Bush says that Gerontion's "consciousness is less insulated than Prufrock's was from eruptions from below." Prufrock is a character whereas, as Maud Ellmann says, "Gerontion is not a 'character,' but a dull head among windy spaces, a space where reading and rewriting recommence."[6] Like "Prufrock" and unlike other poems in the "Prufrock" volume, "Gerontion" works by incorporating allusions and near-quotations, but they are more completely emptied of resonance.

Both poems pose a problem to anyone anxious to find literal meaning – exactly what did Prufrock want to say to this woman? – but the question of literal meaning is left further behind in "Gerontion." The words are startling, and more so because they subsume the action they describe. Though it is difficult to say what meaning they contain, they function with less verbal slither. Though less happens in the narrative sense, the poem as a verbal construct encompasses wider, more general themes: it has a harder edge and religious and historical dimensions which "Prufrock" lacks.

Both the "Prufrock" and "Gerontion" volumes contain, as well as those I have been discussing, a number of poems in a different mode which may seem at first not to fit in with Eliot's "entelechy." The 1920 volume, following "Gerontion," is filled out with poems in quatrains or in French. Sweeney, the protagonist of three of the quatrain poems, by contrast with Prufrock the failed idealist, embodies the brutal vulgarity of solely naturalist values. The other poems differ from "Prufrock" in that the proportions of pathos and satire are reversed; their structural principle is not a quest that fails, or has failed beforehand, revealing itself in the speaker's reverie, but a more or less static situation seen satirically. Vulgarity overtakes suffering, laughter replaces sympathy.

In "Sweeney Erect" and "Sweeney Among the Nightingales," Sweeney is set against the worlds of Classical mythology and literature. In "Mr Eliot's Sunday Morning Service" he joins in a more complicated counterpoint between the Christ of the Greek theologians, of Pre-Raphaelite iconography and of New England culture. In "Burbank with a Baedeker: Bleistein with a Cigar," Sweeney as Bleistein is matched against Prufrock as Burbank. In "Whispers of Immortality," the dissociation of sensibility represented by the fleshly modern Grishkin is compared to the way Webster and Donne might have seen her. In "The Hippotamus," the earliest-written and tonally the simplest, Sweeney's values are represented in a humorous animal counterpart.

The satirical quatrain poems complement the erotic disappointment at the heart of "Prufrock" and "La Figlia Che Piange," and the allusions and the show of cleverness contrive a distance in which Eliot's persona is able to enlarge. They are not wholly unprepared for, of course. Other poems in the *Prufrock* volume step outside the flow of reverie to comment on manners and mores. "The 'Boston Evening Transcript,'" "Aunt Helen" and "Cousin Nancy" nicely fix the emotional and spiritual precariousness of New England culture; "Mr Apollinax" introduces among these decorous figures a Sweeney-related, satyr-like figure (based on Bertrand Russell), with mischievous effect; a prose-poem, "Hysteria," and "Conversation Galante" might be considered as exercises in modes outside the mainstream; as might the four exercises in French in the 1920 volume.

Two things appear to have helped bring forward this new aspect of Eliot's writing. Firstly, his friendship with Ezra Pound led to their conscious joint-experiment in rhyme and regular strophes, based on Théophile Gautier's *Emaux et Camées* and the Bay State Hymn Book.[7] Pound articulated their aim as being greater objectivity, to prevent their verses from sinking in the flow of their participant's musings. His own "Hugh Selwyn Mauberley" is the counterpart to Eliot's quatrains. Secondly, the criticism which Eliot was writing at the time that he put together the 1920 volume affected his verse profoundly. His discovery of Elizabethan and Jacobean dramatists like Webster, Tourneur, and Middleton not only supplied particular allusions but the nature of his reading affected the way such allusions were employed. Often, quite ordinary words and phrases are lifted from their context to make echoes and almost new meanings multiply in new contexts; what could mark dependence is made to communicate greater self-sufficiency. It is a ventriloquial technique which marks off "Gerontion" and the poems that accompanied it in 1920 from the poems published in 1917.

The perceptions Eliot arrived at or was working towards at this time, with Pound's help and through his own critical writing, represent a steadying and deepening of his sense of purpose. When he wrote about tradition and the individual talent, he described how his allusive method works; when he wrote about a dissociation of sensibility taking place in the seventeenth-century mind he described the subject of his own poetry; when he wrote of the objective correlative in *Hamlet*, he defined its method. Eliot's enlarging consciousness of the direction of his achievement is reflected in the way poems connect in a dialogue with other poems, and later poems go back to earlier ones – especially to "Prufrock" – in order to advance. The enlargement of his poetic concerns represented by the 1920 volume left him poised on the brink of writing *The Waste Land*, in which more various elements than ever before miraculously, and again with Pound's help, came together in the same poem.

In retrospect, then, Eliot saw his achievement as having a direction, an entelechy, which took "Prufrock" as the starting-point to be built upon; the 1920 quatrain poems represent a broadening of scope which is reflected in "Gerontion" but not fully assimilated until after. In this view, the quatrain poems represent a kind of enabling digression: they are not on the main highway, but they allow the main highway to broaden. Indeed, some readers have felt they go too far, that they become too difficult, that the tissue of allusion and quotation becomes too heavy for the burden of meaning and replaces it with something merely grotesque and disgusting. "Sweeney among the Nightingales," for instance, describes a situation from within and without, what Sweeney is and what he represents. The parallel with Agamemnon universalizes the description and makes it condemnatory, but it can be argued that the poem is too slight to bear such a weight of meaning, that it almost sinks beneath the parallels and perspectives and multiple allusions and close-packed cleverness. This was certainly the view of many early readers, in days before exegetes had done their work and compendia like Grover Smith's[8] were to hand.

The sense of shock and real difficulty felt by Eliot's early readers is a reminder of qualities familiarity can overtake. Always, as real originality is understood, its status alters in the process. Informed understanding follows on the first state of bewilderment, and comprises a process of containment by hindsight which often suppresses what is troubling and simplifies what is diverse. Eliot's career is only an extreme instance. His status as a classic rests on a recognition of the central, continuous tendency whose paradoxical authority I have been discussing. This is sharply at odds with the way his early writing struck readers as provocative or outrageous when it appeared. It is salutary to recall how monuments of our civilization once appeared to threaten it, and also what is lost when the threat is conquered. It is instructive to consider how Eliot adjusted his style (and his values) in a way which secured their assimilation.

Eliot's writing-career runs parallel to that of his readers in that, as the significance of what he had done impressed itself on him, he chose among opportunities – that is, simplified his past – in order to proceed. It was a retrospective judgment which brought together, but also diminished; it provided outline, like any rear-view mirror, by cutting off the world beyond its edges. Specifically, his career moved less consistently in the direction of spiritual pilgrimage than he chose to stress in "The Frontiers of Criticism"; his first volumes contain not only the beginning of the tendency with which his career continued but they also built towards a crossroads. Robert Frost's poem, "The Road Not Taken," supplies an image which keeps the present argument clear.

It is a retrospective distortion, therefore, to understand Eliot's quatrain poems as satirical adjuncts to his confessional theme, which helped enlarge its scope but which are disruptive because they head in a different direction. What from one point of view is inconsequential is, from another, a measure of their openness; these quatrain poems display Eliot, in his own terms, writing outside himself. If they are distinguished by qualities which appear marginal to the trajectory of his career, the same qualities, applied to something other than what he was aiming to be, are released into a novel realm. The kind of poetry he chose not to pursue afterwards possesses utterly distinctive qualities.

This kind of poetry is funny, inventive and surprising, and sometimes extravagant. Eliot was himself at pains to distinguish between poems which were not really "serious" ("Whispers of Immortality" and "The Hippopotamus") from those which were ("Burbank . . ." and "Sweeney Among the Nightingales"),[9] but the qualities I have named are shared by this kind of poetry as a whole. It is concerned less with salvation than with the world as it is, and consequently it is never sorry for itself or sanctimonious. It has a zest shared with the polemics of Eliot's criticism, and stands apart from the hesitant tones of disavowal of his other verse. It is concerned not with the rejection of the world, but with being in the world. It attacks targets without apology; anger does not drain away in personal concern and mutual understanding; there is nothing stuffy about it and it is not afraid to be unfair.

The inventiveness and energy and fun express themselves in many ways. Hugh Kenner has some characteristically acute comments on Eliot's handling of the stanza-form, saying "there is a surprise round every corner."[10] "The Hippopotamus" (the earliest) is the most regular in its adoption of the Gautier-stanza of two rhymes. Others rhyme the second and fourth lines (as in the ballad stanza) in different ways. The confined form compresses energy which makes possible odd transitions and juxtapositions.

"Burbank with a Baedeker: Bleistein with a Cigar" is marked by the way rhymes are carried over between stanzas in the first half and the way sense carries over from stanza to stanza in the second. "Sweeney Erect" and "Mr. Eliot's Sunday Morning Service" are distinguished by sharply contrasting points of view, one narrative, the other more strongly thematic. "Sweeney Among the Nightingales" sweeps into a long, elaborating, implicative sentence which runs across eight whole stanzas; "A Cooking Egg" is scooped into tight counterpoint. When these poems are set beside the poems in the *Prufrock* volume which they recall – "The Boston Evening Transcript" and so on – one appreciates that their pace is bound up with, wound up by, the verse form. The stanzas tighten the sense of threat and alarm, build a field of energy which implodes, yet do this in subtly various ways. Points of view are brought into collision so they re-adjust, just as references to surprising backgrounds gain a separate force which reacts upon their original contexts. The stanza-form acts like a particle accelerator, changing the behavior of what comes within its field.

The field of reference is not only wider and more compressed in the 1920 volume, but references operate with different effect. Whereas Prufrock's comparison of himself to John the Baptist or Polonius gains him a certain grim sympathy, the image of flowers growing from a skull in "Whispers of Immortality" (taken from *The White Devil*) is only to be marvelled at. There is no possibility of the allusion being absorbed to build a sense of the speaker's character; the speed with which it arrives and departs maintains it in a limbo of constant surprise. Names and phrases, as in poetry written contemporaneously by Pound, are generalized into the surface of the poem; that is, they flow into the medium and assume a status in which their original character is unimportant.

A good many more kinds of people come to inhabit Eliot's poems in this mode. Whereas the descendants of Prufrock bear a family resemblance which increases as their sense of withdrawal intensifies, Sweeney has a centrifugal identity: he moves away from the Eliotic center and reappears in proliferating guises. Whereas the Prufrock-character concentrates sympathy, the avatars of Sweeney generate fascination and disgust; their animation depends on a degree of animosity. Christopher Ricks has written well on this aspect of Eliot,[11] and it also has something to do with matters touched on by those who remark the relevance of Eliot's American background and of insights provided by feminist issues.

The outsider's vision, which enabled him to rewrite the sense of borrowed lines, also enabled him to draw caricatures. There are social dimensions to his sense of self-awareness which make it both vulnerable and shocking, as in "Burbank with a Baedeker: Bleistein with a Cigar" or Gerontion's vision of international Jewry. It is not simply a matter of individual references which happen to be off-key, but a measured tone of aloofness and pretense, composed with great care and skill, which is pervasive.

Only an outsider in dire need would have chosen to mimic upper-class English patterns of belief and behavior so assiduously, and Eliot's values were not uncontaminated by the roles he chose to play. However, at their best, the snobbery and pretentiousness are neutralized by the pure comedy of his estranged perceptions, as they are in Evelyn Waugh's early novels. Again, the evident sensitivity to physical contact of the Prufrock-protagonist, and his lack of sexual confidence, creates – defensively, through revulsion – such various grotesques as Madame de Tornquist, Doris, Rachel née Rabinovitch. Only a writer so vulnerable could have been so cruelly exact, and the personal grounds biographers have brought to our attention do not make the caricatures less troubling.

Eliot turned aside from such a teeming time-bound world to travel the road of what in *East Coker* is called "deprivation" and "destitution" and is pictured in "Gerontion" as a world of whirling, fractured atoms. He thereafter wrote humor of the same wild, inconsequential kind only as a joke – that is, with a certain archness – in *Old Possum's Book of Practical Cats*. He was unable to complete the play he began about Sweeney in 1924, and the humor which entered the play-writing after *Four Quartets* is somewhat precious and genteel. It seems he was only able to write the way he did here on the brink of a decision to pursue another course. In this respect, what I have called the Sweeney-mode is unique.

There is a comparison to be made with Wordsworth's 1798 contribution to *Lyrical Ballads*. Poems in ballad-stanzas like "Anecdote for Fathers" and "The Idiot Boy" possess a wild unassimilated hilarity which Wordsworth and Coleridge appear to have recognized by a special use of words like "glee" and "joy." Such poems are the opposite of everything Wordsworth is usually celebrated for, which is slow, solemn, sometimes prim, and they fall outside the ambit of his proto-Victorian celebration of man's unconquerable mind. They are in a sense an aberration, but this only enhances their special quality. They are funny, in quatrains, satirical, were prompted by a friend, and perhaps this last is the clue to their success. Persons absorbed by their own problems – namely, Wordsworth and Eliot – were interrupted at a crucial stage of their careers – by Coleridge and Pound – in ways that helped them momentarily write outside themselves.

Pound was instrumental in the creation of Eliot's first two volumes, and a case has been made for seeing *The Waste Land* as a jointly authored production.[12] Pound's relation to Eliot was complementary: besides the material assistance he gave, he provided someone against whom Eliot could fitly measure his difference. He was able to confirm "Prufrock" as starting-point and also able to assist Eliot to take a larger view of what he was doing. In the Sweeney-poems and aspects of "Gerontion" he may be said to have enabled Eliot to do more than Eliot afterwards wanted to remember; and Eliot's way forward beyond *The Waste Land* was, to some extent, a narrowing. Never again did he rise to such a dizzying comedy and pure writing. If it is in Pound's mode, it is writing which remains distinct from Pound's.

Eliot's late proposal that a body of poetry should be appraised in terms of what it is aiming to be is therefore complicated by the double-direction of his early poems. The 1920 volume left him facing in two directions, the direction he shared with Pound being overtaken by the direction he chose to pursue. Pound's response to Eliot's choice was unsympathetic; like Yeats, he shunned the way of salvation which "crawls between dry ribs / To keep our metaphysics warm."[13] Later on, in response to "The Cultivation of Christmas Trees," he wrote: "Let us lament the psychosis / Of all those who abandon the Muses for Moses." Readers of Eliot's early poems should be aware of the choice they present, and presented Eliot in his time, and must arrive at their own judgment.

NOTES

1 "Eliot's Classical Standing," F. R. Leavis and Q. D. Leavis, *Lectures in America* (London: Chatto and Windus, 1969), p. 30.
2 Compare Stephen's telegram in the Library chapter of *Ulysses*, borrowing a thought from George Meredith's *Richard Feverel*: "*The sentimentalist is he who would enjoy without incurring the immense debtorship for a thing done.*"
3 *Primitive* (Santa Barbara: Black Sparrow Press, 1979), p. 31. Oppen changes

"human" to "other," "and" to "or," divides Eliot's single line and omits a comma.

4 In a letter to Harriet Monroe, January 31, 1915; in D. D. Paige (ed.) *The Letters of Ezra Pound 1907–1941* (London: Faber and Faber, 1961), p. 92.

5 *The Invisible Poet: T. S. Eliot* (London: Methuen, 1965), p. 30.

6 Ronald Bush, *T. S. Eliot. A Study in Character and Style* (New York: Oxford University Press, 1983), p. 40; Maud Ellmann "The spider and the weevil: self and writing in Eliot's early poetry," Richard Machin and Christopher Norris (eds.) *Post-structuralist Readings of English Poetry* (Cambridge: Cambridge University Press, 1987), p. 390.

7 *Polite Essays* (London: Faber and Faber, 1937), p. 14.

8 *T. S. Eliot's Poetry and Plays. A Study in Sources and Meaning* (Chicago: The University of Chicago Press, 1956).

9 In a letter to Mary Hutchinson, July? 1919, *Letters* I, p. 311.

10 Kenner, *The Invisible Poet*, p. 85.

11 In *T. S. Eliot and Prejudice* (London: Faber and Faber, 1988).

12 Jack Stillinger, "Pound's *Waste Land*," in his *Multiple Authorship and the Myth of Solitary Genius* (New York: Oxford University Press, 1991), pp. 121–38.

13 "National Culture. A Manifesto 1938," William Cookson (ed.) *Selected Prose 1909–1965* (London: Faber and Faber, 1973), p. 134. The subsequent lines, printed in *Edge* (May 1957), are quoted by Robert Langbaum, "Pound and Eliot," George Bornstein (ed.) *Ezra Pound Among the Poets* (Chicago: The University of Chicago Press, 1985), p. 169.

9

HARRIET DAVIDSON

Improper desire: reading *The Waste Land*

When Ezra Pound read the manuscript of *The Waste Land* at the end of 1921, he objected to Eliot's epigraph from Joseph Conrad's *Heart of Darkness* (1899):

> "Did he live his life again in every detail of desire, temptation, and surrender during that supreme moment of complete knowledge? He cried in a whisper at some image, at some vision, – he cried out twice, a cry that was no more than a breath –
>
> "'The horror! the horror!'"

Pound argued that Conrad was not "weighty" enough for an epigraph, while Eliot, unsure about whether Pound objected to this quotation or to Conrad himself, responded that the passage was the most "appropriate" and "elucidative" he could find (*Letters* I, pp. 497 and 504). Pound won out in the end, for Eliot replaced this quotation with the present epigraph from Petronius' *Satyricon*, a passage in Latin and Greek which in its ancient and mythic references could be said to present the reader with a much weightier, indeed, intimidating opening to the poem:

> Nam Sibyllam quidem Cumis ego ipse oculis meis vidi in ampulla pendere, et cum illi pueri dicerent: Σίβυλλα τί θέλεις; respondebat illa: ἀποθανεῖν θέλω.

The passage from the *Satyricon* is appropriate to the poem in its references to imprisonment and desire for death, and in its connection to the Greek and Roman beginnings of European civilization. But the passage is hardly elucidative, both because the ancient languages themselves need to be elucidated for most readers and because the story of the Sibyl only ambiguously relates to the contemporary situation Eliot evokes in the poem. Indeed, the Sibyl's wish to escape her living death of immortality through a real death is put into immediate contrast with the opening of the poem which seems to yearn for the living death the Sibyl can no longer bear. The story of the Sibyl remains another disjointed piece of this puzzling poem.

More than accessibility was lost with the decision to begin with Petronius rather than Conrad. The change suppresses Eliot's appreciation of his contemporaries, instead impressing upon the reader the seriousness of classical scholarship. And importantly, the reader loses a helpful psychologizing of the emotional tone of the poem in Conrad's depiction of Kurtz's horror at his improper acts, so contrasted with Eliot's images of Prufrockian timidity and propriety. Kurtz's response of horror is not to an empty or even necessarily meaningless life, but to his rather too full embrace of human possibilities quite beyond the bounds of "proper" behavior.

The Waste Land can be read as a poem about the proper and the improper. Eliot's change of epigraph is one of many circumstances that contribute to emphasizing what we might call the "proper" side of this poem, that is, its scholarly apparatus, its respect for tradition, and its recoil from the chaos of life, rather than its "improper" side – its equally apparent lack of respect for tradition and poetic method and its fascination with mutation, degradation, and fragmentation. Proper means not only respectable or correct, but also in its etymology as "own" it means belonging to one thing, connecting the proper not only to social propriety, but also to property and the jealous guarding of boundaries. The poem returns again and again to "improper" sexual desire, temptation, and surrender and their often tragic consequences. The poem also, in its interest in metamorphosis and use of quick juxtapositions, blurs the proper boundaries between things; different characters and voices confusingly mutate into each other. Most obviously, the poem questions the boundaries between poems, liberally appropriating other poets' property as its own. As any reader of *The Waste Land* knows, none of this is done in the spirit of play; the overriding tone of the poem seems to yearn to be rid of improper desires, setting up a deep contradiction within the poem.

This contradiction, along with the poem's lack of thematic clarity and its careful refusal of connections between images, scenes and voices, makes *The Waste Land* particularly open to different interpretations. In fact, it is a measure of the poem's indigestibility that many of the controversies surrounding the poem when it was published in 1922 persist today. Readers in the twenties argued over whether the poem was too radical and meaningless or too conservative and tied to traditional values. New readers are still likely to come away from the poem bewildered by the many voices, allusions, and shifting tones of the poem. And professional critics still argue over the most basic of issues: what voice, if any, dominates the poem, what themes control the poem, and what values are upheld by the poem?

Given these unresolved questions, it seems surprising that the poem has come to seem such a monolithic representative of the long dominant New Critical values. Early New Critical readings of the poem canonized the poem as the exemplar (even origin) of a kind of high modernism that powerfully depicts and rejects modern life, valorizing myth over history, spatial form over time, an orderly past over a chaotic present, and the transcendence of art over the pain of life – what I would call the proper over the improper. Recent, politically minded critics make similar observations to dismiss the poem as the worst, most conservative side of modernism.[1] These interpretations tend to concur that the barren waste of the poem's title is a metaphor for the chaotic life within the poem and that the enormous longing to escape that life implies that a world of greater propriety, of stability, order, and beauty must exist somewhere, usually in a transcendent realm of the past, of religion, or of the aesthetic imagination.

But the power of the poem, I will argue, comes from its refusal to supply anything to appease the longing for propriety. The poem treats myth, history, art, and religion as subject to the same fragmentation, appropriation, and degradation as modern life – nothing transcends the effects of finitude and change brought on by the regeneration of April. The strong binary oppositions in the poem between desert and water, emptiness and crowdedness, suggest that the barren waste can be read as different from, and in opposition to, the chaotic life in the poem, not as a metaphor for it. In this reading, the empty unchanging desert represents what would happen if our wish to escape the uncertainties of life through absolutes, transcendence, or, like the Sibyl, immortality were to be granted. Sadly, the only alternative to the human world of thwarted and degraded desires, loss, change, and confusion is a barren waste. While the poem provides an emotional and often visceral critique of the state of human life, it equally provides a critique of the desire to transcend and escape that life, and it offers no alternatives beyond that life or the persistence of that desire.

Eliot's prose writings of the time, especially his philosophical writings, show very clearly that the young Eliot believed that nothing transcends the finite and particular world. In these writings, particularly his dissertation written for a doctorate in philosophy, he challenges the philosophical notion of a transcendent Absolute, either Ideal or Real, and argues that change and diversity alone are absolute, thus undermining the stability and unity of all ideas, things, and personalities. But Eliot is no relativist; he admits that things, selves, and ideas often seem clear and fixed. Eliot's philosophical position resembles the pragmatism of his professors at Harvard: the world is neither objective nor subjective, nor empirically verifiable, but also not relative for each individual. Instead, selves and objects simultaneously arise out of and create a shared culture, giving us the strange situation in which, "We are certain of everything – relatively, and of nothing – positively" (KE p. 157). Our certainty is only within a particular, historical, cultural context, which will, inevitably, change for better or worse.

His prose presents all this rather matter-of-factly, but the young Eliot's poetry is haunted by the metaphysical uncertainty about the self and the cultural dependence of identity; the poetry is by turns bitingly satiric about social roles and despairing of any more authentic existence. The older Eliot solved his dilemma about the self by embracing the most stable culture and tradition he could find and accepting the identity it gave him, thus becoming a royalist, Anglican, and proper Englishman. These actions are consistent with his rejection of an idea of the authentic self, but they suppress the instability and fragmentation of the actual self and world. His embrace of a conventional British identity and his often reactionary arguments for homogeneous and stable cultures suggest a dauntingly complacent cultural conservatism that effectively hides the experimental and improper impulses of his youth. Just as in The Waste Land the powerfully rendered voice yearning to escape life under the forgetful snow has had a disproportionate effect on subsequent readers, so Eliot's image of propriety has had enormous impact on the study of his poetry (and indeed all literature) up through the 1960s.

The Waste Land strongly reveals the unruly forces of improper desire in its emotional yearning, in its constant return to sexual tragedy, and in its disorienting juxtapositions and displacements. But the textual history of the poem, from draft, to edited version, to published version with endnotes, tends to tame some of the unruliness of the poem. The manuscript draft of the poem, which is even more various than the final poem, includes three long narrative sections cut in the final version by Pound and by Eliot himself. These cuts excise Eliot's rawer side: scenes of drunkenness, whoring, urinating, defecating, and bigotry are removed from the poem and from Eliot's emerging public persona. And with the removal of the manuscript's comic, narrative opening, the poem foregrounds the life-denying voice, which begins by recoiling from spring: "April is the cruellest month."

Perhaps even more important for confusing understanding of the poem are the notes which were not originally attached to it but were added only for the book version.[2] The notes focused critical attention on the scholarly exegesis of sources and allusions, and encouraged the kind of source-hunting that began to take over readings of the poem. Eliot may not have intended them to be taken so seriously, and may even have been playing an elaborate and highly successful practical joke on the academic profession. He was later to write, "I regret having sent so many enquirers off on a wild goose chase after Tarot cards and the Holy Grail."[3] Nevertheless, the notes seemed to offer a key to the poem and to promise a full and scientifically accurate explanation which would overcome its fragmentation and suggestiveness. Regretfully or not, Eliot had endorsed a public image of scholarly propriety and encouraged interpretations which tended to erase the improper side of the poem in favor of its proper, pedagogic side.

Knowing the story of the quest for the Grail or the significance of the Tarot does not, of course, hurt when reading *The Waste Land*. Stories of death and renewal or damnation and salvation, from the Grail legends and fertility myths outlined by Jessie Weston in *From Ritual to Romance*, and from Dante's *Divine Comedy*, greatly haunted Eliot's imagination and contributed to his conversion to Christianity in 1927. But part of Eliot's interest in the anthropological work of Weston and of Sir James Frazer in *The Golden Bough* may have lain in the examination of the many variants and mutations in fertility myths over time. As Weston's and Frazer's work powerfully shows, there is no proper or original form of these myths. In Eliot's own variant on these stories in *The Waste Land*, death is never redeemed by any clear salvation, and barrenness is relieved only by a chaotic multiplicity, which is not only an ironic kind of fertility, but is also the distinctly urban chaos that the young Eliot appreciated as conducive to his work (*Letters* I p. 55). The other lesson of the fertility myths, in which a sacrificial death (often a ritual death by water) is necessary for life to continue, is the connection of life and death. Death is not the only horror, as the Sibyl, incapacitated with age and loneliness after being granted her wish for immortality, well knows. Kurtz's cry of horror at the vision of his wretched life and death is matched by the Sibyl's horror at a sterile, changeless state without life, death, love, or loss.[4]

The Waste Land suggests both horrors. Imagistically, the "little life with dried tubers" (I, line 7) and the dry, unchanging desert contrast throughout the poem with life-giving rain and the drowning sea. The images are supported by two distinct ways of speaking. The lyric voice opening the poem uses highly metaphoric, often symbolic images and speaks in repetitive, stylized syntax, suggesting on the one hand order and propriety, and on the other hand stasis. This voice speaks with authority and finality as it recurs in scenes throughout the poem where the vision of barrenness and revulsion from life is intensely clear and controlled.

This voice contrasts with the babel of many voices speaking in metonymically rendered narrative scenes full of movement and change. These other voices resist categorization, ranging from vivid characters such as Marie, the hyacinth girl, Stetson's friend, Madame Sosostris, the nervous woman, the pub woman, Tiresias, and the Thames daughters, to the non-human voices of the nightingale, the cock, and the thunder, and the voices from literature in the many allusions in the poem. The many abrupt changes and mutations in the voices of the poem often blur the proper boundaries between identities, further increasing the reader's confusion about who is speaking.

Both modes – of sterile propriety and fertile impropriety – cause despair, but neither is repudiated entirely. Much of the drama of this poem comes from the interweaving and crisscrossing of these two modes as desire disrupts order and desire for order sets up paradoxical and unbearable tensions. The poem frustrates the reader's attempts to follow themes or images in an orderly way; rather, in the best modernist spirit, form gives us a lesson in mutability that is well illustrated from the very opening of the poem.

"The Burial of the Dead" famously begins with a desire for stasis and anxiety about the change, growth, and sexuality symbolized by April and the spring rain. The slow, repetitive syntax and hanging participles – "breeding," "mixing," "stirring" – seem to freeze and control the movement in the first seven lines. This despairing opening voice is universal and dislocated; it is not in a narrative, nor does it speak to the reader. The clarity and authority of this voice mark it as the voice of propriety, wanting to maintain clear boundaries and rules, and, at its most extreme, hoping to halt forward movement and stop the proliferation of possibilities in life or language.

As readers of *The Waste Land*, we tend to privilege this voice because we, too, would like clarity and the stability of a proper meaning for this confusing poem. But the desire for stability, the desire to end desire, is always a paradoxical one. If we follow recent psychoanalytic theory, we could say that desire is both *caused by* the lack of absolutes in human life, the inevitable finitude and change, and *causes* change in its restless search for something to relieve this lack. The reader's interpretation, like any desire for order, is really just another proliferation of possibility, not at all a stabilizing of the poem. In this sense all desire is improper desire, disrupting clarity and stability in favor of change and movement. And the figure of desire, that endless movement from object to object, is metonymy.[5]

Thus, in these opening lines the desire for stasis brings about change. Line eight begins as if to continue the rhythm and tone of the preceding lines, but then the syntax suddenly mutates into a chatty and incidental narrative:

> Summer surprised us, coming over the Starnbergersee
> With a shower of rain; we stopped in the colonnade,
> And went on in sunlight, into the Hofgarten,
> And drank coffee, and talked for an hour.   (I, lines 8–11)

Now the participle "coming" is not left hanging to indicate continuing action by the generic "Summer," but is connected to its object indicating an action of limited duration by a particular "us." With the syntactic shift from metaphoric similarity to metonymic contiguity, we have left the angst and symbolic world of the opening lines and entered a realist, fairly neutral narrative world replete with the familiar cultural actions of talking, walking, and drinking coffee. In spite of this simple familiarity, most readers feel anxious when confronted with this new turn in the poem. The clear ideas and syntax established in the opening lines no longer control the poem, and attempts to continue a symbolic reading of these lines founder on the difficulty of turning metonymic details like drinking coffee into metaphoric meaning. Not only the coffee in the Hofgarten, but also the overheard line in German, Madame Sosostris's bad cold, Lil's teeth, the typist's stockings, all seem to function as metonymic details from the culture of the time, and they generate a context and a chain of associations which tend to disperse clear meanings.

The speaker of these lines also seems more particularized than in the opening lines, and in lines thirteen to eighteen the clearly gendered voice of Marie further disrupts the expectation of universality. Her story also ignores the metaphors established at the opening; now snow is associated with memory and desire as she remembers a thrilling sled ride with her cousin. Marie, along with the many other women characters in the poem, is associated in a traditional way with sexual desire, fertility, and generation. But quite untraditionally the poem concerns itself not just with women as objects of desire, but also with women as subjects with desires. Marie, Madame Sosostris, the nervous lady and pub lady of part II, the Thames daughters from part III, all bring their own yearnings to this poem; the female perspective, particular and sexual unlike the ungendered metaphoric voice, insists on the continuation of desire but also shows how often desire leads to frustration, ennui, and violence. The narrative world Eliot gives us as an alternative to the little life of dried tubers is driven by desires, but not often happily. The rather neutral scene in the Hofgarten metonymically moves into the emotionally charged story of Marie which ends abruptly in a scene of loneliness and deadening routine: "I read much of the night and go south in the winter" (I, line 18). Once we enter the everyday world, we also enter the world of loss, unfulfilled desire and, inevitably, death.

The movement from metaphoric enclosure to metonymic movement is repeated twice more in "The Burial of the Dead" – as the metaphoric voice tries to control the improper desires, and the metonymic voice breaks out of this control. First, the horrifying red rock section (I, lines 19–30) returns to a symbolic mode of commanding finality. But it is interrupted by the German allusion to the great story of improper love, *Tristan und Isolde*, by the narrative of desire and loss in the hyacinth girl passage, and then by the comic realism of Madame Sosostris. Second, the "Unreal City" passage (I, lines 60–68) returns to a symbolic, static vision of London as a suffocating hell, but here the symbolic enclosure is burst apart by the narrative address to Stetson and then to the reader. The energy of these final lines transgresses a variety of boundaries in their wild historical mixing, grisly violation of the grave, and dense allusiveness. The allusion to Baudelaire in the last line "'You! hypocrite lecteur! – mon semblable, – mon frère!'" (I, line 76) confusingly blurs the narrator's voice with Baudelaire, Stetson, and the reader. We, too, are metonymically drawn into the chain of desire in our search for final meanings in a poem which suggests these meanings but then denies them any stability.

The function of allusion in *The Waste Land* has been much debated; allusion can be considered a metaphoric device, which depends on similarities between the text alluded to and the present text. But allusion is also a dispersive figure, multiplying contexts for both the present work and the text alluded to and suggesting a cultural, historical dimension of difference. For instance, the jolting allusion to *Tristan und Isolde* in this section has a certain propriety for the poem because of its theme of tragic love and its images of fresh wind and water complementing the stirrings of April. But the reader is first struck by the different, perhaps unfamiliar, language and scene, which needs translation, interpretation, and contextualizing. While it is surely a relief to turn away from the chilling symbolism of the "handful of dust" (I, line 30), the reader ends up in a land of confusing particularity and unfulfilled desires.

The introduction of the impersonal, culturally resonant story of star-crossed love leads the speaker to a more personal and therefore more unbearable memory of love and loss in the hyacinth girl section. But even here the unbearable trauma, figured as silence and paralysis, is diffused by another allusion to *Tristan*: "*Oed' und leer das Meer*" (I, line 42). The image of the empty sea is an objective correlative for the desolate silence of the speaker. But as an allusion to a German opera, the line counters the speaker's sense of emptiness with cultural plenitude, leading the poem and the reader right back out into interpretation (and translation) and away from silence. Positioned in this way, the allusion to Wagner seems to reach in two directions at once: it both supports some emerging themes of the poem in its watery images and story of tragic love, and it also disperses attention away from clear themes to disorderly interpretation. In general, the allusions in *The Waste Land* disperse clear meanings into other contexts, undermine the notion of authentic speaking, and blur boundaries between texts.

I will discuss the middle three sections of *The Waste Land* only briefly before ending with a closer look at the final section, "What the Thunder Said." Section II, "A Game of Chess," seems to be thematically centered on a sterile vision of modern life, especially in lines 135–38. But this vision is countered by the narrative animation of the scenes: the sensuous movement of objects in the boudoir, the hysterical woman's insistent questioning, the playful mutation of Shakespeare to a "Shakespeherian Rag," the pub lady's vivid chatter – all suggest the continuation of desire under the static surface. But desire is also particularly tragic for the women of this section, from the allusions to the love suicides of Cleopatra, Dido, and Ophelia (II, lines 77, 92, and 172) and the rape of Philomela, to the loneliness of the nervous woman and the sad domestic life of Lil. Philomela's story (II, lines 97–103), a picture animated into a narrative, is a paradigm of the simultaneously destructive and creative force of desire. After being raped, Philomela is transformed into the nightingale whose song is often a symbol for the poet. But her transcendence of violence is not eternal: her "inviolable voice" is changed into "'Jug Jug' to dirty ears," as the chain of transforming desire leaves nothing inviolate, nothing static.

"The Fire Sermon" refers to Buddha's sermon on the purification of sexual desire. But this section is ruled by water, primarily the river Thames, first described as "sweet" and later as sweating "oil and tar" (III, lines 176 and 267). The mutating panoply of scenes in this section shows desire unleashed, momentarily in love and beauty, more typically in degradation and despair. But Eliot's notes to "The Fire Sermon" also point to a pattern of music which, like the nightingale's song, arises from desire. At the end when the speaker tries to burn away his desires, the music of the poetry, too, is reduced to syntactic incoherence until only the single word "burning" remains (III, lines 308–11). This ending starkly contrasts with the short, musical lyric which follows it. "Death by Water" counters both spiritual burning and linguistic aphasia with the sea and with easy syntactic connections, especially in its many rhythmic pairs. The peaceful surrender of the body to the water suggests an acceptance of death and change, a gentle *memento mori* in opposition to the anxiety about change at the end of "The Fire Sermon."

But the burning returns at the beginning of "What the Thunder Said" with "the torchlight red on sweaty faces" (V, line 322). This final section returns to a barren waste, an inhuman landscape where repetition suggests a pointless circularity. The continuing force of desire is suggested in lines 346–59 as the imagination tries to break out of the sterility of the desert by thinking "If there were water . . ." Trying to imagine water, the voice metonymically moves from the rock to "a pool among the rock" to the "sound of water" and finally to music once again as these lines culminate in imagining the singing of the hermit thrush in the pine trees and the "drip drop" of water. This magical metamorphosis abruptly stops as the categorical voice of the desert insists, "But there is no water." Still, change cannot be stopped. Immediately after this line, the clarity of the desert dissolves and visions begin to proliferate wildly, from the uncertain vision of "another one walking beside you" (v, line 362), the unclear "Murmur of maternal lamentation" (v, line 367), to the city that "cracks and reforms and bursts in the violet air" (v, line 372). These visions culminate in the surreal scene of a woman fiddling on her hair, of bats with baby faces, and of upside-down towers. This vision is deeply improper, not respecting conventional metonymical association. And the impropriety is a sign that desire has not been burned away.

Instead, the continuation of desire is announced rather forthrightly in the crow of the cock, the flash of lightning, and the welcome gush of rain:

> Only a cock stood on the rooftree
> Co co rico co co rico
> In a flash of lightning. Then a damp gust
> Bringing rain   (v, lines 392–95)

These lines rewrite the formal strategy of the opening lines; here the participle "bringing" is attached to its object, giving a sense of release to the sexual and spiritual desire in these lines. Appropriately, the voice of the thunder is neither categorical, proper, nor clear; it is a meaningless syllable, "DA," which needs to be interpreted, starting another chain of dispersion and obscurity. The thunder is interpreted in the Sanskrit words "Datta," "Dayadhvam," "Damyata," allusions to the fable of the thunder in the Upanishads, a different and perhaps unfamiliar cultural context. The translations of these words into the English imperatives "give," "sympathize," and "control" are further interpreted in the poem in enigmatic lyrics.

Many readers find these three lyrics and the allusive ending of the poem which follows some of the most difficult lines of the poem, and they have been interpreted variously as showing resignation, salvation, or nihilism. The sense of change, variety and movement is strong in these lines, as is the sense of being in a social, cultural world. In the first lyric (v, lines 401–10), the voice is conversational, opening out to the reader in the address to "my friend" and the use of the first person plural words "we" and "our":

> *Datta*: what have we given?
> My friend, blood shaking my heart
> The awful daring of a moment's surrender
> Which an age of prudence can never retract
> By this, and this only, we have existed   (v, lines 402–6)

The surrender to desire, to the shaking heart, *is* life, not the safety of prudence nor the lifeless, "empty rooms" (v, line 410). In the subsequent lyric (v, lines 411–17) both the images of the prison and of the key connect with the Sibyl's lonely prison of immortality; the desire for the key, the clear answer, the end to human troubles, is what ironically "confirms a prison," while the revivifying "aethereal rumors" of twilight represent yearning and possibility (v, lines 414–15).[6] Most importantly and optimistically, in the third lyric (v, lines 418–23) the image of the sailboat both propelled by and controlling the wind and water combines the force of desire and control. In this image order and control are linked to the continuation of desire in the boat's movement across the water.

At the end of the poem, the desire for order and the surrender to the chaotic desires of life remain in tension. The speaker sits by the sea, turning his back on the "arid plain" of the desert. Still he asks, "Shall I at least set my lands in order?" (v, line 426) indicating the continuation of a quest for order and meaning. But the speaker is answered by a series of allusions which are neither properly "my lands" nor in any discernible order. The lines themselves speak of disintegration and disorder, madness and desire. And the variety of voices here, speaking in different languages and different tones, indicates a world rich with possibility as well as confusion, with salvation as well as loss. The ending is deeply improper, not respecting boundaries between poems, between cultures, or between voices. The impropriety suggests the disrupting power of desire in *The Waste Land*. The passionate and paradoxical desire to end desires leads only to the continuation of life in all its variousness, confusions, tragedies, and improper desires.

NOTES

1 See, for instance, Terry Eagleton, *Criticism and Ideology* (1976; London: Verso, 1978), pp. 145–51; also Sandra M. Gilbert, "Costumes of the Mind: Transvestism as Metaphor in Modern Literature," *Critical Inquiry* 7 (1980): 400–4.

2 *The Waste Land* was published in the Fall, 1922 in the *Dial* in New York and the *Criterion* in London. In December it was published in book form by Boni and Liveright with the notes included.

3 Quoted in Hugh Kenner *Invisible Poet* (New York: McDowell, 1959), p. 151.

4 In an essay on Baudelaire written in 1930, Eliot writes, "it is better, in a paradoxical way, to do evil than to do nothing: at least we exist," *SE* (1950), p. 380.

5 See Jacques Lacan's discussion of metonymy and desire in "The Agency of the Letter in the Unconscious, or Reason Since Freud," *Ecrits: A Selection* (New York: W. W. Norton and Co., 1977), pp. 146–75.

6 In his notes to *The Waste Land*, Eliot quotes F. H. Bradley's statement of solipsism in relation to these lines, but in his dissertation of 1916 Eliot is at some pains to refute the possibility of solipsism, saying that the sense of self only comes with a sense of others (*KE*, p. 150).

10

JOHN KWAN-TERRY

Ash-Wednesday: a poetry of verification

While Eliot's prose writings between 1925 and 1945 expound the need for self-transcendence, his poetry can be said to display the *difficulties* involved in this process. As early as 1916, in his dissertation on *Knowledge and Experience in the Philosophy of F. H. Bradley*, he had made it clear that by "self-transcendence" he meant, paradoxically, the struggle to progress from a purely personal experience of contact with the noumenal, the realm that is beyond phenomena and outside the process of time, by entering more fully into the shared world of objects and of time; and by multiplying experiences to pursue the ideal "of an all-inclusive experience outside of which nothing shall fall" (*KE* p. 31). The assumption is that the more comprehensive our experience, and the more unified our knowledge derived from experience, the nearer we come to the total truth.

It is the limited scope of merely private experience that compels us to go out of ourselves, out of even our most intense and timeless moments, into the common world of others and of passing events. No individual can be self-sufficient, "for the life of a soul does not consist in the contemplation of one consistent world but in the painful task of unifying (to a greater or lesser extent) jarring and incompatible ones" (*KE* p. 147). But to "unify" is to incorporate and to transmute, to make what was other our own, and so to get free again of the world of timebound phenomena. The vital difference between the beginning and the end of this process is that what was at first simply one's private experience comes to be confirmed and verified, and established as impersonal and absolute truth. The kind of truth in question, however, as Eliot made clear, is metaphysical, and not the literal truth of science: "It involves an *interpretation*, a transmigration from one world to another, and such a pilgrimage involves an act of faith" (*KE* p. 163). The process of verification does not end then in objective certainty, but can only confirm the faith, the personal desire, which drives us on toward the whole truth which may, or may never, be attained.

Eliot's "Ariel" poems are, in this sense, prayers of faith. In "A Song for

Simeon," Eliot has Simeon say: "Not for me the ultimate vision." And it is interesting to note that Simeon does not connect with the congregation of believers: "Not for me the martyrdom, the ecstacy of thought and prayer." He seems to return, at the conclusion of the poem, to the veracity of individual experience. Perhaps such a moment of experience is like belief in the Second Advent, the *parousia* that the early Christians waited for: a hope based on faith. Verification is thus still to come. It is a matter of faith that one's experiences are "real," not a matter of objective knowledge, and it is a matter of faith that there is a total identity or an Absolute, not a matter of scientific verification. For all the poetry's emphasis on connection and community, and its efficacy against the ravaging work of Time, it does often seem to allow Time the upper hand.

"The Hollow Men" enacts the despairing voyage of verification. Images, tantalizing or terrifying, remain echoes and fragments in mankind's abortive effort to make sense of a history of wisdom and spirituality:

> Between the desire
> And the spasm
> Between the potency
> And the existence
> Between the essence
> And the descent
> Falls the Shadow

Personal experience remains entrapped in immediate actualities and desires, unable to see beyond them, or seeing beyond them unable to authenticate any felt sense of order. The need for verification, plus the fear over the dangers of over-individualization, akin to solipsism, seems to indicate that Eliot has difficulty in treating personal religious experience as a real, self-subsistent object. Connection and verification are important needs themselves, as Eliot informs us in his dissertation on Bradley. And in the prose, he constantly warns against the danger of the purely personal – of solipsism – which allows no relationships of any sort, no social world, and is, in the end, life denying. It does not even allow any definite belief that what one had previously seen is true: it may have only been an illusion – the "mad experiences" of the finite centres of his dissertation. Yet in his essay on "Dante," Eliot informs us that this dissolving of the finite self – which Life cannot offer – is also what he *would have*. He would have it both ways: he would live in the world of Time, though it savages and destroys, causing separation; but he would also connect with all who believe as he does (and this as a strategy to overcome Time) in order, finally to be translated into the beyond. Hence, his senses of what history is contradict each other and battle it out in the poetry. His poetry often teaches us to dispossess the world, even as the prose apprises us of the need to save the world through a renewed contact with the standards that make civilization fecund. It might be said therefore that the battle of Eliot's contradictory ideas of what history ought to be is the battle between subjective experience and the need for a manifestation of reality in the here and now, even while the poetry concedes that the latter desire has real limitations.

Ash-Wednesday (1930), widely regarded as Eliot's "conversion" poem, displays to us the difficulty the Eliotic protagonist has in treating personal religious experience as self-subsistent. While the fallen world and desert of *The Waste Land* has become, in *Ash-Wednesday*, a part of the journey to the Absolute, the very climax of the poem (the garden scene of the fourth section) is fraught with ambiguity and uncertainty. By the time we reach the last section of the poem, the poet's personal experience of transcendent truth seems inadequate and appears to be about to slip out of his grasp, even as he issues a last prayer for help. The lure of the world, it would seem, draws him back – back into the world of time and sequence, the world that he had attempted, in the first place, to negate and leave behind.

The first section begins with a translated quotation from Cavalcanti, and the idea of renunciation is introduced immediately. The poet renounces his love and is thereby stating his readiness for death. This particular sense of loss then modulates into a theme of worldly loss and renunciation in the citation of Shakespeare's Sonnet 24:

> Because I do not hope to turn again
> Because I do not hope
> Because I do not hope to turn
> Desiring this man's gift and that man's scope . . .

We are told: "I no longer strive to strive towards such things." But the tone, then, begins to shift: the first four lines with their syllable-by-syllable emphasis, highlighting the resigned disillusionment the poet would have us know he feels, changes to defiance. The last three lines of the first paragraph become almost strident in tone:

> (Why should the aged eagle stretch its wings?)
> Why should I mourn
> The vanished power of the usual reign?

There is a sense of triumph in his renunciation: it is not now a resignation born from tiredness but one that is made by *choice*. As we look back at the first three lines, we find that they can now be read with a more affirmative sense: "*Because* I do not hope to turn again . . ."

The entire first paragraph, hence, seems to become an indication of the power of the personal will of the narrator. However, a breakdown in his certainty occurs in the more fragmented utterances of the second paragraph, and the situation is aggravated by the appearance of phrases that qualify rather than assert:

> Because I do not hope to know again . . .
> Because I know I shall not know
> The one veritable transitory power

While the prosody is, as in the first paragraph, iambic, the forward movement is contradicted by the content of these utterances. There is a pause after the last quoted line, after which the speaker reveals the actual barrenness of his present circumstances. Fresh knowledge comes to him:

> Because I cannot drink
> There, where trees flower, and springs flow, for there is nothing again

To function in the phenomenal world, "where trees flower, and springs flow," is to function in the realm where there is "nothing."

The opening lines of the third paragraph elaborate upon what he has learnt in the realm of "nothingness." It is a discovery that promises spiritual healing. The verse becomes mellifluous, and a sense of tranquil movement is conveyed through the repetition of various key words, such as "time," and "place," that almost, if not quite, qualifies the austerity of the first two paragraphs. The austerity is not quite qualified because of the *content* of what he has learnt: that the temporal sphere must be left behind (for "time is always time"); that whatever he may have found to be true so far is limited, because it was only true in a moment of time ("what is actual is actual only for one time / And only for one place"). Yet as in the essay on Pascal's *Pensées*, joy – if not an unmitigated joy – comes about from his skeptical realization:

> I rejoice that things are as they are and
> I renounce the blessèd face
> And renounce the voice . . .

Even as he gives up the "blessèd face" and "voice" (they are metaphors for the "Lady of silences" who is the perfect counterpart of the "worldly" woman the poet has renounced), he has begun to have intimations of what the higher perspective holds. Now he knows that the way of self-effort, with the "I" at the centre, cannot reach the higher: "Because I *cannot* hope to turn again." The first line, which initially harbored some prospect of meaningful choice, is here negated completely. The self – that which can make choices and which has some meaning in the fragmented, partial sphere of Time – is of less use in the journey towards the Absolute, for in order to reach that exalted realm, the poet has to "forget / These matters that with myself I too much discuss / Too much explain." As the finite center aspires towards the Absolute, it has to learn to forgo the way of self-effort, for the realm where the Absolute dwells has "air which is now thoroughly small and dry," too rarified for the poet's "wings" to function in and where they would be "merely vans to beat the air."

As the first section ends, the verse returns to the immobility of the opening lines, with its syllable-to-syllable emphasis, though now laden with the knowledge of the *via negativa*:

> Teach us to care and not to care
> Teach us to sit still.

For the first time in the section, a "full-stop" appears: this prayer, then, is where we must stop. We have learnt the Way. There has been an attempt to point us to a new state of being. In the "Dante" essay, Eliot tells us that, in the *Paradiso*, Dante's "insistence throughout is upon states of feeling; the reasoning takes only its proper place as a means of reaching these states." (*SE* [1951], p. 266). The poetry itself, in the case of *Ash-Wednesday*, serves to point us beyond the poetry – the poetry itself is part of the process of "reasoning" that takes place before the reaching of eternity. If we are to take the "Dante" essay as shedding some light on Eliot's own poetic craft, we can say that Eliot does not indulge in images for their own sake. Instead, figures are "serious and practical means of making the spiritual visible," (*SE* [1951], p. 267) as was, he felt, the case with Dante. From this first opening section of *Ash-Wednesday*, we are informed that personal experience of mystical death is one of the first weapons that must be employed to defeat the realm of sequential time, with all its barren actuality. As Balachandra Rajan has noted, "the understanding to be gained in *Ash-Wednesday* must be achieved and not announced . . ." The difficulty, however, as Rajan notes, is that "the settlement when reached cannot endure. Time in its corrosive nature demands the renewal of any conclusion that is achieved in time . . . there can be no harbour and no garden except to equip the mind for a new exile."[1] And this, in a nutshell, is the problem that dogs the poet in the later portion of this poem.

The second section contains the poet's recollection of his spiritual rebirth, not to a new self, but as a dissolution of the self. The poet, whose body is being consumed by the enigmatic "three white leopards," says, almost joyously:

And I who am here dissembled
Proffer my deeds to oblivion, and my love
To the posterity of the desert and the fruit of the gourd.

As always with Eliot, whether in prose or poetry, one sees the distrust of the personal and the desire for the total: "oblivion" is what the poet seeks, and this oblivion can only be found in the region of the eternal. The dry bones of the poet recognize the need for the whole in their "burden," their song or litany of paradoxes. The apparent contradictions indicate how complex is the way to Absolute Being: in giving up a woman of the "world," the poet has, in the first section, begun to gather an understanding of what his worldly desire *actually* is for – in renunciation is the true finding of oneself. Hence, the "Rose of memory" – which belongs to the earthly sphere – leads him to a better way, the "Rose of forgetfulness." More than this, however, is now comprehended by the dissembled poet. Individual vision thus gained by forgetfulness is not enough: the "conclusion" is "now the Garden / Where all loves end." Personal experience must be placed in a larger context. Where all loves end, love begins. The poet has to journey further, higher still, for an even stronger grasp of the Eternal. The bones continue to chirrup in the lines that follow the litany, and the section ends on this note: "This is the land. We have our inheritance." He must go on to further narrow the breach between his realm and the realm of the transcendent other. But the realm of the transcendent other is crossed by the need of the actual. The protagonist in the third section glimpses "The broadbacked figure drest in blue and green" but is "distracted" by "stops and steps of the mind," memories of "brown hair over the mouth blown / Lilac and brown hair."

It is inevitable, when the poet reaches the garden in section four and sees the lady, the representation of the invisible Good that he searches for by way of dispossession, that the vision should reveal its fragility: it is "The *unread* vision in the *higher* dream . . ." Though he has come to virtual contact with the vision to be seen, and come close to "the still point of the turning world" (*BN* II), the new center where dwells Silence, revelation is not without its treacheries. Standing between the yew trees and the lady who wears "white light folded, sheathed about her," is "the garden god," a reminder of the natural world where Time exists and is not redeemed. The meeting of the two worlds is difficult. Here, the Time-filled world is stronger, for the poet does not hear what the presence – the lady – might have said to him: total understanding is denied him, even as the fruition of the negative way seems imminent. The "fountain" (of the Time-filled realm) may have sprung up to meet the eternal, even as the "bird" (of the Eternal realm) may have sung "down," or reached downwards – but it is of no use. He does not hear the true Word, but only empty "whispers from the yew."

The final line is a phrase from the Catholic hymn *Salve Regina*: "And after this our exile." Tellingly, there is no "full-stop"; for the completion of the actual utterance ("And after this our exile, show unto us the blessed fruit of thy womb, Jesus") is impossible. He has not heard nor met the Divine Word of John 1:1, only the mortal whispers of the yew trees. Total identity eludes him, and he is forced back into exile in the finite world where separation from the correct or full understanding of the Absolute is the norm.

When we reach the last section, section six, we find that the opening line of the poem ("Because I do not hope . . .") has undergone another metamorphic change from "Because I cannot hope" to "Although I do not hope to turn again." This subtle shift indicates that whatever positive action the Cavalcanti phrase may have promised, it is now almost devoid of such affirmation. "Although," which in this case seems to mean "admitting," or "not withstanding that," is surely weaker than "because," which indicated that the poet had tried to make a choice. The Cavalcanti phrase, then, has become steadily reduced. Both affirmation and the negative way appear limited.

The poet is left, finally, in "the time of tension between dying and birth" – the temporal sphere, the twilight zone of sequential time where there is no comprehensive understanding of anything. This is "The place of *solitude* . . ." The last line of the poem ("And let my cry come unto Thee."), normally the ritual response in a Catholic mass to the phrase "Hear my prayer, O Lord," taken from Psalm 102, becomes, instead, the cry of an individual who finds out the finitude of personal experience in the face of the power of the time-filled realm of the temporal. Is the eternal only possible in glimpses? Does this make absurd the notion of an eternal history? Eliot, trapped in the existential here and now, is neither able to connect with transcendent truth, nor to make sense of the temporal sphere.

At this point, it may be helpful to consider once again the contradictory urges of Eliot, where history is concerned. One urgent desire on Eliot's part – the part manifested by the "Dante" essay, and *Ash-Wednesday* – is for total transcendence. Poetry, if it is after the same manner as Dante's poetry, should have the power at every moment "to realize the inapprehensible in visual images." (*SE* [1951], p. 267) This should be the moment of triumph for man; when he is fully part of the Absolute, history will be finally left behind. But man is inescapably in history. The closing section of *Ash-Wednesday* shows that man is time-bound. Even as he aspires towards the Absolute, he remains trapped in the fragmented sphere of the this-worldly plane. Hence, one has to make "sense" of history. The prose, with its discussion of tradition, Anglo-Catholicism, religious and secular values, the limitations of Humanism, is just that – an attempt to make sense of sequential history. In Eliot's view the existence of a realm of Eternal possibilities will help us to save history from chaos: order can be achieved now. Even now, we can have some recognition of truth that is eternal. It can be seen from *Ash-Wednesday* that Eliot has a very strong sense of being trapped in the nether world of time. There, there is no significance; total significance can only exist in the eternal realm. The problem is "the place of vision in an ordinary world" (Rajan, *Overwhelming Question*, p. 49). Time offers no significance because it separates one moment from another, rendering everything relative. What stable truth can there be in such a realm?

In *Ash-Wednesday* and the "Ariel" poems, the poet strives for the one moment in history when "the fountain sprang up and the bird sang down" (*AW* IV) and the realm of the timeless successfully connected with the temporal world. This was the important moment in time when Absolute significance could be found on earth: "A moment not out of time, but in time, in what we call history." It offered the chance for Time to be redeemed, to possess meaning: ". . . time was made through that moment." ("Choruses from *The Rock*" VII) This moment must be treasured: it is the cause and being for a faith that the future can be meaningful. Such faith can only be "faith" because this extraordinary event, the transcendent moment of truth which became historical experience, the Word which became flesh, happened.

What is unique is that Eliot, instead of taking this moment in history as the starting point of a meaningful historical movement, simply sees the moment as needing to be repeated, over and over again, in order to redeem the chaos of historical time. History does not move to a close, but needs, instead, renewed contact with the eternal, and it is the function of the artist to do this, to fashion art where the "Visible and invisible" meet (*The Rock*, IX), and point us back to the center, that which the protagonist of *Ash-Wednesday* wanted so badly to reach. A moment that once was must now be repeated: an underlying continuum, between then and now, must therefore be made to exist. The not-now has to be recovered, made present in the here and now. The constant use of Romanist liturgies and litanies in *Ash-Wednesday*, the valuation of the medieval tradition in the "Dante" essay, the valuation of Anglo-Catholicism and the repeated use of Bishop Andrewes' sermons in "Journey of the Magi" and the poems from "Gerontion" onwards: all these "recoveries" are part of Eliot's strategy to redeem the temporal realm through recovery of the past. We can say that his "mystical" poetry, such as *Ash-Wednesday*, is not mere pietism: it seems indicative, rather, of Eliot's need to break out of the trap of sequential history.

How many men can "see," in the first place, that History has been redeemed by the appearance of the Word or the one moment of transcendent reality? Both the "Journey of the Magi" and "A Song for Simeon," for instance, display rather finite renunciations. The narrator of the first poem does not even describe the birth event; he only calls it "satisfactory." While the birth offers potential significance for the world of time, as the narrator ought to see when he enters the "temperate valley" with all its pregnant symbols of what can be at the child's birth, the narrator does not manage fully to break out of the nether world of the temporal and unregenerate realm: he returns to his kingdom, but "no longer at ease . . . in the old dispensation / With an alien people clutching their gods." And, as for Simeon, despite what he has seen – the birth of the Christ child – not for him is the "saints' stair" that the protagonist of *Ash-Wednesday* mounts. In considering "Journey of the Magi," we need to consider how the content of the poem clashes with the – at least – initial form of this poem. The creative repetition of Andrewes' sermon is itself a form of recovery of the meaningful from the past. But how successful can this specific tactic be when weighed against the Magus not fully letting go of the old historical realm, and failing to be "born again" into regenerate history? In presenting eternal history as the way out of the nether world of the sequential, one does encounter some problems. The journey to the goal of full significance is not without its attendant pains and stresses.

The perpetual possibility of the this-worldly plane connecting with the other-worldly plane eludes Eliot in the actual realm. But the business of the poet that he would be is to keep the frontiers of practical verification of Absolute Truth open. The poetry as much as temporal experience will always hope to transcend itself, and perhaps the function of poetry of this type is like the function of philosophy as Eliot saw it:

> A metaphysic may be accepted or rejected without our assuming that from the practical point of view it is either true or false. The point is that the world of practical verification has no definite frontiers, and that it is the business of philosophy to keep the frontiers open . . . And this emphasis upon practice – upon the relativity and instrumentality of knowledge – is what impels us toward the Absolute. (*KE* p. 169)

Eliot's theory therefore posits an experiential order in which the world-views of the individual are incomplete, always in process. Hence there is no stable world-view to consider, save the felt presence of truth. Hence too, all identity is fragile, doubt and uncertainty and disharmony are in the nature of things and are the conditions in which one searches for a unified whole, a felt sense of common destiny and effort, by absorbing these disharmonies into a unified whole that is not to be "real" but ever remains a desire, a faith, an act of mind. Such is the poetry of *Ash-Wednesday* that is evoked with lyrical poignancy in "Marina":

> This form, this face, this life
> Living to live in a world of time beyond me
> *   *   *
> What seas what shores what granite islands towards my timbers
> And woodthrush calling through the fog
> My daughter.

The imagination finds hope and future, not in the timeless moment beyond death, but in the very possibility of "the backward glance," the mind's retrospective reflection on its own mortality. What characterizes such poetry is that the apocalyptic moment is not sustained. And the poet finds the strength for this avoidance of apocalyptic abandon in time itself – a time darkened and deepened by this very insight and that has incorporated the power of mind. The road beyond and away from time and history in fact never ceases to be a temporal road, and if it gives sight of the invisible world, the invisibility refers to the mental inward nature of this world as opposed to the world of the senses; within the language of its evocation, this transcendent world is clearly to be understood in a temporal sense as the continuous futurity of "striving." This heightening vision is not the result of "unmediated vision" but of another mediation, in which the consciousness relates itself to a temporal entity which could be called history, but history understood as the retrospective recording of man's mortality and persistent attempt to overcome the power of time. Such a historical sense is directed towards the world of men rather than towards God, so that the human bond the poet finds is not one of common belief, but the recognition of a common temporal predicament.

NOTE

1 Balachandra Rajan, *The Overwhelming Question: A Study of the Poetry of T. S. Eliot* (Toronto: Toronto University Press, 1976), p. 56.

11

A. DAVID MOODY

Four Quartets: music, word, meaning and value

From the start we are teased into thought. The compact title plays upon severalness and singularity: four works, and yet one work. Not just four works either, but four to the power of their four instruments; and still the title declares them to be a single work. Further, the title declares the words on the pages before us to be musical compositions, like those of Haydn or Beethoven or Bartok. What then are the instruments of these "quartets" which are actually composed of words? And are they truly written in quartet-form? Thus the title proposes its own questions and perspectives. Over the first half-century of the poem's life these have provided the most appropriate and rewarding approaches, and they are still the ones to start out from. They will lead us to other and more problematic questions as we discover the meanings and values generated in the verbal music and are confronted by Eliot's radical revaluations of nature and human society and history. Meaning itself, we gather, is merely instrumental: what matters is what the poem can do in the way of altering our values and redirecting our desires. But then is it conceivable that one could love and love no-one and no thing, as the poem would have us do? Can *love* really be an intransitive verb? And is it not a self-contradiction for a poem to be dedicated, as *Four Quartets* is dedicated, to the ending of everything human and to silence? Must it not speak in spite of itself, and speak to us of ourselves? The further we go into the poem the more we find that its music does not resolve its contradictions but rather becomes the music of a profound and irreducible contradiction.

It took some time for *Four Quartets* to appear as a single long poem. *Burnt Norton* was published first in Eliot's *Collected Poems 1909–1935* (1936), and then reissued as a separate pamphlet in 1941. *East Coker* appeared in the "Easter Number" of *The New English Weekly* in 1940, and then as a pamphlet. *The Dry Salvages* (1941) and *Little Gidding* (1942) like-wise were published first in *The New English Weekly* and then as separate pamphlets. The four poems were collected into one volume and given the comprehensive title *Four Quartets* only in 1943 and in the USA. A further year and more went by before they were thus brought together by Faber & Faber in England. It would seem that Eliot, who was after all a director of the firm, was in no hurry to present them as a single work. Yet once they were so presented Faber & Faber kept *Four Quartets* apart from his other poems for twenty years, until at last in 1963 the 1936 *Collected Poems* was replaced by the definitive *Collected Poems 1909–62*. (The American publishers had included *Four Quartets* in their *Complete Poems and Plays* in 1952.) The effect of the delay, in England at least, was to establish *Four Quartets* as distinct from the rest of his poetry and complete in itself. In fact it is not so much distinct as a direct development from his previous poetry and verse-drama. At the same time it is complete in itself, and can quite properly be considered on its own as a long poem in four parts.

Eliot called the four parts "quartets" while being well aware that such analogies should not be pressed too far. "I should like to indicate," he wrote to his friend and adviser John Hayward in 1942,

> that these poems are all in a particular set form which I have elaborated, and the word "quartet" does seem to me to start people on the right tack for understanding them ("sonata" in any case is *too* musical). It suggests to me the notion of making a poem by weaving in together three or four superficially unrelated themes: the "poem" being the degree of success in making a new whole out of them.[1]

In fact what Eliot is describing would more usually be referred to as sonata-form. "Quartet" suggests rather a quartet of instruments than a way of constructing a work by developing several distinct themes both separately and in relation to each other. But it is clear that in his own mind the themes and their inter-relations are in the foreground, while the instruments appear to be taken for granted. However, if we are to follow the analogy actually proposed by his title, we have to think also of the fact that in quartets in sonata-form the definition and the development of the themes are effected by using the distinctive characteristics of the different instruments. The formal structure is designed to allow the instruments to remain distinct from each other while yet performing together, and so to treat different themes in different ways while weaving them into "a new whole." To be put on the right tack by the title, therefore, we need to make out both the themes and the instruments performing them. But what, to break through the analogy, are the instruments of the poem? Perhaps, since we are dealing with words, and with the performance of words, we might think of them as voices. Or again, since we are dealing with the sense which words make in the mind, we might think of them as different modes of mind. They are "voices," and they are the modes in which the mind of the poem operates as it works out its themes.

Thus, in the first movement of *Burnt Norton*, the theme of Time and its end is introduced in the voice of impersonal thought, seeking a universal truth through abstraction, logical argument, and the resolution of paradox. This modulates in the course of lines 11–19 into a personal voice with a contrasting sense of "What might have been and what has been," a sense arising from experience rather than from abstract argument. Memory and imagination combine in a sustained development of this second theme as a paradoxical experience of the world of light. At its close, ("a cloud passed and the pool was empty"), this voice rises in intensity – and then abruptly gives way to the detached voice of the opening lines. The arrangement of the voices in the second movement is the reverse of the first. It opens with a passage of taut lyrical writing in a symbolist manner, as if memory and imagination were essaying their own statement of the universal truth of sensual experience. Then thought takes over and continues to the end in a sustained exploration of how time and the sensual body might be transcended. "At the still point of the turning world" appears at first to take up the conclusion of the lyric; but the series of paradoxes would have us conceive a realm beyond sense and contrary to sense. In fact the meditation begun in the opening lines of the poem is being resumed. If there is a pattern in earthly experience it is because "the one end, which is always present" may be found "At the still point of the turning world." The meditation unfolds through three distinct sections: eight lines of paradoxes determined by negatives and exclusions are followed by nine lines positively affirming what is to be aspired to; then there is a return to the inescapable complications of a consciousness that is in time and in the sensual body. Here memory and imagination re-enter, but now we find that they have been incorporated into the process of thought and subjected to its perspective and its ends: "only in time can the moment in the rose-garden . . . Be remembered; involved with past and future."

In the third movement the thought does what it will with the world of experience, determining its nature, and then dismissing it with outright satire. With "Descend lower, descend only" the meditation modulates rather suddenly into a third voice, that of prayer or exhortation. The desire and direction of the will which have been present but in suspense from the beginning here reveal themselves as the motive-force behind the thought, from which they effectively take over now that it has done its work and prepared their way. The fourth movement, like the lyric at the start of the second movement, is an account of the world of experience. But it differs from it in being informed by the thoughtful critique of experience, and it affirms the light that is beyond sense. Moreover, it does this with an air of desiring to be with that light, and thus to transcend time. It would seem then that the three voices previously made out, and which have followed one upon another, are here heard in unison, thus producing the fourth voice which completes the quartet. It is wholly characteristic of Eliot that there should be a hierarchy of instruments, that the lower should give rise to the higher, and then be caught up into the ultimate voice and vision. (In the fifth movement of *Burnt Norton* the three individual voices are heard both separately and together.)

In the later quartets the voices are more developed, and the structures more complex. The most remarkable technical feature is that *East Coker* and *The Dry Salvages* are so constructed as to make up a single continuous composition, a double-quartet, which ends as it began upon the subject of life reverting to the soil, and in which the conclusion of *East Coker* is also the introduction of *The Dry Salvages*.

The first two movements of *East Coker* follow the model of *Burnt Norton*, but with the signal difference that the two contrasting voices are both derived from traditional sources. The first assumes the tone and something of the style of Old Testament prophecy; the second adopts the language of a Humanist of the English Renaissance. Already it is clear that what is in question is impersonal wisdom, and the discrimination of one order of wisdom from another. It is also clear that the commitment of the poem is to proceed beyond the wisdom of natural experience. The critique of that wisdom, in the second movement, is designed not so much to dismiss it as to build upon it, and to turn its unsatisfactoriness into a motive for pursuing instead "the wisdom of humility." So "The dancers are all gone under the hill" is effectively an affirmation, indicating the way forward.

It will be characteristic of the poem from here to its end that the different instruments will cooperate rather than contend with each other: the hierarchy of their relations established in *Burnt Norton* holds throughout and is never again in question. That hierarchy is the basis of a direct progression, from the critical discriminations of the second movement of *East Coker* ("That was a way of putting it – not very satisfactory"), through to the complex faith affirmed at the end of *The Dry Salvages* ("Here the impossible union"). The challenge which the poetry sets itself – and it is a profound challenge – is to rise to each fresh call made upon its resources by the determination to proceed from one degree of wisdom to the next. One can mark the progression by the sequence of lyrics: the "periphrastic study in a worn-out poetical fashion" (*EC* IIa); the still rhetorical Good Friday lyric (*EC* IV), in the fashion of seventeenth-century devotional verse; the more meditative Annunciation "sestina" (*DS* IIa), after the form of the love poetry of Arnaut Daniel and Dante; and the surprisingly quiet prayer to the Divine Mother (*DS* IV). Each of these attains a further degree of "the wisdom of humility," to bring the poem to the point where it can speak of the "occupation of the saint." Between the lyrics of course there is the essential work upon which they depend, the process of criticism and meditation, of thought and mental action, seeking to resolve the mind's knowledge and experience into an ultimate integrity.

In the passages of thought and meditation the writing can vary, to some readers' alarm, in quality as well as in kind. For the most part the writing is relatively intense, as we expect of "good" poetry; but there are also drops into a flat prosiness which strike the judicious ear as rather bad. The most noted "lapse" is the river section at the opening of *The Dry Salvages*, but there are others just as "bad" in the third and fifth sections of both parts of the double quartet. Now in fact these sections are no less successful than the rest, given their specific function. The drop in intensity and interest marks the relative meaninglessness, from the point of view of the questing spirit, of the material being dealt with. The style is a form of discrimination – properly understood, style *is* discrimination.

It is obvious that this is so when the style is that of direct satire, as in the vision of an infernal London in *BN* III, or the "To communicate with Mars" section of *DS* V. But more subtle and more telling discriminations are being made by the shifts of style in *EC* III. The first two lines allude to and have something of the grandeur of Milton's – in Eliot's view rather empty – magniloquence. The catalog of those who go into the dark veers towards mock-seriousness, until pulled up by the sharp change of tone in "And cold the sense and lost the motive of action." The serious tone holds for four more lines, to "the darkness of God." But before that idea is developed we are given some relatively prosy analogies from commonplace experience. These are not interesting in themselves, and they are allowed no more attention than they merit. This is not satire; it is merely keeping the commonplace in its place while using it to further the progress of the soul. When it comes to the meaning, and to the meaningful experience, the writing becomes once more fully serious and intent, as in "I said to my soul be still, and wait without hope," and "echoed ecstasy / Not lost, but requiring, pointing to the agony / of death and birth." The final section of this movement, the set of rather dry paradoxes of the negative way to God, stands in perfect contrast to the Miltonic opening, that first sense of our all going into the dark having been profoundly altered. All the dramatic emotion has been squeezed out, and with it the sense of mere fatality. In its place there is a clear idea, stated in the imperative mood, of a way requiring to be freely and positively chosen.

To appreciate the appropriateness of the prosy start to *EC* v we have only to recall (from II) that "in the middle way" is not yet "all the way," and then (from *BN* v, but even more from *DS* v) that the endless struggle with words is meaningless except insofar as the words are in accord with the Word of God. In this section it is simply the trying "to get the better of words" that is in question, not yet the Word itself. The writing changes when "The world becomes stranger, the pattern more complicated"; and when it goes on to speak of Love (taking up the theme from the end of *BN*) there is the sense in its growing intensity of a deepening and totalizing move toward the Word. But next we read "I do not know much about gods" – a dull phrase followed by several lines of turgid periphrases. The writing clears however when it take up the theme of destruction and desolation from the close of *EC*. The point of the prosy beginning was surely to carica-ture the pseudo-learned account of the river, so far as it failed to recognize the divine order in nature. It is not the writing which is inferior, but the order of understanding which it is just there representing.

Getting the better of words is of the essence of *Four Quartets*. Its major design is to so use words as to make them mean what is beyond words; or, to put the same idea another way, to so transform the understanding of the world which is in its words that it will be perceived as the divine Word in action. (The two themes, that of conquering time, and that of getting the better of words, are drawn together, since words are the medium by which the mind may attain the consciousness which transcends time.) The theme of words that must strive and fail to reveal the Word is stated explicitly in *BN* v, briefly restated in *EC* IIb, partially developed in *EC* va – then appar-ently left aside to be finally developed only in *Little Gidding*.

The Dry Salvages appears then to be the exception in not consciously addressing the poem's concern with words and with the Word of God. Yet it is in this quartet that the theme is most directly and fully developed. It begins by drawing attention to words through the empty wordiness of those periphrastic phrases which would tame the destructive power of a great river. That wordiness is to be contrasted with the sober statement of fact, "the river with its cargo of dead negroes, cows and chicken coops"; and with the intellectual apprehension of its belonging with the "daemonic, chthonic / Powers." But those powers are to be understood as annunciations of "the one Annunciation," that is as revelations of the Word in the world. In fact, between "I do not know much about gods" and the naming of the Word – "The hint half guessed . . . is Incarnation" – the quartet is virtually entirely devoted to occult communications. "His rhythm was present in the nursery bedroom"; the sea gives "hints of earlier and other creation," and its "many voices" resolve into the one voice of its "tolling bell" – "the bell of the last annunciation" which becomes its "Perpetual angelus" or bell of "the one Annunciation." In the third movement "a voice descanting (though not to the ear . . . and not in any language)" communicates what can be conceived by the mind in its proper state. The fourth movement is a prayer, to the Lady who conceived the Word, to pray for all who are in the sea's power, especially those who have not received its message. The words of that prayer are plain yet eloquent. The contrast with the opening section of the final movement could hardly be greater. This section is all about communications which serve mere curiosity, and it bristles with recherché words, such as "haruspicate or scry," "sortilege," and "pentagrams." These are words to be treasured for crosswords and scrabble, words which belong in large dictionaries, but do not speak to the spirit. They are dismissed in favor of a very different order of apprehension, where words reach beyond themselves – "Here the impossible union / Of spheres of existence is actual." There words strain and break in the effort to conceive the meaning they have been pointing to. How can the impossible be actual? Yet the syntax affirms what logic would negate, and the conscious mind is impelled to follow the syntax beyond the sense.

When we consider *Four Quartets* as something made of words we find that each instrument has its own idiom. Memory and imagination speak in the language of natural experience, a language of sense-perception and feeling and thence of emotion. Its concern is with what is pleasing, or menacing, to the sensual being. The moment in the rose garden is its domain, with its bird and flowers and leaves full of children; also the moment in the historic village of East Coker ("Wait for the early owl"); and the endless experience of the sea in *The Dry Salvages* ("No end to the withering of withered flowers"); and the first impression of the winter's day at the beginning of *Little Gidding*, while "The brief sun flames the ice, on pond and ditches."

The critical mind, the poem's second voice – taking the voices in the order of their hierarchy – speaks the very different language of philosophy, a language purged of sense experience and emotion, and given to exact definitions and sharp discriminations in pursuit of an understanding of things in general. Its sense is the sense of thought, and its concern is with what fulfils or frustrates the mind. Yet its primary material is provided by the "first world" of natural experience. This it may treat satirically and merely dismissively, as in *BN* iii and *EC* iii when it can find neither daylight nor darkness in it; or as in *DS* va where its news communicates nothing the mind cares to conceive. Where the sense experience engages its interest however, it sets about converting it to its own sense, by explicating what it means to the mind, and by altering its emotional value to accord with the mind's valuation. The transformation is mainly effected through setting up and resolving paradoxes, as in "So the darkness shall be the light, and the stillness the dancing," or "In windless cold that is the heart's heat."

While the idiom in which the criticism of experience is carried on is characterized by paradox, the idiom of the third voice – the voice of the mind contemplating what its thinking has established – is characterized by a form of metaphysical conceit. The paradoxes are mental ladders by which the mind ascends from a merely natural sense of life to a spiritual understanding of it. In the conceits any contradiction between a lower and a higher sense has already been resolved. Their function is to concentrate the mind upon the meaning and to make it real, to conceive it. An example of a paradox which has been resolved into a conceit would be, in *BN* iv, "the light is still / At the still point of the turning world"; and another, in *BN* v, would be "as a Chinese jar still / Moves perpetually in its stillness." The Good Friday lyric (*EC* iv) is altogether an exercise in conceits; and in *The Dry Salvages* there is the sustained conceit of the sea's annunciation of "the one Annunciation"; and there is also the effort, which goes beyond such conceits, to conceive "the impossible union / Of spheres of existence." Much of *Little Gidding* is in the conceited mode, from "Midwinter spring" through to "And the fire and the rose are one." Its climactic lyric –"To be redeemed from fire by fire" – carries the mode to its fullest realization.

The fourth voice is distinguished not so much by a specific idiom as by its comprehensiveness. It incorporates the idioms of natural experience and thought and meditation, and resolves them into a medium of spiritual apprehension. It would conceive the Word in the moment of experiencing the world, as at the start of *Little Gidding*, where "Midwinter spring" conveys "pentecostal fire." We are told that it is beyond common sense and notion; and we may gather that it is beyond common prayer. Like "the communication of the dead" it "is tongued with fire beyond the language of the living." It is heard in the most intense passages, at the end of *East Coker*, and in the final movement of *The Dry Salvages* –

> But to apprehend
> The point of intersection of the timeless
> With time, is an occupation for the saint –
> No occupation either, but something given
> And taken, in a lifetime's death in love,
> Ardour and selflessness and self-surrender.

It is characteristic of this idiom to move through the paradoxes in which thought contradicts feeling, and the conceits of the religious sense, to some immediate apprehension of "a further union, a deeper communion." Just there it is in the word *ardour*, placed in apposition to "a lifetime's death in love." The root sense of the word has to do with fire, so that its filiations run back through "a lifetime burning in every moment" to the "purgatorial fires," while anticipating the "refining fire" of *Little Gidding*, its fire lyric, and its final image of ardent love. That image, and the lyric, show how completely the language of natural experience has been transformed and transvalued, to the point where the spiritual sense is wholly dominant. To "suspire" is an out of the way word for "breathe," and one which brings it close to a sigh, and also to the root of *spirit*. The enemy bomber is apprehended as the Holy Spirit, its fire-bombs as his revelations, and death by fire as the only way of spiritual life. It seems the entire world is turned into holy fire. The very earth (French *la terre*, Latin *terra*) is caught up into *terror*, and then made to be whitening flame, tongued as upon Whit Sunday. The word *pyre* is not here associated with cremation and the reduction of dust to ashes, so much as with its root sense of purifying fire. God's love for his creation manifests itself as an all-consuming fire – "And the fire and the rose are one."

When the poet's double declares "our concern was speech, and speech impelled to us / To purify the dialect of the tribe," the sub-text implies that the poem's language should itself be passed through the refining fire. Its diction is in fact remarkably purified. That is to say, the words carry only the sense intended, neither more nor less. If "free" associations enter in at all, it is only in those passages which are designedly "not very satisfactory" – *BN* IIa, *EC* IIa and *DS* va. For the most part the language is unequivocal, as in the double's disclosure of "the gifts reserved for age." Where secondary meanings enter they are invariably part of the clear pattern of meaning, as with the range of words which contribute to the theme of fire: the *bonfire* (or bone-fire) of *East Coker*, *ardour*, *purify*, *pyre*. There are not many *double-entendres*, beyond the obvious variations played upon *end* and *still*. "The *deception* of the thrush" (*BN* I) may be one, where the French sense of *disappointment* might underlie the delusion. *Humility* (*EC* IIb) is reinforced by its association with "humus," bringing the human down to the soil to which it shall revert. Behind *agony* (*DS* IIb) lies the Greek αγον, with its very pertinent idea of an actor who suffers the action of the drama; and *destination* (*DS* III) is of course close to "destiny." *Sempiternal* (*LG* I) seems to comprehend time and eternity in the one word. *Peregrine* (*LG* IIb) was applied in ancient Rome to aliens visiting the city, and was later used of pilgrims visiting it as a Holy City. But these words are not typical of the poem's diction. If its words come to be "tongued with fire beyond the language of the living" it is not because they are extraordinarily highly charged or mysterious. The sense that is beyond sense remains beyond its language.

The poem does not state its ultimate meaning, or not in the form in which we are likely to look for it. It offers neither a doctrine nor a revelation. There is the difference between its beginning and its end, of an alteration of consciousness; but what that amounts to is a different consciousness of the way, and not at all a sense of having attained the end. The poem goes no further than such affirmations as these: "We must be still and still moving" – "To be redeemed from fire by fire" – "in a lifetime's death in love." Or if its complete consort of words does dance together, then it dances in the refining fire to the measure of stillness. Such ideas do not define meanings so much as point in a definite direction. Meditated upon, they orientate the mind on that one bearing. This is what the poem as a whole would do – neither inform nor instruct, but establish a certain orientation.

The clear orientation of *Four Quartets* is towards "God's holy fire" – a phrase out of Yeats's "Sailing to Byzantium" which resonates dissonantly in Eliot's similar and yet so different context – and it is achieved, quite consciously and deliberately, at some cost. The cost is not so great as "not less than everything" – for the poem breaks the absolute silence it aspires to, and breaks it with a virtuoso mastery of verbal music. The mastery of course is directed towards the discovery of the spiritual sense of things. But because the spiritual sense is beyond any sense which words can make, the art has to work in a mainly negative way, creating space for "the dumb spirit" by excluding whatever is not in accord with it. The art, at its finest, is necessarily an art of alienation and negation. Words and things have their specific density refined out of them; the natural world is made strange, and entered into most fully when it is least itself; human relations are reduced to the most elementary; and history becomes a buried pattern of prayerful moments.

Consider the treatment of *light* in *Burnt Norton*. It is the ground of the quartet as earth, water, and fire are the elements upon which the later quartets are based. It is introduced obliquely, in an entrancing illusion, as "water out of sunlight," the surface of which "glittered out of heart of light." I cannot tell whether "a grace of sense, a white light still and moving," in the second movement, refers to such an experience or to any experience. The most direct account of light is given in the third movement, in its absence, and again as a source of illusion:

> neither daylight
> Investing form with lucid stillness
> Turning shadow into transient beauty
> With slow rotation suggesting permanence

That would be "plenitude," we are given to understand; but at the same time it is evident that it would be a fullness without substance – leaving perhaps "the bitter tastelessness of shadow fruit" (*LG* ɪɪb). Only when the sun has been carried away, and the flash of light from the kingfisher's wing has gone, is a real and lasting light allowed, and this is of course the light of a purely metaphysical conception, the light that is "At the still point of the turning world." It is not only light, but the entire sensible world that has become a remote abstraction in this conceit.[2]

The natural world figures positively only in very simplified terms, and even so it is consistently denatured. It is what is not seen or heard, or what is not actually there at all, that gives the rose-garden its fascination. It is the same with the midwinter spring time, with its blossom of snow, a bloom "neither budding nor fading." And the children in the apple-tree who recur in the final lines are only "heard, half-heard." When nature is in the negative however, it is registered as firm fact: "Then a cloud passed, and the pool was empty," or "Dung and death," or "the river with its cargo of dead negroes." The lyric of *Little Gidding* ɪɪ would comprehend all of nature in the definitive death of the four elements.

The perception of human living comes to be governed by the Biblical "dust thou art and unto dust thou shalt return." The dust moving in a shaft of sunlight is a strikingly disillusioned image to counter the moments of "plenitude." In *East Coker* the dance of earthly fertility is turned into a dance of death, and earthly life is redirected towards "The life of significant soil." In *The Dry Salvages* the sea casts up only evidences of death, and means nothing but death to those who put to sea, and the fear of death to those who think of them, unless this death is understood as a birth agony. It is only the dead who are allowed to come alive. The Dantescan passage in *Little Gidding* ɪɪ is a masterpiece of dead speech. The first half of it uses English as if it were a dead language – not as Milton sometimes wrote English, as if it were Latin, but as if English itself were no longer spoken among the living. So long as the living poet speaks the writing is like an exact reproduction of poetic speech, perfectly correct and yet synthetic. It is a tissue of reminiscences of past poets' meetings with the dead, not only Dante's but Shelley's ("The Triumph of Life") and Yeats's (*Purgatory*, "All Souls' Night" and many other poems) –

> Over the asphalt where no other sound was
> Between three districts whence the smoke arose
> I met one walking

This is not natural speech, and quite appropriately not, given the dramatic situation. But when the dead master speaks, and especially when he speaks of the last gifts of life, his communication is indeed tongued with purgatorial fire and becomes powerfully eloquent –

> And last, the rending pain of re-enactment
> Of all that you have done, and been; the shame
> Of motives late revealed . . .

The emphasis there upon "shame," natural and unforced, is an effect of living speech and responsive art. The poetry is at its most vital when it can embrace mortality – so long as mortality is understood to be a refining fire.

Among the themes being woven together in the poem love must count as of the first importance, but "love of what?" becomes the critical question. The entry into the rose-garden of memory introduces the theme of love; yet there the invisible guests are as formal and distant as elders, and it is the mystery of light and the laughter of children which mark the intense experience. Was the moment in the rose-garden after all simply a moment of childlike happiness? The later moments of remembered ecstasy are of the same order: "Whisper of running streams, and winter lightning, / The wild thyme unseen and the wild strawberry"; or "music heard so deeply / That . . . you are the music." What characterizes these moments of ecstasy is the being taken out of oneself, but not any entering into a relationship with another or with others. Adult human relations are first treated in *East Coker* I, initially as "The association of man and woman / In daunsinge, signifying matrimonie," but then as "the coupling of man and woman / And that of beasts." For a positive sense we have to turn to the second movement of *The Dry Salvages*, where – after looking in vain for the ecstasy of love among "The moments of happiness" – we hear that "the moments of agony" are better appreciated "In the agony of others" in which (rather than in *whom*) we are involved. This is the use of love, then, to give an abiding experience of another's agony! That might lead on to "a lifetime's death in love," if the meaning of the agony were understood. But the love would not now be directed towards another person, but towards the only union that the poem will endorse, "the impossible union" of the human and the divine. It is towards this union that "The soul's sap quivers" in *Little Gidding*, and towards which it is drawn by the Love who devised the tormenting and refining fire of human experience. In this way the desire which is "Not in itself desirable" is made at one with the Love which is its "cause and end" (*BN* v).

The idea of that Love dominates the treatment of human love throughout the poem. It is the reason why the poem has so little to say of desire, except that it is undesirable; and why it maintains that love would be "love of the wrong thing." It is why "disaffection" (*BN* III) and "detachment" are preferred to desire and love. In a sequence of remarkable transitions in *Little Gidding* III we are told that detachment means "not less of love but expanding / Of love beyond desire." But neither desire nor love are much in evidence there. "Attachment to self and to things and to persons" is a coldly detached way of putting it; and so too is likening attachment to the stinging nettle flourishing in the hedgerow. Again, "attachment" to one particular person is merged into attachment to people in general, as if it were of no special interest, as has indeed been the case throughout the poem. But even the attachment to others has been unfeeling, as in the treatment of "the quiet-voiced elders," or in the meeting with the "familiar compound ghost." Such detachment from human feeling makes it easy for the passage to shift from the idea of love and desire to "love of a country," and from that to "History"; and then to have everything loved – the persons and the places of the poem, so far as they have been loved, and "England" as the present moment of History – vanish into "a pattern of timeless moments." This can appear a renewal and transfiguration only from the viewpoint of the Love which consumes love. In that view the only significant moments are those of holy dying, so that the whole of an individual's life can be condensed and refined to just those moments in which the destructive fire is consciously known and accepted as the fire of Love. The whole of history is then condensed to those few significant moments (which are essentially all one and the same moment). Picked out in what has become an otherwise featureless web they appear to constitute the sole pattern of temporal existence, the pattern in which the rose of desire becomes fire, and the fire becomes the Rose named Love.

Four Quartets thus systematically subverts and inverts "normal" humane values. Its wisdom is the negative wisdom of humility; its love is concerned only to conceive the Word heard in humble submission to death; and its history would record nothing but the deaths in that Love of saints and martyrs. Now it succeeds as a poem precisely to the extent that it succeeds in realizing its extraordinary values. And it does very effectively weave those themes together to make life's usual fulfilments appear mere vacuity, and the evacuation of that vacuity a fulfilment. Yet it is not a complete success – indeed it exists as a poem only by virtue of its imperfection. It aspires to an absolute beyond words and speech, but, caught "in the form of limitation," it must use words and speech to reach towards the silence of the divine Word. And its "imperfect" speech keeps it within the reach of the human, and maintains an essential humanity within it. Its orientation is not humane, and nevertheless it is a human achievement and one which speaks to our humanity.

For there is more to the poem than its conscious meaning, and more to our experience of it than our final analysis. While it would measure its own rightness by becoming simply "an epitaph," it has nevertheless had to admit too much of the living world to allow that. The hedgerow "blanched for an hour with transitory blossom / Of snow" does something more and something other than point to "the unimaginable / Zero." That image is a finely registered perception of something actual, and the poetry makes it actual to the reader as a product of nature, sense and human creativity. Even the declaration that "the communication / Of the dead is tongued with fire beyond the language of the living" is charged with an energy and excitement that belongs to the realm of human utterance. And the poem itself everywhere manifests the human need and power to shape experience and knowledge into a commanding form. Reading it, we are engaged by, and then engaged in, its quest for a comprehensive organization of the world in the mind. Whether we follow it all the way, or find it a dead end, it still extends and refines our common language and understanding, and contributes to our common quest for an intelligible order. Even its final celebration of the end of the human has a developed humanity in the precision of its words and rhythm —

> And all shall be well and
> All manner of thing shall be well
> When the tongues of flame are in-folded
> Into the crowned knot of fire
> And the fire and the rose are one.

There is a further dimension to the humanity of those lines and of the poem as a whole. Beyond their speaking of "tongues of flame" in the simple words of common speech, the lines incorporate other voices — specifically Julian of Norwich and Dante — and through them a long tradition of ascetic mysticism. And there is not only the Christian or western tradition, but also the far-reaching eastern tradition behind Krishna and the *Bhagavad Gita*. The orientation of the poem is in fact very far from being alien to humanity. Its guiding views and values are as established as any which humanity has conceived, and to deny their power would be both futile and a diminishment of ourselves. There are contradictory imperatives in human existence, one being the need for and impulse towards its fullness and abundance; and the other being a need for and impulse towards "a condition of complete simplicity." There is also a profoundly limiting tendency — manifest in *Four Quartets* itself — to exalt one of these as an absolute imperative and to repress the other. But both imperatives exist, and both belong to humanity, the ascetic "negative" no less than the life-affirming "positive."

Even as it seeks to transcend the human realm, the poem thus remains in and of that realm. It strains it in one particular direction, but it does not depart from it. Its key-note can be found in the bridge-passage which leads from *East Coker* into *The Dry Salvages*:

> Old men ought to be explorers
> Here or there does not matter
> We must be still and still moving
> Into another intensity
> For a further union, a deeper communion
> Through the dark cold and the empty desolation,
> The wave cry, the wind cry, the vast waters
> Of the petrel and the porpoise.

The syntactic structure is extremely fluid and open, giving a continuous development through the sequence of separate statements. The first line is musing, reflective. The second, a definite assertion, carrying the mind from "ought to be" to "must be"; and here the sense becomes emphatic, with the strongest beat so far upon "still," and with an echo of that in "still moving" as the meaning shifts and doubles. (Within the continuing motion there is the stillness of arrest, an effect like that of "still life.") The move in fact is into a realm of abstract nouns and intensive adjectives. This is where the aspiration towards the absolute is most clearly stated, but it is the adjectives which carry the stress of desire, while the nouns can only indicate the direction. The movement of desire finds its effective notation in the known world, in that aspect of experience which answers to the motive of the exploration. And the rhythmic pattern which had been developing, marked by two increasingly weighted strong beats in each phrase – "still moving," "further union," "deeper communion" – is continued through the rest of the sentence, finding its resolution in the broader movement of the closing half-line where the two beats are distributed one to each of the two phrases. All of this is to use and to shape and to charge the common language with a very specific intent. But it is an intent which finds itself thoroughly at home in the language. The language lends itself to it as to something that is in its nature, which is to say in its history, as a permanent tradition. All that is new is the immediacy and individuality of the voice, making what is perennial appear original and personal.

That voice of course bespeaks not so much an individual person as an organization of mind, a musical organization of the mind's resources in a form which, while drawing deeply upon traditions, is genuinely not like any other in English literature. Cleo McNelly Kearns, near the end of her contribution to this *Companion*, speaks of the poem as the culmination of a certain tradition and the point of departure for a new mode. It remains to be seen whether others will carry further the specific form and mode of *Four Quartets*. To do so would require no less a commitment to the unattainable absolute, and no less a humility to submit wisely to the inescapable conditions of human life and language. But this much is sure, that the eternal note of desire that will not be content, and which seeks rest in motion, silence in utterance, and fulfilment in annihilation, has been heard in our time in a new form.

NOTES

1 Letter dated September 3, 1942, as given in Helen Gardner, *The Composition of "Four Quartets"* (New York: Oxford University Press, 1978), p. 26.
2 Compare the reverse process in "The worlds revolve like ancient women / Gathering fuel in vacant lots" ("Preludes" IV).

12

ROBIN GROVE

Pereira and after: the cures of Eliot's theater

As a dramatic performance, the character "T. S. Eliot" had one of the century's most successful runs. Formidably stylish, like Edith Evans's Lady Bracknell, it was exotic yet lifelike, as critics said when Olivier played Othello, and should have been extensively recorded on film. The grave voice and firm though melancholy gestures, head inclined a little to the side, were expert renditions of presence. Even the costume was capable of taking on small character-parts: as witness the heavily lapelled overcoat, the reliable shoes and umbrella, the wardrobe of identical three-piece suits ("Nothing ever quite to excess," his tailor is reported as saying). The Eliot costume, moreover, was animated by a range of interested parties, some of whom contributed anonymously to journals like the *Times Literary Supplement*, while others published poems in their own name with Faber and Faber, or signed letters under this or that *nom de plume*. Eliot the ventriloquist has been admired by plenty of commentators now, just as he himself admired artists able to carry off the difficult trick of vanishing into their own performance. Whether it was Nellie Wallace and Little Tich in the music-hall, offering "an inconceivable orgy of parody of the human race" (*The Criterion* 1.2: 193), or the Diaghilev Ballet's leading dancers ("Massine, the most completely unhuman, impersonal, abstract, belongs to the future stage," he wrote in 1932: *ibid.*, 1.4: 305), what he seems to have valued particularly is theater's power of removing both spectator and performer out of ordinary life.

Given this interest – sharpened perhaps by needs which led him to perform even "T. S. Eliot" in the masterly fashion he did – he saw in the drama of his day possibilities other than those that it was conscious of itself. When he turned to composing for the theater, he did not jettison the various sorts of commercial entertainment which held the stage. As occasion allowed, he transformed them. In fact, his own dramaturgical career goes on to incorporate quite up-to-date examples, so that *Murder in the Cathedral* reworks the Shaw of *St Joan* for opposite purposes – celebrating martyrdom, rather than attempting to demystify it – while Coward successes such as *Private Lives* prepare the audience for the play – about modern marriage, etc. – which *The Cocktail Party* inventively refuses to become. Likewise with high stylizations, such as the theater of Yeats with its use of mask and mime: Eliot didn't forget what he knew of these, or of the Russian Ballet, when he came to devise *Sweeney Agonistes* or *The Rock*, but instead of heightening his art by the force of their example, he added a characteristically 'twenties mix of low-brow forms – the burlesque, the revue, the music-hall, and so on.

In every case, the established form undergoes a twist or realignment, most usually in the direction of some startling X-ray-like simplification. Thus, inside the jollity of music-hall and dance-band, sinister growths and shadows are discerned. "Any man has to, needs to, wants to / Once in a lifetime, do a girl in. / Well he kept her there in a bath . . .": the jazzy beat of the verse and its chillingly casual syncopations are made to revolve around nightmares. Or *Murder in the Cathedral* might be thought to represent a different simplification again, when Eliot summarizes it as follows, "A man comes home, foreseeing that he will be killed, and he is killed." (*PP* [London], p. 80) At a stroke, the post-Ibsenite drama of "ideas" is compressed into something more dangerous: a single action, inside which power is coiled as it might be in an electrical circuit.

Reading such plays at the end of the century, we have the advantage of seeing them refracted, as it were, through a range of other drama. The poeticizing playwrights like Christopher Fry may be best forgotten, but the Berlin theater of Brecht and Weill casts its own cabaret-light on *Sweeney*, while the miscellaneous materials of *The Rock*, including Cockney turns and choruses and harangues, crop up in later plays – Auden and Isherwood's, for a start – and the horror and loneliness carried by family life finds expression again in Pinter. But there has always been a difficulty in catching Eliot's drama so as to see it whole. To plenty of critics, this is simply because the work does not comprise a unity anyway; for them, a failure of life or nerve, or perhaps a hammering attempt on West End success, splits it only too evidently into "early" and "late." On the other hand, it must be said that the author himself has not helped by allowing his first two plays to disappear into the *Collected Poems*, where *The Rock* survives only as a collection of choric pieces, and *Sweeney Agonistes* as an Unfinished Poem, no less a captive of the printed page than the "Coriolan" sequence. It is difficult to keep their existence as theater-works in sight. But then, the very prominence of Eliot the poet has helped to obscure his drama. Throughout the middle century, his was the definitive achievement ("a very penetrating influence," wrote Empson, "perhaps not unlike an east wind"), and his importance to English verse continues to be so great that we may sometimes forget how much besides poetry he wrote. Yet his active career as playwright spanned quite as many years, so that while "Portrait of a Lady" to *Four Quartets* takes us through three decades, so too does the parabola from *Sweeney Agonistes* (1926–27) to *The Elder Statesman* (1958). If anything, the impulse to theater-activity lasted longer. And as well as dramatic works of various kinds, Eliot wrote *about* drama almost from first to last.

It won't do, therefore, to think of his plays as a fading comet's-tail, or a remnant left over after his true career. It might even be better to consider the printed verse as itself a series of gestures, speeches, quasi-theatrical occasions – beginning with the titles ("The Love-Song of J. Alfred Prufrock"), and going on through monologues, ensembles, scenes in the pub, the rose-garden, and the rest. No one could suppose the advances and hesitations, the implorings and self-mockeries of the voices in "Portrait of a Lady" somehow *un*dramatic. Yet virtually none of the drama of such a poem could be staged. For not only do rings of light upon the ceiling and walls dissolving into smoke and fog comprise its setting, that setting is also constituted out of consciousness – the specified yet unlocatable consciousness which has the scene arrange itself, "as it will seem to do," among the atmospherics of your own December afternoon. So transnatural are the workings of the verse that a whole generation of critics, after Kenner, insisted on the peculiarly verbal composition of Eliot's locales.

Such emphasis on setting as a "literary 'effect'" and character as "the name of a possible zone of consciousness" ("certainly not a person"), meant a steady contrasting of page and stage, a distinguishing between dramatic poetry, and real plays, as available in the theater. Many a commentator's pencil underlined the sentences in "Seneca in Elizabethan Translation" which compared unacted drama ("at one remove from reality") with the acted drama of the Greeks, and discerned behind the drama of words "the drama of action, the timbre of voice and voice, the uplifted hand or tense muscle" (*SE* [1951], p. 68). Not for Eliot the modern bookishness that recaptures physicality for the library, turning whatever is staged back into "text" again: performance-text, "inscribed," "circulated," "erased," and always already written by culture at large. His emphasis instead is on the "concrete visual actuality," and behind that in turn, the "specific emotional actuality" which words reveal only in part.

> The spoken play, the words which we read, are symbols, a shorthand, and often, as in the best of Shakespeare, a very abbreviated shorthand indeed, for the acted and felt play, which is always the real thing.   (*SE* [1951], p. 68)

Yet the opposition of dialogue and action, though adumbrated, is undone by that closing phrase, "the felt play," which, spanning the gap between mind and body, helps us remember the extraordinary capacity of Eliot's writing to incorporate, in words read, the effect of voices heard and actions physically felt. I wouldn't say of his writing, as he does of Seneca's, that "the drama is all in the word, and the word has no further reality behind it." On the contrary, in printed verse, even more often than in his plays, he managed something different.

"Stone, bronze, stone, steel, oakleaves . . .": the noise of that Triumphal March is, if we like to suppose it so, a relentless clop of "horses' heels / Over the paving"; but it is a coming and going of petrification too, as the mimed life of the poem is rigidified instant by instant, its arrest enforced, then reinforced, in the dead echo of the lines. Like a sullen drumbeat, "stone . . . stone" falls between things fashioned (bronze, steel) and things which grow of their own accord. Re-uttered, it rhymes only with itself, and numbs the resonance of its neighbors. The phrasing could hardly be simpler, yet the line is a mimesis, a diagnosis, and a transformation of nature, all at once. And faced with writing so potent, any contrast between "the drama of words" and "the drama of action" seems largely beside the point.

Instead, drama of various kinds, one wants to say, called out his powers from the start; and what is striking in Eliot's long concern with it is his emphasis on leaving ordinary states of perception behind: either by the way of exaggeration, like the "torrential imagination" he admired in Marlowe, or the "fierce grotesquerie" of Tourneur (SE [1951], pp. 119; 185), or by art's other way, of relinquishment and excision – as when he calls for poetic drama to offer "some quite new selection or structure or distortion," a "reduction of detail . . . a stripping" (SE [1951], pp. 112; 159); "a world which the author's mind has subjected to a complete process of simplification" (SW [1928], p. 68). "There is a brutality," declares the essay on Ben Jonson, "a lack of sentiment, a polished surface, a handling of large bold designs in brilliant colours, which ought to attract about three thousand people in London and elsewhere" (SE [1951], p. 159). The essential thing for the playwright, the essays insist, is to achieve some rhythm which may be "imposed upon the world of action," some form to arrest "the flow of spirit . . . before it expands and ends its course in the desert of exact likeness to the reality which is perceived by the most commonplace mind" (SE [1951], pp. 112; 111). Characteristically, there is a concealed sexual drive to the phrasing; and characteristically too, the scorn embraces, not just commonplace ways of seeing – such as the reader might employ – but any flow and expanding of spirit that leads to the desert of lifelikeness.

Being like life is what Eliot strenuously advised drama, post-Pinero, to avoid, since life, he seems to have felt, is a pretty poor thing to reproduce.

So, it must look all the odder that midway through his career as playwright he appears to double back and turn, if not to realism, then to the production of stage-pieces "in overt competition with prose drama" (*PP* [London], p. 81). In fact, on this particular decision he is flagrantly precise. It was in 1938, he writes, that he was prompted to move his plays toward conversational verse, as "the third voice [*that of a dramatic character*] began to force itself upon my ear" (*PP* [London], p. 92).

Yet the impulse that led him to remember Dickens here, and to phrase his explanation in the words of that other, older author (" 'The voices was very loud, sir,' said Mrs. Cluppins, 'and forced themselves upon my ear' " [*The Pickwick Papers*, ch. 24]), is hardly at the service of naturalism, after all. Rather, the choice the author has ostensibly made – to adopt a style in which characters will speak "for themselves" – is made to resemble a haunting or possession. He didn't choose; if anything, he was chosen. So, even as ordinary life is gathered up, it is denaturalized again – a pattern which is repeated both in the plays themselves and in Eliot's writing about them. At the very moment of his advocating that poetry should be brought "into the world in which the audience lives and to which it returns when it leaves the theater," he presses on towards a vision of "our own sordid, dreary daily world . . . suddenly illuminated and transfigured" (*PP* [London], p. 82). Which actually means that the sordid, dreary and daily are to be left behind. Despite what the essay promised earlier, we are not expected after our night at the theater to return to the low place we ordinarily inhabit; art will have carried us beyond.

> For it is ultimately the function of art, by imposing a credible order upon ordinary reality, and thereby eliciting some perception of an order *in* reality, to bring us to a condition of serenity, stillness, and reconciliation; and then leave us, as Virgil left Dante, to proceed toward a region where that guide can avail us no farther. (*PE* [London], p. 87)

It is an elevated pronouncement; but in the midst of being stirred, we may still remember that the region where Virgil left the poet was Purgatory – and to enter the further condition of serenity, stillness and reconciliation, the usual passage required is death.

Suppose, therefore, that one use Eliot made of the opportunities the action of theater allowed was to devise and perform rituals of extinction.

Now, his late plays are more often praised for virtues of quite a different kind, and the last one particularly, *The Elder Statesman*, is singled out for its reconciliatory spirit. Accounts of the plot would agree in summary that Lord Claverton, the statesman of the title, after an illustrious public career, is brought to seek an inner peace which will match his outward honors, and leaves the stage at last with the healing recognition of his need to love and be loved. The play, wrote the *Saturday Review* of its first performance, "deals with universals and reveals to us a more human T. S. Eliot than before." But what are we to make, the same reviewer wondered, of the sentimentality, the preachiness, the static and outmoded devices of the piece? "Indeed, the most conventional and dated scene comes right at the beginning when we are treated to a love proposal to a young lady named Monica by her very correct suitor, Charles."

Henry Hewes was not the only critic to be struck by a conventionality of theme and treatment, and if those are shortcomings, it is easy to imagine the author would have avoided them if he could. Eliot was near the end of his writing career, and this was his last play, we remember, looking back. At the time, however, *The Elder Statesman* was not the last, but the latest – a rather different thing. Its first production, indeed, was a moment of marked rejuvenation for its author, who declared himself feeling younger at seventy than he had at sixty, and spoke with interest about the possibility of writing "a few more poems in a rather different style." To judge from this interview (*ibid.*, September 13, 1958), Eliot saw his play as another case of "reaching an end and making a new beginning," as had happened with his work several times in the past. Which raises the question of what exactly *is* being brought to an end in *The Elder Statesman*?

Most obviously, Claverton's life. Though his death is not announced on stage, it is (with some solemnity) implied. "He has gone too far to return to us," says Monica, his daughter, in the closing moments; "He is under the beech tree. It is quiet and cold there." In any case, the parallel with *Oedipus at Colonus* (spelt out in Carol H. Smith's *T. S. Eliot's Dramatic Theory and Practice*) keeps the audience aware of the coming, welcomed end.

But Sophocles' ambiguous tragedy is not the only parallel to events. The death of the "old man" and the putting on of the "new" is an experience for all Christian souls, as David E. Jones phrases it in *The Plays of T. S. Eliot*, and similarly religious echoes hover, as when Monica (her name changed from the "Angela" of earlier drafts – perhaps in memory of St. Augustine's mother, and the part she played in his conversion) declares to her fiancé, Charles,

> I've loved you from the beginning of the world.
> Before you and I were born, the love was always there
> That brought us together.
>   O Father, Father!
> I could speak to you now.

The listener in the stalls may catch the Johannine phrasing, but for readers there are further signals given off by line-shift and capitalized exclamation, that one order of experience is being made to extend to another. The text does not hesitate to underline its effects: "It's as if he had passed through some door unseen by us. / And had turned and was looking back at us / With a glance of farewell."

Not just the particular character's extinction, then, but the end of a mortal life spiritually considered: at this point, a further parallel – another possible reading – appears, for while Claverton sees himself as "emerging / From my spectral existence into something like reality," critics have found in the play a similar liberation from the ghosts that had haunted Eliot's career. For the first time, not purgation, martyrdom, or expiation, but love between people becomes the dominant motif. Indeed, the drafts and summaries of *The Elder Statesman*, published in E. Martin Browne's *The Making of T. S. Eliot's Plays*, show this new concern breaking its way through material originally quite different in kind. Only by degrees, does the drama of "THE REST CURE – or alternatively – THE MAN WHO CHANGED HIS NAME" come to incorporate the various passages of love, between Monica and Charles, and between her and her father; and then the result is that the first conception of the play (as a study in mortification) simply fails to fit with the second (a discovery of love in life). Nevertheless, as A. D. Moody argues in *Thomas Stearns Eliot: Poet*, that makes it all the more eloquent as a human document; for what is revalued and abandoned in the final version is, on his reading, little less than "Eliot's life-work."

Yet the odd thing about the play is that at any level it remains so bland, so unshocking. If this is what death, or spiritual awakening, or revaluing one's life-work costs, the expense seems not too great. Claverton in his rest-home is pursued, not by Furies, or even, it turns out, by torments of his own conscience, but by an unsavory businessman and an ex-showgirl who are easily dealt with, once class-confidence – the characters' *and* the author's – supervenes upon their blackmailing menaces to find them rather laughably ill-bred. Indeed, the claims the two accusers have against Claverton are class-coloured from the start, since Gomez, was an Oxford chum of that "plain Dick Ferry" whom Lord Claverton used to be, and went to the bad through the latter's encouraging him in "expensive tastes" (cigars are mentioned), while Mrs. Carghill – who used to be Maisie Montjoy on the stage – was wronged by the same young Dick, and her breach-of-promise action bought off by his father's lawyers so that the up-and-coming man could continue his political climb.

Lucky the statesman who has nothing worse to haunt him. For the close of the 1950s, the plot could hardly be more old-fashioned. Europe may have torn itself apart, Hungary be crushed, Soviet and American empires threaten each other with destruction, Suez heap humiliation on top of dishonor, and Macmillan (1957) have come to power in a year of unprecedented industrial non-cooperation, but not a tremor from public event disturbs the protected *milieux* of the play. Badgley Court is not just a place where the well-off elderly are looked after, it is a rest-home or last haven for decrepit motifs of "successful" West-End drama. These superannuated practices stalk their way through settings so familiar that the very furniture proclaims itself nothing but convention – i.e., an unreality we have temporarily agreed to share. For this is *"The Drawing-room of* LORD CLAVERTON's *London house. Four o'clock in the afternoon"* and from the hall *"voices are heard."* Male and female Young Leads walk on, talking of afternoon-tea. Within moments, enter the trolley, with LAMBERT the servant attached. As if to expose a whole world of appearances, social life reappears as stage-business, with speaking and non-speaking "parts."

It hardly took Eliot's genius to see through the conventionalities of french-window-and-terrace comedy, but it is characteristic of his temperament that the closing movement of his career as playwright should see him confine himself within fictions he was simultaneously encouraging to dissolve themselves away. Maybe we understand it as a means of "imposing an order" on "our own sordid, dreary daily world," while at the same time pointing beyond the order, the transparently artificial drama, the playwright had devised. "It is possible," the essay on Marston suggests, "that what distinguishes poetic drama from prosaic drama is a kind of doubleness in the action, as if it took place on two planes at once." Even in "emptiness and irrelevance," in the very "shadow-show" of rhetoric and gesture, we may glimpse "a pattern behind the pattern into which the characters deliberately involve themselves; the kind of pattern which we perceive in our own lives only at rare moments of inattention and detachment, drowsing in sunlight" (*SE* [1951], pp. 229, 225, 232). But that is to give a higher value to the shadow-show of *The Elder Statesman* than it is ready to support. At best, one can come to believe that the staginess of feelings and speeches is part of the working of the play. Indeed, the more "sincere" the writing – as in speeches about the lover lost for words "like the asthmatic struggling for breath," or "brushed by the wing of happiness," or "only a beginner in the practice of loving" – the more its poetry sounds like declamation, a style in which emotions are impersonated rather than expressed. So we are not to put our trust in the theater's pretences, though they may be the best we have. After all, what else are they but make-believe, a scene already scripted, where anything may sound like histrionics, and nothing is for real? Far from representing a new "humanity" of treatment, *The Elder Statesman* might be seen as a final dismantling of the play-world's canvas and struts.

But then, exploiting the staginess of theater had been integral to Eliot's drama from *The Family Reunion* onwards. Coming to his plays, we might wonder at first why the sense of locale is so thin, compared to the compacted Englishness of Hardy, Betjeman, Larkin, where living leaves its print on objects almost by the way – or compared even to the busy authenticity striven for by Barrie and Shaw in stage-directions; but the point is that Eliot's places are constructed not so much to look "like life," as to operate like theorems or machines. All four of the plays between 1939 and 1958 take as their setting the three-walled stage-box of the genteel home, and subject it to some ritual of extinction. In the first of them, Wishwood, the unchanging country-house, "a cold place" in the north of England, broods over the family reunion of destinies, and, as in classic detective-fiction, the two acts are set, the one in the drawing-room, the other in the library, amid a circle of witnesses, some cognizant, some ignorant of the meaning of events unfolded before them. *The Cocktail Party* (1949), closer to the entertainments of Freddy Lonsdale and Noel Coward, takes place in a London flat with a refrigerator for keeping next-to-nothing in, a telephone, and doorbell, points of emptiness, absence and exit; after which the action shifts to Harcourt-Reilly's consulting room, similarly equipped to negotiate with the outside world through house-telephone and bell to summon the secretary – except that those devices carefully make the distinction between outside and inside even more unclear. Modern Living itself, amid the reflecting surfaces of this up-to-date decor, strikes the macabre note. By contrast, the settings for *The Confidential Clerk* (1953) are more heavily furnished, as befits that play's *fin de siècle* opulence of plot: writing-desk, piano, armchairs, typewriter, silver-framed portraits, solid door, for knocking on. But here too the telling gaieties of the relevant convention (W. S. Gilbert, reworked by Wilde) are summoned up, only to falter and drop away. In every case, the enclosed living-space of these dramas acts like a sealed chamber from which the air is inexorably pumped out.

One escapee is all that is allowed each play: Harry, Celia, Colby. For the rest, if they do not die, the drama shows small interest in how even the best of them might go on living, once their purpose in awakening the hero is achieved. Mary, Agatha: what of *them*? For a moment, *The Confidential Clerk* may gesture towards larger possibilities (as with Lucasta and her B. Kaghan), but the touch of feeling between them is lost to the simpering dénouement of Colby's predicted vocation (organist; piano-teacher; reading for orders; "a precentorship! a canonry!"). Mostly, the subsidiaries disappear into darkness, or remain suspended in the limbo their natures have confirmed, like Sir Claude, with his "collection" arranged on shelves, or the Chamberlaynes's uncomprehending marriage-duet.

To undo the place where the prosperous of the world are at ease, and thereby expose the evasions on which their home was built, was perhaps no bad endeavor in the middle-class theater of the English forties and fifties. Old-fashioned, yet salutary – like Ibsen's mission to the stuffy suburbs of bourgeois Norwegian life. But there is more to Eliot, and he does not fail to let us know it. The plays are not social drama only; they mean *something else* all the time. Beneath their drawing-room manners, what they mean is Sin, and Expiation, Vocation, Sacrifice; the Way.

"It's hard to make other people realize / The magnitude of things that appear to them petty," Lord Claverton complains, and this peevish note, like a draught from an ill-fitted window, seeps through the writing now and then. Something is in the air. Hardly a name but has meaning: Lucasta Angel, who is all the two words suggest, and "flighty" as well, we're told; or Violet, Ivy, the aunts of *The Family Reunion*, contrasted in their vegetative consciousness with Amy (the soul hardened into will) and Agatha, in whose name the Good is echoed, almost inaudibly, from far-off. It is almost a relief to learn that pereira, brought up in the first line of *Sweeney Agonistes*, does exist, a fever-reducing medicine, called after the English pharmacologist, Jonathan Pereira (1804–53). One always felt that there was more to the mysteriously sinister name. Or there are flirtatious scurries of dialogue, as in the joke that opens *The Cocktail Party*: "You've missed the point completely, Julia: / There *were* no tigers. *That* was the point" – which dares the listener (not missing the point) to recall worlds where tygers do spring (Blake's forests; Gerontion's juvescence of the year). There are elaborate wheezes like the to-and-fro about Julia's glasses, without which she "simply can't see a thing," and whose missing lens makes her a variant of the Seer-as-One-Eyed-Riley. The middle plays are full of details that, kept under wraps, give off an air of profundity, their hints steamily rising from the treatment of religion as a secret society, a way reserved for the few. "For the most intelligent and sensitive members of the audience," wrote Eliot about another of his plays, there would be a high-level meaning available, while the remaining spectators would share the "material, literal-minded and visionless . . . responses of the other characters" (*UPUC* [London], p. 153). The contrast between those who see and those who don't, false knowledge and true, is repeatedly enforced, so that Celia Coplestone finds the world she inhabits "all a delusion," while for Harry "It is not my conscience, / Not my mind that is diseased, but the world I have to live in." In such a place, where "reality" is vanity, the most frivolous appearances may be the very ones which demand to be interpreted again – one thinks of Alex and Julia's prattle. *Un*enlightened society, in fact, is understood to be so corrupt that truth must be smuggled in like contraband, as if it were some pure spirit available only through the fifth column of God's spies, specialists in concoction and espionage – a way of doing business not surprising in the War-shadowed years of *The Family Reunion* (1939) and *The Cocktail Party* (1949), but not entirely attractive, either.

Still, *The Family Reunion* at least has its own weird power, rather like a haunted house. In it, nightmares of the "crowded desert" give place to the worse nightmare of the desert "cleared, under the judicial sun / Of the final eye," and that in turn to the helpless moment of release, when "the awful evacuation / Cleanses," and realization comes at last,

> I was not there, you were not there, only our phantasms
> And what did not happen is as true as what did happen
> O my dear, and you walked through the little door
> And I ran to meet you in the rose-garden.   (II, ii)

To be freed, by the way of purgation, from the desert wasteland into a garden of ghosts: that is the essential design, the wished-for metaphysical action, of all four plays from here to the end. For a moment, the poetry, like *Burnt Norton* to which it is clearly related, no longer splits "real" and "unreal" apart, but recreates them as inseparably involved with one another, happening and not-happening together. Yet for the author, as for the redeemed of *The Family Reunion*, even this fulfilment, of rose-garden present-in-absence, is to be relinquished: one more necessary extinction, since nothing lasts – not happiness, nor personal and private agony, transmuted (in that struggle "which alone constitutes life for a poet") "into something rich and strange" (*SE* [1951], p. 137); not even language itself, perpetually brought to the brink of exhaustion by the great writers who use it, "so that it must, after yielding a diminishing crop, finally be left fallow for some generations" (*PP* [London], pp. 64ff.) – and even then, will reawaken to the damage of a lifetime and the impassable triumph of what can never be done better, or even be done again. There is no abiding city to be built on temporal ground, and Eliot does not write another play in the style of *The Family Reunion*.

He wrote that "every attempt is a wholly new start." Perhaps; yet looked at from a different angle, it might also seem that each is an effort to restate what cannot be shaken off. For in all of the plays so far, what is pivotal, for better, for worse, is the family. Not content with one such grouping, in fact, each play provides a *double* family, to offer on the one hand true knowledge (the Eumenides and Agatha; the Guardians of *The Cocktail Party*; Mrs. Guzzard in *The Confidential Clerk*), or on the other hand, complicity and spiritual death, as in Lord Claverton's old specters, or Amy's tyranny of love, or the false choice of merely human affection which Harry, Celia, and

Colby in varying ways reject. The terms shift, but the patterns are strangely alike, resemblances springing up amongst them as between blood-relatives and generations. Childless himself, but be-familied, Eliot was intensely conscious of what it was to be the heir of parents and past – to have to earn a tradition, to have to be a Hamlet, a Coriolanus, or to take up the awful destiny of killing the old priest in order to become new lord of the sacred wood. Killing a priest forms the outward and visible drama of his first full-scale play.

Not only that, but *Murder in the Cathedral* (1935) has its own double family too. The female side is segregated and humbled, as "women of Canterbury" – "charwomen," the author once called them (*PP* [London], p. 91) – while the males are celibate, priests of the cathedral, congregated around their Archbishop. This bisection leaves the men free to articulate "higher" needs and fears, those of *ecclesia*, mostly, while to the female chorus who feel "the strain on the brain of the small folk" falls the job of apprehending death and evil as, more than anything, bodily disgusts. For them, the nightmare vision is of nature turned to an oppressive sexuality: the air heavy and thick; earth pressing up, heaving to parturition; a sickly smell and sticky dew; nauseating tastes and textures to the touch; things ingurgitated to live and spawn in the bowels. Eliot thought of his chorus as "excited and sometimes hysterical women" (*PP* [London], p.81), but as they trace the sin which is spun in the plottings of princes, and find it "woven also in our veins, our brains . . . woven like a pattern of living worms / In the guts of the women of Canterbury," it is clear they are women *in order to* have these living worms inside them. For sin soils – sexually: flows under feet and over sky, in at the ear, the mouth, till

> Nothing is possible but the shamed swoon
> Of those consenting to the last humiliation.
> I have consented, Lord Archbishop, have consented.
> Am torn away, subdued, violated,
> United to the spiritual flesh of nature,
> Mastered by the animal powers of spirit,
> Dominated by the lust of self-demolition . . .
> By the final ecstasy of waste and shame

Although, theologically considered, the priests are as implicated as anyone else in humanity's fallen state, they don't talk this way. It is the women who, suffering a kind of self-rape (they *consent* to be violated?), are victims of evil and, in the play's terms, carriers of it too, revulsed and yet intimate with corruption, while the Knights – for all their blustery self-exculpation – are merely a murdering machine.

Nowhere, then, in the world outside himself can Becket find his way of purgation patterned, or even pointed out. In this, he is unlike the spiritual heroes of the later plays. He returns to his city like Shakespeare's Coriolanus in triumph, streets packed to suffocation, frenzied plaudits, clambering crowds, but his pride, says the Messenger, wills "subjection to God alone" – no one else being grand enough, it appears. Solitary from the start, and looking down on his people from a loftiness even God might hesitate to match ("They speak better than they know, and beyond your understanding. / They know and do not know what it is to act or suffer"), he sweeps forward through temptations progressively more inward, until the victory is gained: "Now is my way clear, now is the meaning plain": i.e., he has conformed his will to God. We know, because he says so. Or maybe, the doubt springs up, he has conformed God to his will, and chosen martyrdom vaingloriously after all.

There is simply no way anyone could tell. Whatever Becket's motives, an audience can never be sure of them; only God can see his heart, while we are left to hear his chosen words. "I shall no longer act or suffer, to the sword's end," he orates. Yet how can an actor *not* act? the theatergoer enquires. To proclaim, "I give my life / To the Law of God above the Law of Man" can only sound as if the speech is *meant* to be overheard. Contrariwise, however, what would silence tell? Problem here, as Winnie says in *Happy Days*. *Murder in the Cathedral* may not compel as an affirmation of faith, despite its powerful moments, but it still intrigues, just because its irresolvability is complete. Having directed us towards a light into which we cannot peer, the drama leaves us simultaneously exalted (God has given us "another Saint in Canterbury") and pleasurably skeptical (the pious have been taken in by another holy fraud – acted out, what is more, on the sacred site of the martyrdom itself).

Because, the *locus* speaks. Becket's *agon* is performed not in the home or "apartment" where the four later plays take place, but in the divine arena instead. (Originally, in the Chapter House of the cathedral, fifty yards from the spot where the Archbishop died.) Here, the audience is not buying entertainment, invisible onlookers at a history unfolded within the lighted and furnished space of the proscenium stage; rather, the true action – the nature of the hero's choice – has become inaccessible to view, while it is the spectators who are scrutinized, questioned, prayed for, and harangued, "You, and you, / And you, must all be punished. So must you." And this tense relationship, as between schoolroom and dominie, leaves its mark on the stage-works from first to last. (One remembers Lord Claverton proposing to sit "side by side, at little desks" with his son, to "suffer the same humiliations / At the hands of the same master." Not much of a model of education, one has to say.)

In the case of *The Rock* (1934), belief in the audience's infirmity goes so far as to determine genre itself, the pageant or Cochrane-style revue being a form which has *already* judged its spectators deficient in staying-power. And while Eliot and E. Martin Browne, in a program summary, describe it as portraying the Church "opposed, ignored, or interfered with by the secular tendencies of the present age," the pageant itself finds so little value in secular life at any time that it is a mystery, to this Christian reader at least, to know what "the Church" in its other-worldly isolation could possibly be built *out* of. Certainly, the ROCK, *led by a BOY*, proposes to show "the work of the humble," but as with the small folk of *Murder in the Cathedral*, the effect is to patronize instead, and to prove "living" not good enough unless perfected (i.e., not human at all). Until perfect, it is only "Living and partly living," or "weariness of men who turn from GOD" (Chorus III), and the denigrating cadences tell us what we ought to feel.

Yet in the very stiffness of its preaching robes, its stylized fragmentariness, and incorporated variety-acts, *The Rock* is at least not a routine English play. With Chorus in "stone-coloured masks and dresses, standing in a solid and motionless block about the central figure" (*Church Times*, June 1, 1934), it takes its place among popular-highbrow experiments of the day – Stravinsky's *Oedipus Rex*, for example (book by Cocteau, staged New York, 1931, with singers encased in sculpture), Yeats's Plays for Dancers, or early Auden/Isherwood entertainments. Miss Latrobe's pageant in *Between the Acts* had plenty of precedents, for its absurdity, its giant historical ambition, its pastiche, and lyricism, and the odd convincingness with which, in the moment of its performance, it images its own audience reflected back to themselves on bits and pieces of shaky looking-glass.

But that is nowhere near so disruptive as the work which at the start of Eliot the dramatist's career is so peculiar that it is not even called a play, but a "melodrama" – an "Aristophanic" melodrama at that (only comedies by Aristophanes survive), and published among the Unfinished Poems (though it is not clear that it is a poem, or that *more* is what is needed). *Sweeney Agonistes* first appeared as two pieces in *The Criterion*: October, 1926, "Fragment of a Prologue," and January, 1927, "Fragment of an Agon," at which point was added the further heading, "[From *Wanna Go Home, Baby?*]." The present inclusive title seems not to have been decided upon till some years later. As if to ensure that we do not miss the Fragments' proportions, though, *The Criterion* prints the double epigraph, from *Choephoroi* and St. John of the Cross, twice over. So each time we make our way into the company of Dusty and Doris via these pagan and mystical passages, as if through a labyrinthine corridor of careful stage-directions:

ORESTES: *You don't see them, you don't – but I see them: they are hunting me down, I must move on.*   Choephoroi.

Hence the soul cannot be possessed of the divine union, until it has divested itself of the love of created beings. St. John of the Cross

The mental music of those unharmonized quotations forms the setting or aural space within which the melo-drama will occur.

This highly original staging on the page, then, disciplines itself to ask for no embodiments beyond those we get, since names, echoes and non-vocal noise are actors, quite as much as anyone in make-up and costume could be. In the same way, even repetition becomes an agent, an operative moving part, as when the Doris-Dusty first exchange ("'How about Pereira?' 'What about Pereira?'") turns out to have paralleled the monosyllables of the epigraph: *You don't see them, you don't – but I see them.* There is nothing in common, there is everything in common, between the brassy knowingness of the women's to-and-fro ("'I don't care.' 'You don't care!'") and the seesawing pattern from *Choephoroi*, where horrified knowledge divides the "you" from the "I," the visionless from those who have seen what is hunting them down. We tell ourselves that Orestes' tragedy belongs to a different world from that of Doris and her pal in their rented flat; when the parallel steps forward, it is startling, as if a figure had materialized from empty air. The telephone has a part also, "Ting a ling ling / Ting a ling ling" dead on cue, and is treated like the Messenger of legend who, bringing bad news ("That's Pereira"), must be executed at once: "Well, can't you stop that horrible noise? / Pick up the receiver." The door speaks, or more exactly KNOCK is given ten lines to itself; but we are never told that anyone comes in, since nobody is there to enter and there is no scenery on which an entrance might supervene. It is enough to *name* DORIS. DUSTY. WAUCHOPE. HORSFALL. KLIPSTEIN. KRUMPACKER., each set of letters finalized by a full-stop, like inscriptions on a classical tomb. If they make themselves known when their voices are raised, it is as presences at a seance might do.

In this disembodied fashion, then, *Sweeney Agonistes* may come to seem the most dramatic of all the Eliot plays: farcical, gruesome, and rendingly sad. The wonderful thing is how completely it includes in its tiny compass the range of its author's theories, interests and talents. It is of its twenties time, right down to the black entertainers ("SWARTS AS TAMBO. SNOW AS BONES") you meet in early Waugh novels, or could see on stage, in Josephine Baker numbers. (The enthusiasm for non-European performers like Katherine Dunham, or Ram Gopal, continued through the next decade.) Yet look up the entry "Tambo: a tambourine player," in the *OED* ("a negro minstrel troupe . . . seated on chairs, at the ends are Bones and Tambo"), and what comes to mind is Senecan drama as described by Eliot, where characters "behave like members of a minstrel troupe sitting in a semicircle, rising in turn each to do his 'number,' or varying their recitations by a song or a little back-chat" (*SE* [1951], p. 69). New Orleans amidst London amidst ancient Rome: one cultural occasion transparent to another – as in a Cubist painting, or just as he hoped would happen in his other, more elaborately allusive plays.

At the same time, the grotesque intensity of every element in *Sweeney* brings it close to that "farce of the old English humour, the terribly serious, even savage comic humour . . . prodigious caricature" which intrigued him in Marlowe (*SE* [1951], p. 123), and in Jonson and Marston too. Likewise, when the pub-scene of *The Waste Land* took Lil's pain and set it to ragtime – "He said, I swear, I can't bear to look at you . . . I said . . . I said," sounding like dance-steps, twitchy-compulsive, in Eliot's recorded rendition – a new form of modern satire-tragedy was made: then developed further, in these two monumental Fragments. From *Sweeney*, one understands how the discarded "American" opening of "The Burial of the Dead" ("First we had a couple of feelers down at Tom's place") might actually have fitted in: *Wanna Go Home, Baby?* indeed. But one begins to see, too, how omnivorously Eliot drew on available material, popular song, or cabaret turns, or Vachel Lindsay's jazz-poems, while still transmuting everything he touched. "A kind of satire over-exploited in recent years," Morton Zabel called it in 1933. It isn't, as it happens; but the walk-up Dusty and Doris inhabit, with car-parking round the corner, and newspapers reporting the horrors of the day, is a precisely identified milieu, constructed out of the emptily smart second-hand of that transatlantic idiom the girls share with Loot Sam Wauchope and Klip, Krum and the Cap; and as with the setting of "Portrait of a Lady," its particular reality could only be lessened by an attempt to put it on the stage.

Yet compared to the vernacular art of Marie Lloyd, Ernie Lotinga, or Nellie Wallace (*SE* [1951], pp. 456–57), the "popular" style of *Sweeney* is actually another form of élite appropriation; and the brilliance which enables it to rise beyond the need for flesh and blood performers, is at the same time a sort of death – one to which the author, with his interest in liturgy, the possibility of "a mute theater," and other ways of freeing drama from the actor (*SW* [1928], p. 67; *SE* [1951], pp. 47, 113–14), had long been drawn. Beckett, by contrast, even at his minimalist extreme, remains a playwright of the moving mouth, of action, however reduced, sounds of shingle, of music, of breath itself; the *sound* of silence – whereas in "Fragment of an Agon" it is enough for the break in the discourse, the mental disconnectedness, simply to be written down:

SWEENEY: Birth, and copulation, and death.
DORIS: I'd be bored.
SWEENEY: You'd be bored.

We do not have to hear the abyss between the lines, it has been registered already. No doubt Eliot's idea that *Sweeney* might be accompanied by drum-beats was a period touch (Lifar's Icarus would dance to unaccompanied drum), but it was also a way of de-voicing the drama, of over-riding if not drumming out the performer's work with the lines.

To annul his actors will seem a strange aim for a playwright, but suspicion of the body is the other side of fascination with the powers it may possess: as when the poet yields to a rhythmic impulse out of which the demon-embryo of a poem is conceived. Eliot's preoccupation with pattern and ritual in drama – what he would often call "rhythm" – tugs it between body and soul. In *Sweeney*, physical presence is not even necessary to the play's success, while in later works, setting, action, actors, are there to be *seen through* to the higher reality beyond. At first, quite explicitly, as with the immobile Rock, or the symbolic figuring of *Murder in the Cathedral* (the wheel of action and suffering in the Knights circling Becket with their swords), then more surreptitiously, as the plot thickens and the "religious" significance with it, audiences' eyes must be opened. Never without benefits – to have had Eliot as a contemporary must gladden all of us, as readers of the language he so intensified – but the dualism he suffered from has been blighting. Higher/lower, sacred/profane, the old oppositions construct so much of his thinking for him, it is sometimes hard to remember how unnecessary they are. Perhaps the antidote, as he himself half-recognized, half-resisted (*SE* [1951], pp. 317–22), is in Blake: the Blake whose Devil recognizes no Body distinct from the Soul – "for that call'd Body is a portion of Soul discern'd by the five Senses, the chief inlets of Soul in this age" – and whose Everlasting Gospel has God himself declare, in triumphant paradoxes of Incarnation,

> 'Thou art a Man, God is no more,
> 'Thine own Humanity learn to Adore'

What a difference it would have made, for a dramatist working in the space and time of theater, to have been able to give effective assent to that.

WORKS CITED

Browne, E. Martin. *The Making of T. S. Eliot's Plays*. Cambridge: Cambridge University Press, 1969.

Empson, William. "The Style of the Master," Richard March and Tambimuttu (eds.) *T. S. Eliot: A Symposium*. London: PL Editions Poetry London, 1948.

Hewes, Henry. "T. S. Eliot at Seventy," *The Saturday Review* 41 (September 13, 1958): 30–32.

Jones, David E. *The Plays of T. S. Eliot*. London: Routledge & Kegan Paul, 1960.

Kenner, Hugh. *The Invisible Poet: T. S. Eliot.* New York: McDowell, Obolensky, 1959.

Moody, A. D. *Thomas Stearns Eliot: Poet.* Cambridge: Cambridge University Press, 1979.

Smith, Carol H. *T. S. Eliot's Dramatic Theory and Practice.* Princeton: Princeton University Press, 1963.

Zabel, Morton D. "Sweeney Agonistes," *Commonweal* 17 (April 19, 1933): 696–97.

13

JAMES LONGENBACH

"Mature poets steal": Eliot's allusive practice

"The borrowed jewels he has set in its head do not make Mr. Eliot's toad the more prepossessing": so wrote an early reviewer of *The Waste Land*, affronted by the bold allusions from which Eliot's poetry was built.[1] Those allusions, reinforced by Eliot's own notes to *The Waste Land*, have never ceased to affront; even today they account for Eliot's still formidable reputation as a "difficult" poet, and several generations of source-hunting critics have reinforced that impression.[2] Eliot sometimes played this game himself ("Immature poets imitate," he quipped early in his career, "mature poets steal" [*SE* [1950], p. 182]), but other times he was dismayed that readers found the surface difficulties of his poems prohibiting. And while it's true that knowledge of Eliot's models and sources does enrich a reading of his poetry, it is ultimately more important to understand the nature of Eliot's allusive practice – to ask not only *what is the source?* but *why does Eliot allude?* and *how do we experience the allusion?*

Eliot's poetry does not contain more allusions than that of Milton or Spenser; a representative passage of *Paradise Lost* will typically require many more footnotes than a passage of *The Waste Land*. But especially in his earlier poems (the poems written after *The Waste Land*, we will see, work rather differently) Eliot forces his readers to feel the weight of his allusions very strongly. The allusions do not seem to reinforce an otherwise approachable meaning but instead seem essential to the structure, not immediately perceivable, of the poem. If we catch the allusion in Yeats's "Easter 1916" –

> And what if excess of love
> Bewildered them till they died?

– to Shelley's "Alastor," in which the doomed young poet is "sickened with excess / Of Love" when he has a vision of ideal feminine beauty, then our sense of Yeats's feelings about recklessness, both political and amorous, are enriched. If we do not catch the allusion, our reading of the poem still feels secure. But when we confront these lines in Eliot's "Gerontion" –

> Signs are taken for wonders. "We would see a sign!"
> The word within a word, unable to speak a word,
> Swaddled with darkness.   (lines 17–19)

– we feel the weight of something missing in the lines. But once we know that Eliot alludes to Matthew 12:38 ("Master, we would see a sign from thee") and Lancelot Andrewes's sermon on that passage ("the Word without a word; the eternal Word not able to speak a word") then we begin to see that "Gerontion" is about, among other things, the difficulty of acquiring certain knowledge and passing on that knowledge to future generations. Teasing out the allusions, we, as readers, become part of that difficult process of transmission. If we do not know the references, we may feel excluded; indeed, that feeling is crucial to the ultimate power of our sense of understanding. As Christopher Ricks has recently said: "Whatever else Eliot effected by these early poems, he ruffled people, and there is something missing from any criticism which comes across as entirely unruffled, as if rufflement were for other people."[3]

Readers are forced to account for Eliot's allusions in special ways not because of their frequency or obscurity, then, but because the allusions in Eliot's earlier poems are structural. Still helpful is the account offered by Robert Graves and Laura Riding in *A Survey of Modernist Poetry* (1928), probably the first study that could be thought of as "post modernist" since it self-consciously considers Eliot's generation "with historical (as opposed to contemporary) sympathy." As both poets and literary critics themselves, Graves and Riding describe the relationship of modernist poetry, its critics, and its readers as a "vicious circle": put off by the unfamiliar difficulties of new work, most readers ignore it, leaving the work to literary critics, who further alienate readers by making the work seem like "a high-brow performance for a snobbish cult." In response, "the modernist poet, left without any public but the highly trained literary connoisseur, does not hesitate to embody in his poems remote literary references which are unintelligible to the wider public and which directly antagonize it." Offering an extended reading of Eliot's "Burbank with a Baedeker: Bleistein with a Cigar" (one of his most densely allusive poems), Graves and Riding become caught in this vicious circle themselves: dutifully explicating the references to Byron, Shakespeare, Browning, and Ruskin, they throw up their hands at Eliot's epigraph. And rightly so: its six quotations are taken from Gautier, Mantegna, James, *Othello*, Browning, and Marston – but whatever the sources, Eliot seems here to exaggerate his own arrogance in order to ruffle his readers. Duly ruffled, Graves and Riding suggest that the epigraph might be written "by some obscure diarist or by Mr. Eliot himself: we cannot be bothered to discover whom." Here Graves and Riding, as literary critics, refuse to play Eliot's game; however, though they conclude their reading of "Burbank" by admitting that it "is aristocratic writing, and its jokes are exclusive," they finally join forces with Eliot as poets, insisting that these jokes are "exclusive [only] if the reader has no capacity or interest for sharing them: the Baedeker is common to all men."[4]

Graves and Riding sometimes blamed Eliot for the difficulty of his poetry and other times blamed his historical moment – his readers. This double attitude is common throughout the critical history of modernism. (Louis Vauxcelles, the critic who coined the phrase *les fauves* – the wild beasts – to describe Matisse's circle of painters, also used the phrase to describe the audience who rejected the paintings: he could not decide who was more arrogant.)[5] And it seems to me that we must maintain a similarly double attitude towards Eliot's allusions – at times resenting their exclusiveness and at other times sympathizing with their power and with the cultural predicament that precipitated them. It would be shortsighted to insist that exclusiveness was not one of Eliot's goals, but it would be equally shortsighted to dismiss the poetry in turn, ignoring the personal and cultural factors that made Eliot feel, as he once said, "that poets in our civilization, as it exists at present, must be *difficult*" (*SE* [1950], p. 248).

Eliot himself would have agreed with Graves's and Riding's characterization of the cultural predicament of modernist poetry. In 1918 the *Times Literary Supplement* published "Professionalism in Art," an attack on the professional that upheld the rights of the dilettante: "Decadence in art is always caused by professionalism, which makes the technique of art too difficult."[6] Eliot responded in the *Egoist*, claiming that the ineffectual position most writers held in his culture was due to their spurning the authority of professionalism: "An attitude which might find voice in words like these [in the *TLS*] is behind all of British slackness for a hundred years and more: the dislike of the specialist."[7] Eliot self-consciously made his poetry difficult, the property of a specialist, in order to increase the status of poets: the response of the early reviewer to *The Waste Land* represented an attitude Eliot condemned, but it was nevertheless a response which *The Waste Land* was in some ways calculated to produce. Eliot needed to provoke that outrage in order to differentiate his work, along with that of Pound and Joyce, from the literary culture of Arnold Bennett or the Georgian Poets. Allusion was one of the badges of Eliot's professionalism.

While the *TLS* writer condemned a writer's interest in "technique," Eliot responded that the properly professional poet must be devoted to his technique: "Try to put into a sequence of simple quatrains the continuous syntactic variety of Gautier or Blake, or compare these two with A. E. Housman" (Eliot, "Professional," p. 61). Eliot's choice of well-turned quatrains as an indicator of a writer's seriousness was not casual, for in 1918 Eliot was himself laboring on poems in quatrains like "Burbank with a Baedeker." Packed with allusions, the form of these poems was itself allusive, meant to recall the rigor of Gautier or Blake and reveal the weakness of the more popular Housman. Pound wrote poems in quatrains during this period as well (eventually collected in *Hugh Selwyn Mauberley*), and he remembered why he and Eliot made a self-conscious decision to throw over their earlier work in free verse and champion strict form: "at a particular time, at a particular date in a particular room, two authors, neither engaged in picking the other's pocket, decided that the dilution of *vers libre*, Amygism, Lee Masterism, general floppiness had gone too far and that some counter-current must be set going . . . Rhyme and regular strophes."[8] This was a decision made by professionalized poets who wanted to increase their power as specialists. The strategy was paradoxical: though their poetry lacked status in the literature culture of their time, Pound and Eliot were repulsed by the increasing popularity ("dilution") of their once radical work in free verse, and sought to increase their status by remaking their poetry in more difficult and unpopular forms. Pound once admired the highly developed "art of allusion" in the Japanese Noh theater: "These plays, or eclogues, were made only for the few; for the nobles; for those trained to catch the allusion."[9] When they sat together in a particular room, at a particular date, Eliot and Pound were hoping to perpetuate this attitude in their own work.

Eliot was much preoccupied by ideas of tradition in these early years of his career, and, bolstered by his essays, his poems helped to emphasize the important figures in his tradition, both in their forms (invoking Gautier and Blake in the quatrain poems, Pope and Dryden in the drafts of *The Waste Land*) and in the texts to which he often alluded: Dante, Shakespeare, Webster, Marvell, James, and Baudelaire. Conspicuously absent from Eliot's tradition are Milton, the Romantics, Tennyson, and Whitman, all of whom Eliot dismissed in his most well-known early essays. For years Eliot was read through the lens of his own ideas about tradition, so that in the 1970s, when later readers began to stress the fact that Eliot's poems did allude to the writers he publicly spurned (especially Tennyson and Whitman), the received Eliot began to seem contradictory or even underhand. The song of the hermit thrush in the final movement of *The Waste Land* clearly alludes to Whitman's "When Lilacs Last in the Dooryard Bloom'd," but Eliot's notes send us to Chapman's *Handbook of Birds of*

Eastern North America – almost as if to suggest that his birdsong is "natural" and untainted by literary allusion. Faced with these peculiarly selective and evasive notes, John Hollander has suggested that it "is almost as if a kind of suppression were at work in the texture of recognition and avowal" – a prime example of what Harold Bloom has called the "anxiety of influence."[10] Like most post-Enlightenment poets, Eliot surely suffered that anxiety, and productively so; but other more conscious motives also shaped his selective recognitions of allusion. Describing his "general programme of literary criticism" to Richard Aldington, Eliot explained that "any innuendos I make at the expense of Milton, Keats, Shelley, and the nineteenth century in general are part of a plan to help us rectify, so far as *I* can, the immense skew in public opinion toward our pantheon of literature" (*Letters* I, 460). While Eliot's very practice of allusion was designed to enhance his status as a professional poet, his acknowledgments of them (Dante but not Whitman) were designed to emphasize the particular sense of tradition that underwrote his modern "pantheon of literature." In more ways than one, then, Eliot's allusions were part of a self-consciously political program. Whitman and Tennyson were crucial, Eliot knew, to his personal life as a poet; but they could not be part of his public mission to alter the terms of his literary culture.

Having recognized the cultural factors that shaped Eliot's practice of allusion, however, we should also remember the ways in which allusion *was* a crucial aspect of his personal life as a poet. Despite the ways in which Eliot manipulated allusions in his poems, the practice of allusion came naturally to him, and he often expressed his deepest feelings through allusion. Consider this sentence in a letter to his friend John Quinn, expressing frustration over his effort to enlist in the army during the First World War: "Everything turned to red tape in my hands" (*Letters* I, 254). Eliot alludes here to a favorite sentence in Flaubert's *Bouvard et Pécuchet*: "Ainsi tout leur a craqué dans la main." Eliot felt deeply that this line expressed something crucial about modern life, and its syntax infected Eliot's way of thinking: he also alluded to the line in a description of the detached skepticism of Henry Adams ("the pleasure of demolition turned to ashes in his mouth"), and he quoted the line in essays on Marvell and on Stendhal and Balzac.[11] Considering that three of these four references came within six months of one another (between November 1918 and May 1919), it seems that Flaubert's sentence weighed heavy on Eliot during the First World War. And through the very act of allusion, Eliot was constructing a continuous tradition that would help to mend the condition Flaubert so aptly described to him.

The paragraph of Eliot's essay on Marvell that ends with the quotation of

Bouvard et Pécuchet begins (after several lines quoted from "To His Coy Mistress") with these sentences:

> It will hardly be denied that this poem contains wit; but it may not be evident that this wit forms the crescendo and diminuendo of a scale of great imaginative power. The wit is not only combined with, but fused into, the imagination. We can easily recognize a witty fancy in the successive images . . . but this fancy is not indulged, as it sometimes is by Cowley or Cleveland, for its own sake. It is structural decoration of a serious idea.   (*SE* [1950], p. 255)

As much as Eliot's poetry, this passage builds its argument by allusion. To understand the argument fully, we must know not only Cowley and Cleveland but Dr. Johnson on wit and Coleridge's differentiation of imagination and fancy in the *Biographia Literaria*. Whether writing poems, critical prose, or personal letters, Eliot exercised a natural propensity to think through allusion.

It did take Eliot some time to transform that propensity into a structural principle for poetry. In comparison to "Gerontion" or the poems in quatrains (dating from 1917 to 1920), Eliot's earliest poems ("The Love Song of J. Alfred Prufrock," "Portrait of a Lady," and "Preludes," among others) contain fewer allusions. After writing these poems around 1910–11, Eliot devoted several years to his doctoral studies in philosophy, and he wrote no poetry until 1915, when he produced several minor poems influenced by the satiric edge of Pound's work ("The *Boston Evening Transcript*," "Aunt Helen," "Cousin Nancy," and "Mr. Apollinax"). Among these poems, "Cousin Nancy" was the breakthrough: its structural use of allusion was unprecedented in Eliot's work (and alien to Pound's). The first two stanzas offer an ironic portrait of Miss Nancy Ellicott, who "smoked / And danced all the modern dances." Commenting on her rebellious attitude, the final stanza introduces a note absent from the other poems of 1915.

> Upon the shelf kept watch
> Matthew and Waldo, guardians of the faith,
> The army of unalterable law.   (lines 11–13)

The diction of that final pentameter is completely at odds with the nervous rhythms throughout the rest of the poem: it stands apart even if we do not know that Eliot stole it from George Meredith's sonnet "Lucifer in Starlight," which describes Satan's fall from heaven. If we do recognize the allusion, an immense field of reference is brought to bear upon Cousin Nancy's rebellion, and we are swept from Meredith to Milton to the Old Testament. Whether this field of reference aggrandizes or trivializes Cousin Nancy's "modern" rebellion remains a teasingly open question.

Around the time that Eliot wrote "Cousin Nancy" he was completing his Ph.D. dissertation on the philosophy of F. H. Bradley. Eliot was dissatisfied with Bradley's conception of the Absolute (a synthesis of all diversity and contradiction) because, despite Bradley's intentions, it did not rescue the individual from the condition of solipsism. Instead of relying on faith in the Absolute to bring individuals together, Eliot proposed a theory of the gradual unification of discrete "points of view":

> [F]or the life of a soul does not consist in the contemplation of one consistent world but in the painful task of unifying (to a greater or less extent) jarring and incompatible ones, and passing, when possible, from two or more discordant viewpoints to a higher which shall somehow include and transmute them. (KE, 147–48)

While this passage is nothing so premeditated as a theory of Eliot's use of allusion in "Cousin Nancy," it does help to characterize the effect of that poem's final line: through allusion, the poem undertakes the "task of unifying" disparate worlds, combining discordant viewpoints (Nancy Ellicott's, Meredith's, Milton's, Satan's) into a richer and more complicated perspective on "modern" life.

Eventually, after he had written more poems, Eliot was able to reshape these ideas into a more self-conscious theory of allusion. In "A Note on Ezra Pound" (1918) he contrasted the "deliberateness" of Pound's allusions with the "speed" of Joyce's: "James Joyce, another very learned literary artist, uses allusions suddenly and with great speed, part of the effect being the extent of the vista opened to the imagination by the very lightest touch." In this context, Eliot's sympathies lay more with Joyce than Pound, for the final line of "Cousin Nancy" is designed to open just such a vista. In a related context, Eliot's sympathies were clearly with Pound, for earlier in "A Note on Ezra Pound" Eliot characterized Pound's "historical sense" in terms he would later recast for himself in "Tradition and the Individual Talent."

> A large part of any poet's "inspiration" must come from reading and from his knowledge of history. I mean history widely taken; any cultivation of the historical sense, of perception of our position relative to the past, and in particular of the poet's relation to poets of the past . . . [T]his perception of relation involves an organized view of the whole course of European poetry from Homer.[12]

Behind this passage stands Eliot's discussion in his dissertation of the "task of unifying" points of view to make new "wholes": in poetry, both Pound's and his own, the task would be accomplished by allusion.

In "Cousin Nancy" this happens on a small scale. With the multiple allusions in *The Waste Land*, Eliot approached something like "an organized view of the whole course of European poetry from Homer" – though the words "organized" and "whole" beg questions that remind us of the political or polemical dimensions of Eliot's practice of allusion. In the "Unreal City" passage which concludes the first part of *The Waste Land* (lines 60–76), for instance, Eliot begins by alluding to Baudelaire's "Les sept Vieillards," moves on to the *Inferno* ("I had not thought death had undone so many"), then to the hour of Christ's crucifixion ("a dead sound on the final stroke of nine"), to the Punic Wars ("You who were with me in the ships at Mylae!"), to Webster's *White Devil* ("Oh keep the Dog far hence that's friend to men"), and finally back to Baudelaire's preface to the *Fleurs du Mal* ("You! hypocrite lecteur! – mon semblable, – mon frère!"). All these references are folded into what begins as a naturalistic description of the City of London (Eliot even goes so far as to offer a footnote describing the bells at Saint Mary Woolnoth as "a phenomenon which I have often noticed") but then becomes an increasingly horrific city of dreams. The allusions, by relating modern London to medieval Florence, ancient Greece, and nineteenth-century Paris, suggest that this condition is neither unique nor insurmountable. In *The Waste Land*, the question that had seemed open in "Cousin Nancy" (do the allusions demean or bolster the present?) may be answered more conclusively: the wide field of references are folded into the present to remind us of historical continuity and show us the way out of our predicament – they are "fragments . . . shored against my ruins" (line 431).

Throughout *The Waste Land* Eliot's allusions generally do not seem simply ironic (contrasting past and present) because they are presented in dramatic contexts: the allusions are spoken by dramatic voices in particular scenarios, and the aural quality of the poem often makes the echoes seem less learned than ghostly – as if other voices were speaking from the past. In a 1934 essay on Marston, Eliot sketched a theory of dramatic "doubleness" which describes effects he had already achieved in *The Waste Land*:

> In poetic drama a certain apparent irrelevance may be the symptom of this doubleness; or the drama has an under-pattern, less manifest than the theatrical one. We sometimes feel, in following the words and behavior of some of the characters of Dostoevsky, that they are living at once on the plane that we know and on some other plane of reality from which we are shut out: their behavior does not seem crazy, but rather in conformity with the laws of some world that we cannot perceive.[13]

Eliot's plays often achieve this effect when characters step outside the action and begin to speak as if from a different script or as if possessed by a logic other than that of the dramatic action, a logic the audience has yet to perceive. In *The Waste Land* Eliot achieves the effect in ways even more subtle and more spooky than in his plays – through his sudden yoking of various voices, fragments, and allusions. For instance, Eliot begins the third movement of the poem, "The Fire Sermon" (lines 173–202), with natural-istic description of the Thames, but that logic is quickly disrupted by the presence of "nymphs" on the riverbank. The landscape then becomes urban and modern, strewn with bottles, sandwich papers, cigarettes, and the sudden juxtaposition with the lovely refrain from Spenser's "Prothalamion" ("Sweet Thames, run softly, till I end my song"), so unsuited to that land-scape, does not seem merely ironic; rather, it makes us wonder if there is some other presence in this desiccated landscape – and a power in the verse to perceive it – that we cannot fathom. The subsequent allusion to Marvell's "To His Coy Mistress" ("But at my back in a cold blast I hear" – itself disrupted by a further voice which gives us "The rattle of the bones, and chuckle spread from ear to ear" instead of the expected "Time's winged chariot hurrying near") and the reference to the myth of the Fisher King build the sense of an inexplicable "under-pattern" in the verse to an almost unbearable pitch. As Eliot suggests in his essay on Marston the lines do not seem merely irrational; they are all the more frightening for appearing part of a hidden logic that we do not yet understand. By the end of the passage we are swept from allusion to allusion, through motor cars to Mrs. Porter, and finally to the utterly inexplicable epiphany of Verlaine's children chant-ing in the dome: "*Et O ces voix d'enfants, chantant dans la coupole!*" As in the passage from "Gerontion" I glanced at earlier, this alien logic may be grasped: knowing that Verlaine's sonnet describes Parsifal's arrival at the Grail castle helps us to see that Eliot's manipulation of the Grail myth at least partially unites these disparate voices and allusions. But even when all the references are glossed, our knowledge does little to reduce the uncanny power of these lines, especially when they are read aloud.

This power is often retained by the allusions in the poems of the latter half of Eliot's career, written after *The Waste Land*, as are the personal and historical aspects of the allusions. Missing in the allusions of *Four Quartets*, however, is the audacity that is especially strong in the earlier quatrain poems. Generally, Eliot does not seek to ruffle his readers with allusion in the later work: he wants them to acquiesce to the poems' argument more easily. Depending on a distinction between "conscious" and "subliminal" allusions (allusions that are consciously meant to be recognized and allu-sions which appear more unconsciously), A. Walton Litz points that after *The Waste Land* Eliot's allusions "do not insist upon conscious recognition in the way many of the earlier allusions do." Alluding to Lancelot Andrewes in "Gerontion," Eliot forces his readers to feel the lack of the information which the glossed allusion provides. In "Journey of the Magi" (1927), in contrast, Eliot quotes from another of Andrewes's sermons, now dropped into quotation marks (lines 1–5); and as Litz suggests, "the relaxed lines from Andrewes flow into the continuous narrative of the poem, establishing a voice rather than appealing for intertextual engagement."[14]

Another way of accounting for this change in Eliot's allusive practice would be to say that in the later poetry, culminating in *Four Quartets*, the allusions no longer have the same structural function they did in the earlier poems. Rather than sustaining the argument of the poem on their own, they contribute to an argument that is usually otherwise apparent; and the allusions themselves often seem less like cryptic fragments than generous quotations. In *East Coker* Eliot adapts passages from St. John of the Cross –

> In order to arrive there,
> To arrive where you are, to get from where you are not,
> You must go by a way wherein there is no ecstasy.   (lines 137–39)

and from Sir Thomas Elyot's *The Boke Named the Governour* –

> Two and two, necessarye coniunction,
> Holding eche other by the hand or the arm
> Which betokeneth concorde.   (lines 32–34)

These lines are not dropped into quotation marks, and readers do not especially need to be aware of their sources; more important, once again, is the tone established by the lines and then extended by Eliot's own verse. Writing to John Hayward, Eliot explained that the "public intention" of the quotation from Sir Thomas Elyot "is to give an early Tudor setting, the private, that the author of The Governour sprang from E. Coker."[15] In Eliot's terms, the "public" aspect of the reference (its diction and tone) mattered more than the "private" aspect (awareness of Sir Thomas Elyot's connection with East Coker). Had the reference been made in one of Eliot's early poems, readers would more likely need to know the "private" aspect in order to understand the argument of the poem.

Christopher Ricks suggests that while allusion in *The Waste Land* had often been "an act of hostility, demanding surrender from the enemy," it became after his conversion to Christianity (which took place about the time that "Journey of the Magi" was written) "an act of self-surrender" (Ricks, *Eliot and Prejudice*, p. 258). This eradication of the aggressive edge of his allusions was part of a general shift in Eliot's career. While he was composing the essays that went into *The Sacred Wood* (1920), Eliot depended on Whitman and Tennyson in his poetry but, for political reasons, could not acknowledge his debts in his essays. In the later poems, Eliot alludes more openly to poets whom he loved: he is no longer engaged in that struggle to justify his generation's "pantheon of literature." In the early "Burbank with a Baedeker: Bleistein with a Cigar" Eliot alludes to Tennyson's "The Sisters" ("They were together, and she fell") –

> Princess Volupine arrived,
> They were together, and he fell.   (lines 3–4)

– in order to diminish both Burbank and Tennyson. But in his 1936 essay on Tennyson (*SE* [1950], p. 291), Eliot praised as "great poetry" the encounter with Hallam's ghost in the seventh poem of *In Memoriam* (ending with the line, "On the bald streets breaks the blank day"); and in his own encounter with the "familiar compound ghost" in *Little Gidding*, he remembered the line:

> The day was breaking. In the disfigured street
> He left me, with a kind of valediction,
> And faded on the blowing of the horn.   (lines 149–52)

These lines also recall the opening scene of *Hamlet*, and the lines preceding them (meant to recall Dante's terza rima) are overflowing with more particular echoes of Dante, Shakespeare, Milton, Swift, James, Mallarmé, and Yeats. Compared with the "Unreal City" passage of *The Waste Land*, however, we see that in *Little Gidding* our comprehension of the passage does not depend so crucially on our knowledge of the sources. In *Four Quartets* the allusions are more like Yeats's allusion to Shelley in "Easter 1916": they enrich our understanding rather than make it possible in the first place.

Despite this difference, these passages from *The Waste Land* and *Little Gidding* are similar in that they both record ghostly apparitions; and they both reinforce that uncanny sense of the past through echoes of a literary tradition. Another important continuity in Eliot's allusive practice may be found in the way Eliot alludes to himself in both *The Waste Land* and *Four Quartets*. Reading *The Waste Land*, we begin to make sense of its juxtaposed fragments by listening for echoes of earlier passages: when we encounter the phrase "Unreal City" for the second time (line 207) we have a sense of what it means, and that sense is then expanded. Even these almost purely musical lines from "The Fire Sermon" –

> Twit twit twit
> Jug jug jug jug jug jug
> So rudely forc'd.
> Tereu   (lines 203–6)

– become meaningful when we recognize them as echoes of the opening lines of "A Game of Chess": their sexual connotations help to link the seduction scene of "The Fire Sermon" to the rape of Philomel referred to in "A Game of Chess" ("'Jug Jug' to dirty ears" [line 103]). This kind of self-echo is of course common to all manner of literary texts (a good example may be found at the end of Joyce's "The Dead," where phrases uttered earlier in the story return in Gabriel's final reverie with new significance); but in a text like *The Waste Land*, which dispenses with any over-arching narrative coherence, much greater weight is placed upon these self-echoes: through them, we construct a different kind of coherence out of Eliot's juxtaposed fragments.

In *Four Quartets* Eliot depends on allusions to his own poetry in even more complicated and self-conscious ways. When John Hayward questioned the phrase "Autumn weather" in a draft of *Little Gidding*, Eliot replied that the phrase was necessary because it referred

> back to Figlia che piange ... but with less point than the children in the appletree meaning to tie up New Hampshire and Burnt Norton (with a touch, as I discovered in the train, of [Kipling's] "They" which I don't think I had read for 30 years, but the quotation from E. B. Browning has always stuck in my head   (Gardner, *Composition*, p. 29)

For Eliot, the phrase was heavy with echoes of his own poems as well as Kipling's "They" and Barrett Browning's "The Lost Bower." He set out to make *Four Quartets* the culmination of his career, folding in allusions to his earlier poems at the same time that he built one quartet on top of another, establishing musical and thematic continuities through allusions to the previous quartets. This strategy culminates in the end of *Little Gidding*, where lines from *Burnt Norton* ("Quick now, here, now, always"), *East Coker* ("We shall not cease from exploration"), and *The Dry Salvages* ("Between two waves of the sea") are wound together into a passage ending, "And the fire and the rose are one."[16]

These lines show Eliot alluding to a life of allusiveness; but they would never provoke the response of that early reviewer of *The Waste Land*. Between the writing of that poem and the composition of *Four Quartets*, Eliot's literary culture changed dramatically, and so did Eliot's place in it; the terms of Graves's and Riding's survey of "modernist" poetry no longer apply, and one could argue that, at least within the narrow terms of Eliot's career, *Four Quartets* represents a "post-modernist" poetry. While the motivations behind Eliot's allusions changed, however, and while the effect of the allusions on his readers changed in turn, Eliot's propensity to think and feel through allusion remained constant in all his work.

NOTES

1 F. L. Lucas, *"The Waste Land," New Statesman* 22 (November 3, 1923): 116–18; rpt. in Michael Grant (ed.) *T. S. Eliot: The Critical Heritage* (London: Routledge, 1982), vol. 1, pp. 195–99.

2 The most useful and generous of these remains Grover Smith, *T. S. Eliot's Poetry and Plays: A Study in Sources and Meaning*, 2nd. edn. (Chicago: University of Chicago Press, 1974).

3 Christopher Ricks, *Eliot and Prejudice* (London: Faber and Faber, 1988), p. 7.

4 Robert Graves and Laura Riding, *A Survey of Modernist Poetry* (New York: Doubleday, 1928), pp. 258, 103, 236, 242.

5 See Judi Freeman, *The Fauve Landscape* (Los Angeles: Los Angeles County Museum of Art, 1990), p. 56.

6 "Professionalism in Art," *Times Literary Supplement*, January 31, 1918, pp. 49–50.

7 T. S. Eliot, "Professional, Or . . .", *Egoist* 5 (April 1918): 61.

8 Ezra Pound, "Harold Monroe," *Criterion* 9 (July 1932): 590.

9 *Translations of Ezra Pound* (New York: New Directions, 1953), p. 214.

10 John Hollander, *The Figure of Echo: A Mode of Allusion in Milton and After* (Berkeley: University of California Press, 1981), p. 103. Among Harold Bloom's many writings, see especially, "Reflections on T. S. Eliot," *Raritan* 8 (Fall 1988): 70–87.

11 T. S. Eliot, "A Skeptical Patrician," *Athenaeum* 4647 (May 23, 1919): 361; "Beyle and Balzac," *Athenaeum* 4648 (May 30, 1919): 393; Eliot's 1921 essay on Marvell is reprinted in *SE* (1950), pp. 251–63.

12 T. S. Eliot, "A Note on Ezra Pound," *To-day* 4 (September 1918): 5–6.

13 T. S. Eliot, *Essays on Elizabethan Drama* (New York: Harcourt Brace, 1960), p. 173. See James Longenbach, "Uncanny Eliot," Laura Cowan (ed.) *T. S. Eliot: Man and Poet* (Orono: ME: National Poetry Foundation, 1990), pp. 47–70.

14 A. Walton Litz, "The Allusive Poet: Eliot and His Sources," Ronald Bush (ed.) *T. S. Eliot: The Modernist in History* (Cambridge: Cambridge University Press, 1991), pp. 144–45. The distinction between "conscious" and "subliminal" allusions may be usefully compared with Hollander's distinction between "allusion" and "echo" (see Hollander, *Figure of Echo*, p. 64 and *passim*).

15 Helen Gardner, *The Composition of "Four Quartets"* (London: Faber and Faber, 1978), p. 99.

16 For a complete explication of these self-echoes see James Olney, *Metaphors of Self: The Meaning of Autobiography* (Princeton: Princeton University Press, 1972), pp. 275–78.

14

CHARLES ALTIERI

Eliot's impact on twentieth-century Anglo-American poetry

When I was asked to write on the figure of Eliot in modern poetry I thought of several reasons not to accept. On a personal level I could imagine no way that such critical work would not reveal more about my limitations than about Eliot's powers, since I would miss or mistake crucial aspects of his heritage. And on a theoretical level I deeply mistrust any study claiming to speak of influences. Where such studies are not obvious, they tend to rely on loose speculations about specific echoes or to invoke problematic analogies attempting to establish one writer's shaping overall projects for another.

Yet here I am. The theoretical problem quickly became a challenge to test a concept of impact that might avoid the problems worrying me, since impact is less a matter of one poet deliberately engaging another than it is a matter of the currency of ideas and of a logic informing how writers shape ambitions or develop styles. Thus we shift from trying to inhabit the mind of specific writers to attempting to describe a theater in which Eliot becomes a stimulus focussing a range of possible investments in versions of his work. And then we also shift the personal stakes. My fears did not subside, but they were outweighed by the opportunity to take responsibility for my own love of Eliot: I could ask how and why the now dominant account misses much that was, and is, culturally vital in Eliot's work; and I could use the reception of Eliot's work by other poets to make clear what in his work does not yield to appropriation or modification, but marks instead his still distinctive modernist voice.[1]

I

From a historical perspective we must say that there have been many T. S. Eliots, linked at best by family resemblance. But for our purposes we must be content with two basic characters bearing that name, each the hero of a quite different story. The first story dominated for four decades. It cast Eliot as the American poet who brought Anglo-American poetry into the modern

age by forcing it to encounter urban life, by refusing sentimental idealizations in pursuit of the mind's intricate evasions and slippages, and by
intensely engaging the various modes of victimage fundamental to contemporary culture. But this story never quite escaped its demonic other –
now told both by those who think Eliot's modernism was an élitist destruction of still viable poetic traditions and by those like the LANGUAGE Poets
appalled by his conservatism in every domain. Here Eliot becomes a colo-
nizing modernist forcing on poetry the anxieties and powerless learning of a
dying white European culture and imposing a style that could provide no
alternative to the paralysis it recorded.

Let me start with this second story, then try to define its limitations. Its
first strong statement occurs in William Carlos Williams's 1920 "Prologue"
to *Kora In Hell*: "Upon the Jepson filet Eliot balances his mushroom . . . If
to do this, if to be a Whistler at best, in the art of poetry, is to reach the
height of poetic expression then Ezra and Eliot have approached it and *tant
pis* for the rest of us." But it took *The Waste Land* and thirty more years of
brooding to foster Williams's retrospective statement that most fully established the case against Eliot as the prematurely established Goliath against
which young Davids must prove themselves:

> I felt at once that it had set me back twenty years, and I'm sure it did. Criti-
> cally Eliot returned us to the classroom just at the moment when I felt that we
> were on the point of an escape to matters much closer to the essence of a new
> art form itself – rooted in the locality which should give it fruit. I knew at
> once that in certain ways I was most defeated.[2]

For Williams, Eliot's major weakness was his relying on an abstract sense of
culture, ungrounded in any actual communities or practices so that it
became a constant source of snobbism on the one hand, anxiety and paralysis on the other. Without a sense of the local there could be no objects for
consciousness which could directly engage the full energies of one's
medium; there could only be the infinite regresses of the mind seeking to
find within its own activity some rest or cure of the ground.

Such sentiments may have cost Williams dearly, since he spent much of
his later career working against the grain of his own talent in the hope that
he could rival Eliot's status as culture hero and poet–theorist. But he also
saw clearly the basic outlines that future versions of this story would take –
from Yeats on Eliot's merely "satiric intensity," to Auden's desire to replace
a poetics of image and gyre by one devoted to principles of care and of
community, to Karl Shapiro's critique of Eliot's élitist bookishness, to the
strange conjunction leading two rival anthologies in the early 1960s, each to
justify itself by opposition to Eliot on impersonality and his effects on the

New Criticism. Then in recent criticism we find much the same lines redrawn in somewhat different languages – for example in Hugh Kenner's claims for Pound over Eliot on the grounds that where Eliot has only the symbolist mind in endless pursuit of itself Pound binds poetry to the facts of nature and history, in Marjorie Perloff's contrast between a poetics of symbolist lyric closure and a pursuit of Rimbaud's indeterminate and over-flowing transformative energies, and in almost everyone's worries about Eliot's conservatism in politics and in religion.[3] And finally there is emerging a sociological version of these same principles that emphasizes the ways in which Eliot's modernism served larger establishment interests. As Orwell shrewdly observed, Eliot could make a radical modernism in the arts feasible for arbiters of cultural taste and for literary education because he connected it not only to the very tradition it challenged but also to an adamantly conservative politics.[4] Eliot's experimental traditionalism managed to expose the tenuous cultural role of the cultural establishment in the very process of offering it new tokens of its hegemony.

But even if one accepts all these criticisms, as I do, I think one must also ask if such a summary can come even close to understanding what Eliot actually meant to twentieth-century poetry. These critical attitudes grasp what is limited in Eliot, but not what seemed to become possible through him. For that we must turn back to the first story – to grasp its elements, to understand why these elements lost their force in modern culture, and perhaps to see beyond the now dominant versions of those elements. Let us then balance Williams's reaction to Eliot with Hart Crane's. As irritated as Williams by Eliot's pretensions as well as by his pervasive despondency, Crane none the less realized as early as 1919 that for even an alternative poetry to be fully modern it would have to go "through" Eliot "toward a different goal":

> You see it is just such a fearful temptation to imitate him that at times I have been almost distracted . . . In his own realm Eliot presents us with an absolute impasse, yet oddly enough he can be utilized to lead us to, intelligently point to, other positions and "pastures new."

Then another letter puts the case more specifically, "I would apply as much of his erudition and technique as I can absorb and assemble toward a more positive, or . . . ecstatic goal."[5]

One could find similar statements in poets like Auden, Tate, Jones, and Lowell. Part of their excitement was technical. Eliot simply provided new ways of assuming voices, registering details, adapting speech rhythms and putting elements together within poems. But his greatest genius, and greatest impact, lay in the ways that he allowed poets to cast technical experiment as significant cultural work struggling to make poetry a dynamic force for cultural change. As Louise Bogan put it, Eliot "swung the balance over from whimpering German bucolics to forms within which contemporary complexity could find expression."[6] And as almost all early commentators on Eliot remarked, this sense of cultural work took two basic forms: Eliot showed that poetry could enter the city, enter those sites most obviously subject to everything destructive in modernity, and thus could provide intimate access to the costs of consciousness at odds with itself as it tried to engage what modernity seemed to demand. But even more important was the complex relation between the states of victim and visionary that in Eliot's poetry seemed inseparable from one another. Forced to take responsibility for his own historicity, Eliot could not escape the danger of exposing how deeply he, and perhaps the poetic imagination itself, had become complicit in what they proposed to cure. But the greater the sense of victimage, the more intense the haunting prospect that there would emerge an imaginative site where we could at least glimpse an "infinitely gentle, infinitely suffering thing," able to resist our ironies.

To study Eliot's impact is to analyze the appeal and the threats presented by the basic sites which this feeling of being a victim enabled him to construct. As an initial mapping I want to concentrate on the force and the fate of Eliot's two most influential critical concepts – his claims about the dissociation of sensibility that had dominated European thought since the seventeenth century and his insistence on an impersonality that could combat that dissociation by treating art works as objective correlatives rather than as personal expressions or rhetorical performances. This should help clarify the appeal of both stories about him, and it should allow us finally to turn to how the poetry itself both extends the force of those enabling concepts, and retains capacities to affect poets even after the ideas have become antiquarian curiosities.

It seems impossible now to recover the immense appeal of the first of these concepts, perhaps because for us only questions about individuals, not about cultures, seem to have any urgency, or any consequences for action. But for Eliot's age his critical claims about the dissociation of sensibility set the stage for everything else, primarily by foregrounding the interplay between suffering and vision dramatized in his poetry. First it made victimage heroic by posing the modernist poet as one who lives fully the deep contradictions plaguing the West since the seventeenth century. Even more important, it dignified the poet's positive roles by affording a principle for cultural analysis that based a culture's health on the states of spirit or psychic economies that it could sustain. Facing Hart Crane's breakdown, Tate would think not of economic matters, not even of psychoanalytic, biographical contexts, but of the general cultural collapse of any possible harmony between thinking and feeling: Crane's career becomes a "vindication of Eliot's major premise – that the integrity of the individual consciousness has broken down."[7] And then, once the health of the psyche is understood as a spiritual reflection of cultural conditions, poetry takes on enormous significance as a possible means of at once registering disease and testing the possibility for cure. Therefore while Eliot could find a vantage for criticizing Romanticism as little more than puritanism basing its inwardness on nature, he could also appeal to the fundamental emotional consolation Romanticism offered: only by narcissistic self-absorption could one turn one's own anxieties into representative cultural symptoms that one could then hope to combat by imaginative means.

This relation to Romanticism gave Eliot a position for writers much like that which theorists of abstraction occupied for modernist painting. By criticizing the very ideal of representation the painters set themselves up as combatting not simply previous styles but a general cultural plight created by the willful egotism of Renaissance ideals, with their corresponding denial of the demonic and daemonic forces which resist representation. Eliot gave poets a comparable sense of their own world-historical task by inviting them to combat what seemed the very formation of Europe's psyche. Each poet's sufferings were not simply personal; they were representative – impotence conferred power. And each poet's efforts to express the complexity of contemporary life became a possible remaking of what we could take ourselves to be and of what futures we could imagine for the race. Writing need no longer be a matter of personal expression or the exchanges of refined sensibilities or the exploration of the powers of aesthetic contemplation. The imagination was neither a mode of escape nor an instrument for aesthetic pleasure. Through it writers had the power to invent and test aspects of psychic economies charged with the need to find means of facing up to the terrors of modernity, and propelled by the dream that some ways of facing up might actually open new paths for a culture stuck in destructive habits. Thus Eliot's foregrounding of the dissociation of sensibility did for poetry what Marx's concept of alienation did for historical analysis: the terms of suffering became the keys to understanding how deep change might be possible.

But how does one combat this dissociation? One must begin by grappling with its most destructive manifestations – which for Eliot consisted in substituting a faith in personal feelings for what Bradley had taught him were the more comprehensive frameworks that enclosed the person within complex social and intellectual webs. Therefore Eliot tried to idealize principles of impersonality that would force people to see themselves from the outside, and hence to recognize both the limits of their imaginary projections about themselves and the structural forces binding them to those projections. And, more important, impersonality might help free art from our ideas of sensibility, since rather than assume we could identify with speakers, we would confront "impressions and experiences combine[d] in peculiar and unexpected ways."[8] Perhaps by an "escape from personality" we might find different ways to experience both our dependencies and our powers as historical agents. Thus Eliot applied to modern cultural wars the formalist impulse developed by Kant and given lyrical force within symbolism: instead of connecting art directly to the expressive desires of its maker, the work is asked to serve as a distinctive mode of thinking. The formal syntax does a good deal of the motivating that moves the text from detail to detail, and it, not some expressive will, has the power to elicit complexes of feeling which may allow some freedom from those narrative structures contaminated by the dissociation of sensibility. Consequently one can claim for the poem both an extraordinary subtlety and an extraordinary comprehensiveness, since the principles of closure can be as capacious and discriminating as in any other mode of impersonal, and hence transpersonal, thinking.

Now a second difficult question emerges. How can these projections beyond the personality take on cultural force? As we try to respond, we find ourselves having to confront serious problems both within Eliot and within those who tried to mediate his work, so that our story about stories about Eliot comes full circle and we see why the negative version managed to prevail. Eliot's own early poetry could only manage impersonality as an aspect of the dissociation of sensibility, so that rather than providing a cure it became the deepest symptom of the disease. For when the mind seeks such distance from the energies that put it into motion, it finds it almost impossible to escape what I call the "pathos of reflective distance" characterizing his first two volumes. There the intensity and clarity of Eliot's lines oddly isolate the speaking from the speaker, perhaps from any possibility of correlating an agent's investments in a particular life and particular body with the structure for reflection that persons must employ – hence the "shadow" in *The Hollow Men*. Eliot seems fascinated by those moments in which the mind is paralyzed by its own lucid grasp of itself, so that it simultaneously has the last word and realizes that it has no word that can mediate the person's own specific investments in the very processes being enacted. Notice, for example, how chilling, how disembodied, the incredible precision of these lines from "Gerontion" that seem to insist on the gulf between the imperative to think and the possibilities of investing in the mind's actions:

After such knowledge, what forgiveness? Think now
History has many cunning passages, contrived corridors . . .
She gives when our attention is distracted
And what she gives, gives with such supple confusions
that the giving famishes the craving . . .
                    Think
Neither fear nor courage saves us. Unnatural vices
Are fathered by our heroism. Virtues
are forced upon us by our impudent crimes.

With Eliot's work so slippery, and so ready to undo his positive projections, a serious burden falls on those heirs most drawn to his enterprise. Like Crane they felt they had to use impersonality against dissociation without succumbing to an idealization of irony that only repeats the dissociation in more virulent form. And many of them wanted to develop a full theoretical and pedagogical account translating Eliot's idiosyncratically intricate and subtle mind into principles that could put his blend of wishes and insights on what seemed a firm foundation. In both cases Eliot's power of concrete imagination gave way to Eliot the culture figure, and there began both the kind of representation and the need for reaction which made him ultimately a widespread object of resentment. The work of the New Critics makes the process obvious. In systematizing Eliot they also oversimplified him – consolidating his power but also ultimately offering a sacrificial victim for those who recognized the need to overthrow this version of that power. Where Eliot treated the poetic site as a literal construction of possible modes of agency, these critics emphasized the textual, semantic properties of the site. That then led to casting the force of agency within the poem almost entirely in semantic terms that occluded the cultural roles Eliot hoped his impersonality might open up. Impersonal authorship (later to become *textualité*) allowed a multiplying of meanings through a focus on paradox and elaborate conceit. But then to explain how these meanings might be integrated, New Critical theory had to rely on tracing formal relationships and locating their resonance in terms of tragic ironies which only art could provide as the mark of its distance from the life where differences constantly slip into inescapable rigid oppositions. Even the excruciating tensions generated by the pathos of distance became fundamentally semantic properties so that the dynamic divisions between voice and intelligence become less important than the capacity of an ironic authorial presence to contain the whole within certain patterns and mythic echoes. So what seemed capable of transforming life became confined to aesthetic attitudes. The passionate becomes the bookish; and criteria of intensity and intricacy give way to concerns for comprehensiveness and tragic composure.

II

To get back behind New Criticism, and to recapture the specific impact of Eliot's passions on generations of poets, we must now shift from the domain of ideas to that of concrete lyric effects. Once again we must deal with several Eliots – minimally the very different figures who fused symbolist abstraction with the desiccated impressionism of poems like "Preludes," who explored mythic landscape in *The Waste Land*, and who struggled in *Four Quartets* to bring a new personal directness and intensity to the modernist lyric. And we must cover a great deal of material in a small amount of space, so I will have to be quite elliptical, trusting to the reader's familiarity with Eliot and his critics for the evidence that my generalizations are well founded.

For Eliot's initial impact we must place ourselves within the world of late Victorian and Georgian poetry, as if for the first time confronting the opening of "Prufrock":

> Let us go then, you and I,
> When the evening is spread out against the sky
> Like a patient etherized upon a table;
> Let us go, through certain half-deserted streets,
> The muttering retreats
> Of restless nights in one-night cheap hotels . . .

It is the wary indirectness that seems most striking, as if for the first time poetry took account of a cultural situation in which the straightforward interpretation of situations and the direct assertion of emotions had come to seem hollow, impotent, and self-deluding. The very effort to address one's audience and define social relations objectively seemed instead to require registering the displacing force of one's own unmastered desires. And then subjective personality takes on a new, and terrifying force. To come to self-consciousness is to find oneself irreducibly in dialogue with one's projections of an other, equally part of one's subjective life, and equally destabilized. The poem's speaker does attempt to harmonize those psychic roles by turning to description, hoping that the gesture outward might provide common ground. Yet even the effort at description is so warped by the speaker's divided psyche that the attempt at communication only intensifies the pressure from within. Prufrock needs metaphors to express that scene, only to find the metaphors imposing their own violent displacements. This process of displacement begins casually, with the vague figure of evening "spread out against the sky." But that vagueness is enough to open the gates for Prufrock's disturbed sensibility: "spread out" generates a bizarre pathetic fallacy in which the evening takes on the agency of an etherized patient. Then the descriptive focus returns, only to have the half-deserted streets modulate back into both literal and figurative retreats evoked by Prufrock's loneliness.

In this world there is no possibility of adequate description of self-possession through one's art. Fact turns into image, and image forces upon the scene all the pains of the agent's experience of subjectivity. This, we might say, is lyric poetry's rendering of the realities of dissociated sensibility, realities that require turning the poet's skills to the undoing of any dream of thinking as mastery. Instead the poet's self-consciousness is inseparable from the poet's pathos. The fusing of city and psyche traps the artist in an "inner world of nightmare" that demands an aura of intimacy and vulnerability leading ultimately to confessional styles as foreign in principle to Eliot, as they are close to some of his work in affective range. Who is Berryman's Henry but Prufrock with American edges? And Lowell and Plath make powerful use of Eliot's model by which the extremities of voice become a guarantee of access to the deepest registers of the psyche.

So we find in poetry a new pathos, based less on self-exposure than on an excruciatingly fine intelligence at odds with itself. And we find that promise of a new intimacy inseparable from the challenge to take on the mind's intricate dialogues with itself. This intimacy in turn offered three significant sets of resources for those reading Eliot carefully, resources which his subsequent work would both extend and modify. First, this work opens Anglo-American poetry to a strange conjunction between an extraordinarily precise diction (almost parodic in the quatrain poems, but deeply telling in "Gerontion" and later work) and a wide range of expressive effects, much as contemporaneous German painting used its suspicions about realistic representation to broaden the psychological materials that could be given painterly renderings. For Williams, self-consciousness about syntax became the bearer of modernist foregrounding of the medium. That innovation, however, could be seen as limiting poetry to modes of perception and immediate valuation. But Eliot's precision of diction opened several directions – from introducing new complexities to persona poems, where diction is character, to sustaining the kind of discursive lyricism explored by Auden and Tate. More important, poets could make that extravagant attention to diction also a license for an extravagance of vision. Thus we find Auden, according to Edward Mendelson, discovering that since a modern poetry could be "comic and grotesque," "the extravagance of his personality was for the first time free to disport in his verse."[9]

Eliot's second major innovation extends this tension between precisions and extravagance into complex authorial states. Imagine precision as an objectifying strategy, extravagance as the irreducible pressure of subjective fantasy. Then notice what happens when each pole goes to an extreme: the objective takes on an excess that comes to appear an inescapable residue of subjective intensities, and the subjective seems driven by forces from beyond the self that it cannot control. In Eliot's characteristic lyric states these poles of subject and of object continually slide into one another, so that it seems impossible to make any firm distinctions between scene and act, or figuratively, between foreground and background. Poetically the impact of this is as obvious and as widespread as it is important: all descriptive impulses had to pass through the intricate evasions of the psyche. For now though the quickest way to appreciate what is involved is to turn to Eliot's basic concept for these effects – the concept of objective correlative.

Like the other major modernists, Eliot saw that if there cannot be clear objectivity about the world, art must turn constructivist. It must promise not truth but completeness by trying to make visible those psychological energies which constantly displace what both descriptive and mimetic versions of the dramatic attempt to stabilize; and it must hope that such an art can so define authorial agency that its contingency within history will seem less of a burden, more a principle of testimony. Poetry then had to be impersonal and complex – not because such attributes secured the authority of culture but because the poet needed means of resisting the illusory authority of both the poet's descriptive capacities and his or her seductive personality. For Eliot the ideal of an objective correlative offered a way of showing how a constructivist aesthetic could none the less bear a profoundly self-divided and even self-cancelling poetic imagination. By conceiving of the poem as an objective correlative for emotions, rather than a direct expression of them, Eliot could envision writing as an effort to render psychic forces in conflict, without having to succumb to any single version of a speaking presence working, as Prufrock does, to secure imaginary versions of the self which in fact miss half of what is happening in the very process of seeking closure.

The result is what we might call a new immediacy, a new literalness, and a new abstract intimacy for poetry, all of which require resisting traditional ideas of self so that the concrete textures of poetry can provide richer imaginative alternatives. Similarly, the New Critics' ideals of organic unity prove a poor substitute for the density of internal relationships Eliot's poetry establishes, since those ideals make semantic categories more important than the density and complexity Eliot focused on. But the best poets saw better than the critics, as we can observe in the way poems like Crane's "At Melville's Tomb," begin from a point of view so deeply internalized that entering it requires a leap of imaginative faith:

Often beneath the wave, wide from this ledge
The dice of drowned men's bones he saw bequeath
An embassy.

Even more eloquent testimony to the difference Eliot makes in this regard comes from a novelist, Virginia Woolf:

The [new modern] poets express a feeling that is actually being made and torn out of us at the moment. One does not recognize it in the first place; often for some reason one fears it; one watches it with keenness and compares it jealously and suspiciously with the old feeling that one knew. Hence the difficulty of modern poetry; and it is because of this difficulty that one cannot remember more than two consecutive lines of any good modern poet.[10]

The objective correlative is inseparable from Eliot's ideal of impersonality. But by coming to impersonality along this route I think we can appreciate how Eliot's version of it constitutes the third major factor in his impact on other poets. Impersonality is not primarily a defensive strategy or élitist displacement of the social by abstract cultural contexts. Rather it provides a means for elaborating and intensifying the fluid intimacy that Eliot achieves by imagining poems as literal sites where complexes of feeling play against fantasies of selfhood. This is most evident in *The Waste Land*, where we might say Eliot tried to make the impersonal play the dramatic role usually granted to specific speakers. Here the entire effort is to get beyond single lyric personality to a mode of reflection treating the scenic level of the poem as the direct rendering of collective experience. One might say that the ideal of impersonal complexes of feeling, or, better, of the effort to win impersonality from the ego's efforts to impose itself as the arbiter for the energies of personality, provides the necessary link blending the various modes of Eliot's earlier work into the state somewhere between obsession and prayer that characterizes the mythic mindscape of *The Waste Land*. In the earlier writing we find Prufrock's psychological pathos conjoined with poems like "Preludes" that tease out the unbearable tensions between what can and cannot be objectified; then we see those states abstracted into the surreal spaces of the quatrain poems. *The Waste Land* does not quite integrate these modes, but it does put them into conjunctions that reveal the unsatisfied desires underlying them and the possibility, almost entirely destroyed, of a spiritual life available in the interstices of all our expressive vehicles. Literalness to the emotional complexes beneath our ideas of selves opens for poetry the possibility of a romance of the negative, of the interstitial, important to poets like John Ashbery, Ann Lauterbach, Louise Gluck, and Jorie Graham.

Such literalness can take on substantial metaphysical and political implications, now free of the forms of coherence imposed by what Charles Olson would call "the interference of the lyrical ego." On the simplest level impersonality is inseparable from those experiments in juxtaposition that allied Eliot with the collage principles being elaborated in the visual arts.[11] Juxtaposition announces a break with traditional modes of correlating information, both on the level of public argument and, more important, on the level of personal psychological investments. Then it forces us to ask what modes of coherence can take their place. This is not a question that can be answered directly, without turning juxtaposition into simply a vehicle for other forms of argument. Instead the question works as a pressure which makes us attend to the edges of what is conjoined, as if there one could enter modes of relationship deeper than any descriptive language could provide. If we look backward from John Ashbery, the contemporary poet who I think is most responsive to Eliot's example, we can postulate for Eliot something like a semantic transformation of symbolist ideals of the music of poetry: we are invited to listen for what crosses the gaps in the poems and sets up rhythms of feeling, so that the ontology of music takes on a kind of semantic force, seeming to approximate the mind's own deep structure of needs.

In Eliot's poetry this music sustains a dramatic play in which ghostly echoes both open and bridge the constant unmaking of sense into pregnant gaps which we cannot but attempt to fill, even as we know that our efforts can do nothing more than reveal partial understandings opening ourselves to experiencing meaning as a mode of grace. Perhaps only the Joyce of *Finnegans Wake* fully understood the moral and psychological implications of Eliot's mythic method. But all the most ambitious modernists, from Crane, to David Jones, to Seamus Heaney, to Merrill's pastiche version of Eliotic musical necromancy, would take up the basic quest to have ghosts fill the necessary gaps in our experience of meaning. And an even larger contingent would learn from Eliot how the allusions elicited by these ghostly presences highlighted the historicity of their own poetic activity. Allusions necessarily position the author within a set of historical factors: they afford a means of denying the traditional atemporality of lyric states while also invoking that condition as an aura of possible depths underlying the historical differences that the allusions indicate. And allusion foreground's the poet's accepting the historical task of constructing ideal readers, or at least of reminding real readers of a dimension for idealization within their actual practices. Allusions create the sense that there is a common cultural perspective from which the different levels of historical existence within the poem can be understood and assessed, while also challenging poets to push their readers beyond conditions of immediate response so that they will reflect on their own positioning within history, and hence compose a site beyond the immediate event.

Finally I must just touch upon a feature of Eliot's exploration of impersonality which would take us in an entirely different direction. Ultimately Eliot rejected both impersonality and its attendant culturalism because he saw that by seeking comprehensiveness one only insured a constant emptiness, frustrated by endlessly receding spiritual possibilities. There could be no adequate ground discovered in seeking cultural universals, and there could be no redemption glimpsed in the sudden configurations gathered among fragments. Redemption required complete commitment of one's contingent being, in the hope that faith could then deepen. Poetically that required using one's awareness of the limits of impersonality to ground a poetry so deeply personal that it could speak directly and seriously about its underlying belief structures. Therefore with the *Four Quartets* Eliot's impact no longer lay in any specific relational principles or fusions of the subjective and objective or exploration of distinctive imaginative sites. And this poetry did not bring stylistic imitations. Rather it had the more comprehensive effect of persuading poets like Jones and Spender and Tate and Lowell that Christianity could be a viable antidote to modernity's dissociated sensibility. In effect Eliot's struggle to be modern gave him the authority to define the limits of secular modernity and, more important, to use modernism's construction of ideal readers to define what Christianity might involve. The poet-maker had to give way to the listener, to one who can first hear what is contingent in voice and circumstance, and then bring to such hearing an intensity that attunes one to forces that extend beyond such contingency. Self-division in space and patience in time each opens us to an otherness paradoxically necessary for any satisfying view of individuality.

III

So far I have considered only general tendencies that Eliot established within modern poetry. An adequate analysis of his impact also requires studying how a range of poets use those examples, especially when that effort determines how they shape their stylistic options or change the overall ambitions of their work. However here I have only enough space to make some observations about three quite different concrete relations to Eliot – in the work of Hart Crane, John Ashbery, and Jorie Graham.

Crane's relationship to Eliot offers the purest example of impact one is likely to find. Discovering Eliot in 1918, as he was trying to understand how he could be a poet, he took Eliot as constituting what a modern poetry in

English could be. This is the last stanza of Crane's "Black Tambourine" (1921):

> The black man, forlorn in the cellar,
> Wanders in some mid-kingdom, dark, that lies,
> Between his tambourine, stuck on the wall,
> And, in Africa, a carcass quick with flies.[12]

These are Eliot's quatrains; the voice has Eliot's strange distance that cannot quite escape identification; and, while not quite matching Eliot's "Sweeney Among the Nightingales," the poem has his distinctive stress on the image not for its perceptual qualities but for the way it projects a world suffused by feelings at once displacing and intensifying its objective properties. Here Crane seeks to capture within the object the intensity by which the subject comes to perceive his situation.

Even more Eliotic is the dialogue in the last stanzas of Crane's "Chaplinesque" between pitiless objectivity and the dream of locating an "infinitely gentle, infinitely suffering thing":

> And yet these fine collapses are not lies
> More than the pirouettes of any pliant cane:
> Our obsequies are, in a way, no enterprise.
> We can evade you, and all else but the heart:
> What blame to us if the heart live on.
>
> The game enforces smirks; but we have seen
> The moon in lonely alleys make
> A grail of laughter in an empty ash can,
> And through all sound of gaiety and quest
> Have heard a kitten in the wilderness.
>
> (Crane, Weber [ed.] *Complete Poems*, p. 11)

Since Eliot was completing his *Waste Land* at the time Crane wrote this, he would not have been pleased by this kitten serving as the voice that sounds from the wilderness. Yet Crane almost gets away with such sentimentality because he bases his quest for a heart (and Hart) on his power to wield Eliotic fragments and Prufrockian phrases as instruments for finding within contemporary culture, rather than the past, a figure on whom to base his lyrical desires. Moreover his use of Eliot's blend of precision and strangeness proves the perfect lyric analogue for the intelligence that suffuses Chaplin's erratic pathos, as if Eliot gave Crane a way to locate a version of Whitman in Chaplin's too ample pockets, and thus to establish a mode of sympathy that the Eliotic aspects of the poem hold at an ironic distance.

Unfortunately this voice could not suffice. Having opened this space for sentiment or romance or shareable transformative sympathies, Crane had to give it features far more resonant than this kitten figure could provide. So he had to turn to his own version of *The Waste Land*'s mythic method, seeking what his "Marriage of Faustus and Helen" called an imagination that "spans beyond despair, / Outpacing bargain, vocable, and prayer" (Crane, Weber [ed.] *Complete Poems*, p. 33). Responding to Eliot meant elaborating long poems on lyrical principles, and that meant seeking to build from allusions and the dense folding of distinctive levels of experience, ritual patterns which promised to release aspects of the secular world from their contingency, and hence from their pathos. One might even hope to make this very process of bridging the basis for a uniquely American vision outpacing Eliotic prayer.

However, a poetry so bound to Eliotic myth-constructing strategies may not be able to outpace prayer. Once one begins to seek underlying patterns as one's ground for values, the alternatives may remain religion, self-delusion, or despair. Or so at least it seems if we turn to the two contemporary poets I want to look at, each trying very different strategies for completing Crane's secular application of symbolist poetics to contemporary realities. For these poets, as for most contemporaries still in reaction to New Critical theologizings of Eliot's poetics, Eliot would matter not for his cult of pattern but for the opposite, for demonstrating a *via negativa* by which the most important psychic forces could work themselves free of interpretive practices developed to sustain the authority of empiricist analyses.

Take John Ashbery as our first example. When he mentions Eliot it is usually to establish distance between them, concealing how much they share (especially in the echoes of *Four Quartets* carried by the repetition of notions like "end" and "way" when Ashbery's "A Wave" meditates on love). Eliot becomes an emblem for the modernist anxieties that Ashbery hopes to transform. Thus he claims that Eliot is "wrong" in imagining hyacinths in bowls as somehow tragic: "life is life, no matter how artificial, how contrived the context." And, speaking of R. B. Kitaj's own use of Eliot, Ashbery remarks that Eliot seems to back away from his own discovery that the contiguity of fragments is "all their meaning," since meaning can only be understood as paralleling "the randomness and discontinuity of modern experience." Because "meaning cannot be truthfully defined as anything else," there simply is no escape from a horror of fragmentation and a sense of inescapable tragedy. There is only an openness to contradiction within and without, a "moving and not wanting to be moved, the loose / Meaning, untidy and simple like a threshing floor."[13]

And yet when we look at how Ashbery goes about developing lyrical values within these contradictions we find a remarkably positive embodiment of Eliotic stances. Ashbery's sense of fragments in social experience is complemented by a compelling concern for completeness in the rendering of the life of mind. As with Eliot, and with the best New Critical idealizations of Eliot, completeness is not a matter of attributing meanings to the world but of allowing the psyche to trace its own intricate turnings and doublings. This means refusing to bind oneself to the ego's demands for idealized images of itself. And it demands pushing poems to the point that they almost collapse under the burden of history embodied in the voices that play through it. But in encountering that limit Ashbery develops his own blend of Eliot's personal discursiveness in *Four Quartets* with the unceasing distanced self-consciousness of his earlier modes. The result is a strange quasi-discursiveness and disembodied, fleeting yet insistent personal presence that refuses any consolations by projected self-images. As Ashbery's discursiveness dissipates under the demands of the desire staging it, we find a commitment to capturing the full intricacy of consciousness inseparable from a Prufrockian dispersal of focus within the alternate meanings that metaphors introduce. However now the accepting of fragments allows even Prufrock to engage a "you," itself constantly shifting between referents as the modes of expression open different aspects of the speaking voice. For Ashbery can so transform Eliot that we realize the very notion of presence has much less to do with what one sees, or believes, than with how one manages to find release from the burden of trying to make the self more than the continual shifting of positions. Ultimately complexity of mind makes it possible to affirm an absolute simplicity for affective life – "ridiculous the waste sad time / stretching before and after."

Jorie Graham is more transcendentally inclined, echoing Eliot in part because she is adamant in refusing what she considers the banal secularity of the generation of (male) poets immediately preceding hers. Yet she refuses any thematic allegorizing or traditional spiritual foundations for that transcendence, contenting herself instead with the power to undo, and perhaps extend, our sense of sense by the force of her focused negative excess. The parallels to Eliot, and differences from her immediate predecessors, are most evident in two related domains – the sense of self she projects and the ways in which she uses cadence and gaps to sustain a personal pressure within fundamentally reflective, discursive meditations. Eve is Graham's model for personal agency because she finds her strength in her difference from Adam's righteousness, "liking that error, a feeling of being capable *in* an error."[14] It is only in this sense of one's own strangeness and contingency that one can locate a power not subsumed under some decorum or practice or demand from another. Then Graham employs this principle of error to open access to something beyond appearances. Here for example she identifies with Persephone returning to earth for the first time and imagining how the trees might reach beyond themselves to a perfection possible only if one can also identify with the unimaginable:

> that would bend more deeply into it inventing (if they could)
> another body, exploded, all leafiness, unimaginable

> by which to be forgiven by which to suffer completely this wind.

These are not Eliotic sentiments. But they depend for their force, as his *Four Quartets* do, on elaborate cadences and strategic silences as well as on a capacity to find plenitude within suffering which directly echoes Eliot's prayer to let his cry come unto God because he manages to identify with Mary's suffering. In fact one realizes through Graham how Eliot's rendering of gender is far more complex and open to internal multiplicity than are those we find in Yeats, Pound, and Williams. It ought to come as no surprise then that her most ambitious effort to locate herself within history is also her most overtly Eliotic poem. "Pollock and Canvas" equates the painter with the Fisher King, whose wound, and consequent refusal of mastery by the brush, becomes the only means of redeeming a land where the prevailing art kills what it tries to define. So she turns to Pollock for guidance in facing up to the contradictory pulls exerted by an ideal of the end of beauty: how can we at the end of one dream of beauty, repudiated completely in his destruction of illusionist space, still posit beauty as an end, and hence still desire the woman whom we know we can no longer contain within our paintings? There proves no answer, only the demand to let questions themselves carry a new definition of desire, cast out into an "open" free to take its own forms:

> Where does the end
>   begin?
> where does the lifting off of hands become
>   love,
> letting the made wade out into danger,
>   letting the form slur out into flaw, in

> conclusiveness? Where does the end of love
> begin? . . .

> Where is the border of *stopping* and *ending*?
>   And the land was waste but the king did not die . . .
> and the meaning of the rose rises up
>   (shedding the meaning of the rose)
> and the memory of the rose rises up
>   (shedding the memory of the rose)
>   (Jorie, *End of Beauty*, pp. 86–88)

IV

Close as Graham is to Eliot's *Quartets*, however, there remains an enormous distance between them – one which tells us almost as much about ourselves as it does about Eliot. For it leads us to the question of what in Eliot seems inimitable, and why. Crane provides a good beginning here because in so many respects he does capture Eliot's force. He embodies the anxiety over fragments and flat objectivity basic to Eliot, and he seeks the same abstract immediacy based on consciousness facing its own inescapable contradictions. But he does not linger on details enough to let them break through into obsessive states, nor does he let cadence and repetition and abstract pattern develop the full sense of invested intimacy that Eliot's characters come to bear. Similarly, Crane's kitten cannot wield the power of Eliot's "infinitely gentle, infinitely suffering thing," because Crane cannot muster the self-confidence, or self-torment, to generate so slow, so sensuous, so deliberate, and so painful a phrasing. And Crane must yield to an abstract hope that in Eliot is immediately countered by a defensive despair.

Ashbery affords a different set of contrasts. He is one of the few contemporaries to recover Eliot's versions of personal intimacy. Where most poets offer autobiographical melodrama, or flat narratives faintly hinting at deep dark personal tensions, or protracted engagements in the mysteries of memory, Ashbery maintains Eliot's blend of diffidence with a tremendous pressure of personal need within what seems discursive statement. Because of this sense of self, Ashbery is also brilliant at elaborating his own versions of Eliot's intricacy of self-consciousness, his internal play of metaphoric registers and tones, and (occasionally) his tortuous precision of diction. But no one among Eliot's heirs can muster the inhuman absoluteness of the "Son of man" passage in *The Waste Land* or the hallucinatory intensity of the concluding sections. And while a range of poets like Tate, Warren, Lowell, Jones, Heaney, and Crane could capture Eliot's sense of ghost-haunted history, no one but Eliot could combine that with the sense of immediate textures and tonal shifts that Ashbery manages to bring out as the other half of Eliot's projected incursiveness. Yet Ashbery can only be inclusive in his way by weakening the pressure of history and by treating heterogeneity as a matter of the psyche far more than as a matter of social forces. Some Ashbery, especially *Houseboat Days*, is obsessed by history, but only as a dump for metaphors and a reminder of poetic and personal belatedness. There is no sense of apocalypse or deep causal factors shaping psychic life – indeed Ashbery's strength is largely his insistence on weakening and relativizing history so that we are allowed neither nostalgia nor the modernists' idealized ambition.

Graham brings out contrasts that show off the accomplishments of Eliot's later poetry, largely by reminding us of how close the religious Eliot is to the kinds of values that women poets are now trying to foreground – for example in his refusing the traps posed by specular self-images, and in his abstract immediacy so intensely fusing subject and object that no clear distinction becomes possible. But her personal states make far more use of Eliot's gaps than they do of his ghosts, since history enters her work only in highly abstract ways. Similarly, she must provide a dynamic syntax expressing her personal presence primarily by imposing an ecstatic mode, as if the sources of eloquence were always hovering behind the language without quite growing out of the specific linguistic structure. Compare the repetitious features of Graham's cadences with Eliot's amazing pull between the insistence of rhythm and the fluidity of syntax:

> Time present and time past
> Are both perhaps present in time future,
> And time future contained in time past . . .
> What might have been is an abstraction
> Remaining a perpetual possibility
> Only in a world of speculation.
> What might have been and what has been
> Point to one end, which is always present. (BN 1)

Finally, the contrast with Graham invites an Eliotic irony: perhaps the strength of his syntax derives in large part from the fact that Eliot need not make the presence of ecstatic states the measure of the poem's possible significance. He can be content with using poetry as testimony for ideals and principles that lie beyond poetry, informing it and given historicity through it. Graham, on the other hand, wants a transcendental register without being able to trust any ideas about that transcendence (although her more recent book *Region of Unlikeness* sounds much of contemporary thought in quest of those ideas). Therefore she cannot just testify to the power of certain principles – her poems must constitute both the idea and its efficacy, and hence they are haunted by a pressure to make gestures of breathless excitement bear much of the burden in giving content to what cannot actually be said. The more ridiculous appears the sad waste time stretching before and after, the more desperate poetry may become to do more than perhaps anyone can with the present.

NOTES

1 I see this essay as an opportunity to ally from a different perspective with those now attempting to show how thin this dominant negative account is and how much we lose if remain content with it. The critics whom I think provide the best lines for such a recovery are Michael Levenson, Ronald Bush, and, for the

contemporary currency of Eliot's ideas, Richard Shusterman. Also important from a different perspective is Gregory Jay's demonstration of how much of Eliot can fit into poststructuralist thematics.

2 Williams, *Autobiography*, p. 174. The quotation above is from Williams, *Selected Essays*, pp. 22–23.

3 Yeats's critique is most emphatic in his "Modern Poetry." The view of Auden derives from Edward Mendelson, *Early Auden*, pp. xx; 28–31, 131ff. For Shapiro see his *Defense of Ignorance*. The two anthologies I refer to are Hall, *Contemporary American Poetry*, and Allen, *New American Poetry*; and similar claims are made by Poulin, *Contemporary American Poetry*. Kenner's views are outlined in his *Pound Era*, and explicitly argued in "The Possum in the Cave." Perloff makes her basic argument in *Poetics of Indeterminacy*, then uses Eliot as a figure of closure to contrast with a more capacious postmodern openness to the world in her *Poetic License*.

4 Orwell is quoted in a very useful book for my purposes, Raffel (ed.) *Possum*, p. 35.

5 Hart Crane, letters to Alan Tate and to Gorham Munson, January 1923, in Weber (ed.) *Letters*, pp. 114–15.

6 Bogan in Raffel (ed.), *Possum*, p. 37.

7 Raffel (ed.), *Possum*, p. 38.

8 I echo in my description passages from Eliot's account of impersonality in "Tradition and the Individual Talent," in his *SE* (1950), pp. 7, 9–11.

9 Mendelson, *Early Auden*, pp. 28–29.

10 Virgina Woolf, "A Room of One's Own," as cited by Amy Clampitt, "Prefaces." Tate is almost as eloquent in his essay "Narcissus as Narcissus."

11 David Antin elaborates this point in his "Modernism and Postmodernism."

12 Weber (ed.) *Complete Poems*, p. 4.

13 I refer to essays on Nell Blaine and Kitaj in Ashbery's *Reported Sightings*, pp. 237–37, 301–2, 306–8; and for the poetry, to Ashbery's *Selected Poems*, p. 88.

14 Jorie Graham, *End of Beauty*, p. 7. The passage below is from p. 63.

WORKS CITED

Allen, Donald, (ed.). *The New American Poetry, 1945–1960*. New York: Grove Press, 1960.

Antin, David. "Modernism and Postmodernism: Approaching the Present in American Poetry," *boundary 2*, 1.1 (1972).

Ashbery, John. *Reported Sightings: Art Chronicles, 1957–87*, David Bergman (ed.). Cambridge, MA: MIT Press, 1991.

Selected Poems. New York: Viking, 1985.

Bush, Ronald. "T. S. Eliot and Modernism at the Present Time: A Provocation," Bush (ed.) *T. S. Eliot: The Modernist in History*. Cambridge: Cambridge University Press, 1991, pp. 191–204.

Clampitt, Amy. "Prefaces: Five Poets on Poems by T. S. Eliot," *Yale Review* 78.2 (1989): 196–99.

Crane, Hart. *The Complete Poems, and Selected Letters and Prose*, Brom Weber, (ed.). Garden City: Anchor, 1966.

Letters of Hart Crane, Brom Weber (ed.). Los Angeles: University of California Press, 1965.

Graham, Jorie. *The End of Beauty*. New York: Ecco Press, 1987.

Hall, Donald, (ed.). *Contemporary American Poetry*. Baltimore: Penguin, 1963.

Jay, Gregory. *T. S. Eliot and the Poetics of Literary History*. Baton Rouge: Louisiana State University Press, 1983.

Kenner, Hugh. *The Pound Era*. Berkeley: University of California Press, 1971.

"The Possum in the Cave," Stephen J. Greenblatt (ed.). *Allegory and Representation*. Baltimore: John Hopkins Press, 1981, pp. 120–44.

Mendelson, Edward. *Early Auden*. New York: Viking Press, 1981.

Perloff, Marjorie. *The Poetics of Indeterminacy: Rimbaud to Cage*. Princeton: Princeton University Press, 1981.

Poetic License. Evanston: Northwestern University Press, 1990.

Poulin, A. Jr. (ed.). *Contemporary American Poetry*. Boston: Houghton Mifflin, 1st edn., 1968.

Raffel, Burton (ed.). *Possum and Old Ez in the Public Eye*. Boston: Archon Books, 1985.

Shapiro, Karl. *Defense of Ignorance*. New York: Random House, 1960.

Shusterman, Richard. *T. S. Eliot and the Philosophy of Criticism*. New York: Columbia University Press, 1988.

Williams, William Carlos. *Autobiography*. New York: New Directions, 1967.

Selected Essays of William Carlos Williams. New York: Random House, 1954.

Woolf, Virginia. *A Room of One's Own*. New York: Harcourt, Brace, Jovanovich, 1957.

Yeats, William Butler. "Modern Poetry," (1938) in his *Essays and Introductions* (London: Macmillan, 1961).

15

JEAN-MICHEL RABATÉ

Tradition and T. S. Eliot

We have become used to all sorts of temporal paradoxes which can be found thriving not only in Pynchon's rockets whose screaming one hears *after* an apocalyptic Fall, but also in domains ranging from contemporary physics to Biblical theology as revised by new textual exegesis. This would define the plight of the "post-modern" sensibility as a cruel or playful awareness of our being aftercomers, inheritors of a culture others have shaped, and so of living as much in the past as in the present. As Eliot puts it: "It seems, as one becomes older, / That the past has another pattern, and ceases to be a mere sequence" (*DS*, v). However, this insight is not one he gained upon reaching mellow maturity, since it can be shown to have been the founding stone which helped him build his poetics. For it was as a "young man" that Eliot boldly put forward the idea that if one views European literature as a simultaneous whole, the first logical consequence is that the past is altered by the creation of novelty: "Whoever has approved this idea of order, of the form of European, of English literature will not find it preposterous that the past should be altered by the present as much as the present is directed by the past" (*SE* [1951], p. 15). This notion of a systematic order, of an organic unity of literature is now identified as a dominant aspect of modernism, and finds equivalent formulations in Pound and Joyce. Astute critics have rapidly taken up the hint. Thus, following the Joycean idea of a "retrospective arrangement," Fritz Senn has been able to show how a reading of *Ulysses* ineluctably influences our perception of Homer's *Odyssey*.[1]

What has undergone a considerable modification, of course, is the concept of "influence," which has to be radically rethought if it is to be of any use, or else replaced with new terms such as "serial rereadings." Now texts appear always to be engaged in a struggle with each other as to which provides the more comprehensive frame of reference. If this aptly describes the current critical issue, does it mean that we have to accept the full brunt of Eliot's critique of a traditional concept of tradition and his promotion of a new concept? Can we, heirs that we are, caught in the spirals of these serial rereadings, adhere to the thesis developed in "Tradition and the Individual Talent" without believing in an ideal order of European literature, without following Eliot in his famous linking of royalism in politics, classicism in literature, and Anglo-catholicism in religion? If so much of our contemporary mental world has been shaped by Eliot's poems and essays, while so much of his literary theory has fallen into disrepute, is there a proper way of "criticizing the critic" (no less than the poet) when we wish to evolve a theory of reading that can make literature "our own"? Or is this desire for propriety and appropriation, hence for a point of view of mastery and dominance, also spurious, redolent of nostalgia? Are we in a circle, and if we are, how can we start finding a way out? If such a circularity can be shown to be identical with a workable concept of "tradition," a concept which can be elaborated by using Eliot's first statements as points of departure, then we may hope to gain a fresh awareness of the workings of literature in general.

THE METICULOUS METIC

All his life, Eliot seems to have hesitated between two roles, that of the barely "Europeanized American' (according to Huxley's harsh phrase), haunted by the "rank ailanthus" of St. Louis, and that of the "native son" returning to his pre-American roots and attempting to decipher the illegible tombstones in East Coker churchyard. In a letter describing the original impetus behind the writing of "Tradition and the Individual Talent," he explains his position to Mary Hutchinson:

> I have now got started on a long subject which I have not now either time or energy to carry out – instead of replying simply to a question of civilisation and culture. I think two things are wanted – civilisation which is impersonal, traditional (by "tradition" I don't mean stopping in the same place) and which forms people unconsciously . . . and culture – which is a personal interest and curiosity in *particular* things – I think it is largely the *historical sense*, which is not simply knowledge of history, a sense of balance which does not deaden one's personal taste, but trains one to discriminate one's passions from objective criticism. (*Letters* I, pp. 317–18)

Such a dialectical interaction between culture and civilization anticipates the later distinctions elaborated in *Notes Towards the Definition of Culture* whilst making plain that "tradition" needs the individual's "historical sense" in order to bypass too strict an opposition between the objective and the subjective elements in culture. Eliot is clearly summing up here the main tenets of "Tradition and the Individual Talent," whose formulations are nearly identical, but with the difference that, in the essay, "tradition" appears to be on the side of "culture" and not of "civilization":

> Tradition is a matter of much wider significance. It cannot be inherited, and if you want it you must obtain it by great labour. It involves, in the first place, the historical sense, which we may call nearly indispensable to anyone who would continue to be a poet beyond his twenty-fifth year. (SE [1951], p. 14)

Before developing the numerous implications of the "historical sense," I shall return to the letter to Mary Hutchinson because it makes a very open, unguarded admission, which clashes with the usual picture of a young Eliot flaunting his culture and his impeccable manners when facing a British audience. In a passage in which he acknowledges his ignorance in psychological matters, Eliot adds:

> But remember that I am a *metic* – a foreigner, and that I *want* to understand you, and all the background and tradition of you. I shall try to be frank – because the attempt is so very much worth while with you – it is very difficult with me – both by inheritance and because of my very suspicious and cowardly disposition. But I may simply prove to be a savage.
>
> (*Letters* I, p. 318)

Here, a "tradition" limited to the British view of the world is apprehended from the outside, with a curious mixture of awe and enthusiasm. The admission is not that Eliot feels himself to be a real "savage," but that he fears he might be seen as one, a fear which might compound the social uncertainties of a Prufrock with the discovery of the "horror" which Conrad's Kurtz had glimpsed. From the deleted epigraph to the original draft of *The Waste Land* to the epigraph to *The Hollow Men* Eliot keeps circling around the corpse of an intrepid explorer turned mad because he could not face the burden of the white man's civilization and the horrors of life in general. But then he could reflect: "Poetry begins, I dare say, with a savage beating a drum in the jungle" (*UPUC* [London], p. 155). Thus he brings us full circle, from a negative to an entirely positive admission of the "savage," primitive element in poetic creation.

However, the term "metic" looks more adequate as a self-description than "savage," for it designates not a total foreigner, but a stranger who is admitted to the city (originally of Athens) because of his utility: he pays certain taxes (and Eliot's toils in a bank may be relevant there) and is granted rights and franchises although rarely admitted fully into the communal mysteries. The city is the locus from which the "metic" derives his being and significance. One need not labor the point that Eliot's poetry is primarily a poetry of the city, a city which actualizes the "mythical method" of *Ulysses* while doing away with the classical unities of time, place and action. Indeed *The Waste Land* is not so much a London poem as a poem of the *polis*, its city one which spans the Thebes of Oedipus and Tiresias, Augustine's Carthage, Dickens's London and Baudelaire's Paris.

The impersonal "us" opening *The Waste Land* owes much to Charles-Louis Philippe's *Bubu de Montparnasse*, the novel which became Eliot's guide to nineteenth-century Paris as Dickens was his guide to nineteenth-century London. Philippe introduces his hero as a Baudelairean *promeneur* on the Paris boulevards, "mixing memory and desire":

> A man who walks carries all the things of his life and turns them in his mind. One sight arouses them, another excites them. Our flesh has kept all our memories, we mix them with our desires [*Notre chair a gardé tous nos souvenirs, nous les mêlons à nos désirs*]. We wander through present time with our baggage, we move forward complete at any instant.[2]

The notion of a young man walking with a "heap of broken images" circling around in his mind is precisely what Eliot means by a "tradition" which encompasses a feeling of the presence of the past. This provides him with the phenomenological basis of an endless problematization of memory and perception. What type of "intentionality" can structure or synthesize the discontinuous fragments? Are they "related" or unified simply because they happen to be catalyzed within a mind? The Bergsonian "stream of consciousness" might be the cornerstone of Eliot's theory of tradition, especially when rephrased in the more technical language of Bradley: "The present of ideal construction, the present of meaning and not simply of psychical or physical process is really a span which includes my present ideas of past and future." (*KE*, pp. 54–55)

The philosophical "I" becomes the "we" of the inhabitants of *The Waste Land*, a shift which is not without its problems, given the tendency towards solipsism of the Bradleyan monads. A banal enough reason for this shift could be that we are plunged into the middle of the modern urban world with its multitudes of faceless individuals. But the reference to Dickens may suggest a deeper way of accounting for this sense of community. An awareness of tradition is necessary to bridge the gap between the individual "finite centres" and a cultural "Absolute." A useful hint is provided by the rejected title for the first part of *The Waste Land*. It comes from *Our Mutual Friend* (a text in which Dickens attempts to reach to the core of London described as "the world's Metropolis" by Mr. Podsnap), and is the phrase Betty Higden uses to praise Sloppy's wonderful mimetic skills: "He do the police in different voices." By this quotation, Eliot attempted very clearly to connect the Greek πολισ (the polity), with "police" and the question of a founding law. This by homophony generates a prefix in poly-which calls up not only "polyphony" but also the famous "polyphiloprogenitive" of "Mr. Eliot's Sunday Morning Service." No wonder that the "metic" has not turned into a "mimetic" capable of imitating all the citizens' voices! However, the miming of all the voices in *The Waste Land*'s polyglot finale stresses the tragedy of a still disunified consciousness, which has not yet found the way to harmonize the straying ends of tradition.

HIGH MODERNISM AND THE BIFURCATION OF "TRADITION"

Eliot's basic insight in "Tradition and the Individual Talent" is probably derived from Pound's famous declaration in the "Praefatio" to *The Spirit of Romance*: "It is dawn at Jerusalem while midnight hovers above the Pillars of Hercules. All ages are contemporaneous. It is B.C., let us say, in Morocco. The Middle Ages are in Russia. The future stirs already in the minds of the few."[3] But Eliot's "historical sense" has a different emphasis:

> the historical sense compels a man to write not merely with his own generation in his bones, but with a feeling that the whole of the literature of Europe from Homer and within it the whole of the literature of his own country has a simultaneous existence and composes a simultaneous order. (*SE* [1951], p. 14)

This requires that the "bones" belong to the individual who recomposes the simultaneity at every moment without losing a combination of the "timeless" and the merely "temporal." In exactly the same way Baudelaire in "The Painter of Modern Life" defines "modernity" as a combination of the ephemeral and the eternal, stressing the "relative and circumstantial" element without which the invariable elements could not be appreciated.[4]

Pound's concept of tradition is normative; Eliot's comprehensive and descriptive, at least around 1920 in *The Sacred Wood*. What matters for Pound is to find the best of what tradition has to offer. The return to tradition as he advocates it should entail a simplification – "A return to origins invigorates because it is a return to nature and reason."[5] Eliot's "historical sense," on the other hand, implies a process of constant addition and complication. If this model rules out any improvement but replaces it with "complication," it is because there is always a consciousness behind the cultural synthesis to be achieved. The progression towards more knowledge is not teleologically orientated, but simply corresponds to the fact that the dead authors *are* what we know. The past insists on being present, demands to be claimed as his by whoever wishes to be taken as a serious artist and not merely an adolescent pouring out his feelings. Such a theory is founded upon a phenomenological subject without ruling out the agency of the unconscious.

For the "historical sense" has to be integrated into an unconscious knowledge which is less a knowledge of the cultural past than a part of the psyche without which my "present" would never take shape or meaning. Such a knowledge could never be suppressed without generating great anxiety. This idea is recurrent in Eliot's essays, and finds a definite formulation in *The Use of Poetry and the Use of Criticism*:

> [Poetry] may make us from time to time a little more aware of the deeper, unnamed feelings which form the substratum of our being, to which we rarely penetrate; for our lives are mostly a constant evasion of ourselves, and an evasion of the visible and sensible world.　　　(*UPUC* [London], p. 155)

Tradition as an awareness of "poetry as a living whole of all the poetry that has ever been written" (*SE* [1951], p. 17) thus reaches apparently insuperable contradictions, which can only be solved through a metaphor, the famous analogy with a "catalyst." This is why the essay on "Tradition and the Individual Talent" changes tack abruptly and veers off into an analysis (in the chemical sense) of how the poet's mind works when imagining and creating.

The difference between Pound and Eliot may account for a considerable tension within high modernism itself, and also explain the divergence in their political attitudes. Basically, the difference in their conceptions of "tradition" lies in a different translation (and "translation" is almost synonymous with "tradition") of *polis*. Pound always sees the *polis* in its original Greek context, a context determined by state or city polytheism and politics. Eliot, following the drift of his inquest into European roots, revives linguistic energies dormant in Virgil, Augustine, and Dante. He deliberately drifts off towards latinity, translating the "city" into the more comprehensive "civitas." But, as Benveniste has shown, *polis* cannot be translated into *civitas* without great distortion.[6] In the Greek mentality, *polis* is a concept which predetermines the understanding of the *polites*, or "citizen." One is a "citizen" because one partakes of the abstract concept of the *polis* which underwrites basic conceptual or ideological "politics." In the Latin mind, the adjective *civis* is anterior to the concept of *civitas*, which means a "city" as a group of people and is distinguished from *Urbs* (reserved for Rome). Since *men* come before the concept in the Latin model, *civitas* refers to a collectivity understood as a mutuality, a collection of reciprocal obligations. Thus Eliot's choice of a quotation from *Our Mutual Friend* to approach the polyphonic paradigm of his universal city is not due to chance.

The crucial point for Eliot is the essence of man, an essence linked to the transcendent principle of divinity. Thus whereas Pound in canto 27 places the Russian Revolution in historical perspectives – the founding of Thebes by Cadmus who sowed the dragon's teeth, and Napoleon's new Roman empire – Eliot, in citing Hesse in the notes to *The Waste Land*, and in his *Criterion* commentaries, condemned it for explicitly refusing a Christian foundation.[7] Again, in contrast with Pound's gathering "from the air a live tradition" (canto 81), Eliot's vision of the ideal City leads him to attempt a "gathering" which is etymologically and institutionally synonymous with "religion." Thus Eliot's main divergence from Pound stems from the fact that if he did not have to grasp and gather his tradition "in the air," it was because he meant to find it "in his bones," therefore in his "body." This "body" – which remains Eliot's phenomenological basis, the mute substratum needed by a subjectivity wishing to become conscious of an unconscious tradition – is also emphasized by another model for his early critical essays, Remy de Gourmont.

DISSOCIATING THE UNCONSCIOUS

In his 1928 preface to *The Sacred Wood*, Eliot acknowledges the influence of de Gourmont's critical writings, and two epigraphs to "The Perfect Critic" show familiarity with the Frenchman's sensualist theory of style. The idea that a great critic has to "*ériger en lois ses impressions personnelles*" (turn one's personal impressions into laws) contains all the subsequent paradoxes on the need to have a "personality" in order to get rid of personality. The 1928 turning point of Eliot's "conversion" is often described as a departure from de Gourmont's *fin de siècle* skepticism and praise of pantheism. However, one crucial term is retained, the concept of "dissociation." What matters is the significant twist given to the concept, which for de Gourmont is a method of analysis, "analogous to what is called analysis in chemistry" – the dissociation of a material into its various elements "in order to prepare for a new synthesis."[8] His idea is that the critic in his constant care for the language must similarly "dissociate" the usual commonplaces that pass for deep truths. But Eliot used the term quite differently, to signify the disintegration of a unified tradition, as when he blamed Milton and Dryden for ending a period in which feeling and thinking made up a single process. "Dissociation" was thus shifted from a technique of analysis to the name given to a cultural disaster. Instead of being a technique by which sensibility refines itself, it refers to a historical splitting of the communal consciousness.

What is ultimately blamed is the English Civil War, as a prelude to Romanticism. And Romanticism is identified with "excess":

Romanticism stands for *excess* in any direction. It splits up into two directions: escape from the world of fact, and devotion to brute fact. The two great
currents of the nineteenth century – vague emotionalism and the apotheosis of
science (realism) alike spring from Rousseau.[9]

Beyond the obvious misrepresentation of Rousseau, one can see the same
movement at work: any type of excess destroys a just balance between fact
and imagination, feeling and thought. Whereas the early essays still believe
that "analysis" can work as a cure ("The only cure for Romanticism is to
analyse it." [*SW* (1928), p. 31]), Eliot is gradually dissatisfied with the "critical" intellect as such and looks for synthesis as an answer – an answer he
will gradually identify with religion itself. If criticism is not "interpretation"
but comparison and analysis, as Eliot repeats throughout his essays, the pre-
eminence given to Dante over Shakespeare (a value judgment which will
then be qualified, but never wholly modified) is a boost to the synthetic
power of an all-embracing faith:

> Shakespeare takes a character apparently controlled by a simple emotion, and
> analyses the character and the emotion itself. The emotion is split up into
> constituents – and perhaps destroyed in the process. The mind of Shakespeare
> was one of the most *critical* that has ever existed. Dante, on the other hand,
> does not analyse the emotion so much as he exhibits its relation to other
> emotions.   (*SW* [1928], p. 168)

"Synthesis" clearly refers to an integration of the negative drives ("the
contemplation of the horrid or sordid or disgusting") in a scheme which
stresses the "pursuit of beauty." In that sense, the great models after Dante
remain Baudelaire and Laforgue and Poe, more than Mallarmé or Valéry.
They all face what tradition has in store, that is unconscious material which
is to be dissociated, analysed and then synthesized. Eliot often said that the
discovery of Laforgue was that of a brother soul which stimulated his
creative impulse. What must be stressed here is that there is one unbroken
line of thought going from Laforgue to de Gourmont, which concerns itself
mainly with the concept of the Unconscious. Laforgue discovered von Hart-
mann's *Philosophie des Unbewussten* (1869) as early as 1880, and decided to
make this "Philosophy of the unconscious" his personal gospel. He describes the Unconscious as the ultimate ratio of history and of life, as well as
the fundamental source of aesthetic production. In his "Complainte propi-
tiatoire à l'Inconscient," the Unconscious becomes a universal principle in
the name of which the poet attacks God, in a curious parody of the Pater
Noster. Laforgue's insights were not forgotten with his early death, but
were taken up by Remy de Gourmont who published his "Notes on the
Unconscious" in the *Mercure de France* in 1898. Thus two of the main

cultural models chosen by Eliot agree on the idea that symbolism is a movement which returns to a forgotten source of impulses rather than being a
supremely intellectual school. In Laforgue's words, the Unconscious is our
"inner Africa" (*Revue Blanche* 10, 1881–82) which the artist must set out to
explore.

Although in *The Dry Salvages*, Eliot has some fun with the critics who
apply psychoanalytical models too facilely, who "dissect / The recurrent
images into pre-conscious terrors," or "explore the womb, or tomb, or
dreams," he yet seems to point to the possibility of a cultural synthesis that
would not be dissociated from anthropological and psychoanalytical issues.
Quite early, in "The Function of Criticism," Eliot states that "A common
inheritance and a common cause unite artists consciously or unconsciously:
it must be admitted that the union is mostly unconscious." (*SE* [1951], p. 24)
The curious ambivalence felt by Eliot towards psychoanalysis determines
his theory of tradition, and is nowhere so clearly expressed as in the essay
on "Hamlet and His Problems," as it was called in *The Sacred Wood*. The
title seems to have been due to a curious slip of the pen, since Eliot attacks
those who conflate the play and the hero of the play. But had he written
"*Hamlet* and *its* problems," he would have lost the deep personal impli-
cation one can feel in this essay. Indeed, "problem" proves too weak a term,
and reveals that the excess of emotion explodes the barriers separating
subject and object:

> The intense feeling, ecstatic or terrible, without an object or exceeding its
> object, is something which every person of sensibility has known; it is doubt-
> less a study for pathologists. It often occurs in adolescence . . . The Hamlet of
> Laforgue is an adolescent; the Hamlet of Shakespeare is not, he has not that
> explanation and excuse. We must simply admit that here Shakespeare tackled
> a problem which proved too much for him.   (*SE* [1951], p. 146)

What Eliot shows with mastery and embarrassment is that such a
"problem" is both an artistic and a personal contradiction, both layers being
indissolubly bound together. The insight is taken up by Jacques Lacan, who
in his 1958–59 Seminar devoted to "Desire and its Interpretation" focused
his analysis upon *Hamlet* with a surprising reversal of the usual Freudian
idea. Whereas Freud reduced the play to a secondary manifestation of the
Oedipus drama (Hamlet cannot kill his uncle because his father's murder
has realized his own unconscious wish), Lacan reads Eliot's essay and finally
decides that the "inexpressibly horrible" stems from the opacity of the
Queen's sexual desire. Hamlet cannot act, not because of an untenable
rivalry (why could he not be all the more jealous of an uncle who possesses
the object of his desire, if the Oedipal thesis is valid?) but because he is still

dependent on his mother's desire, a sexual desire which he probes with anguished perplexity. A detailed summary of Lacan's complex argument would be out of place here, suffice it to point to really astonishing convergences between Lacan and Eliot. Both share a tragic awareness of life based on a belief in "original sin" connected with the original murder of the Father of the Son (although Lacan's version sticks to the Freudian paradigm and remains basically atheistic); both believe in a tradition which works through death in order to perpetuate a symbolic life. And it is not a coincidence that Lacan should have ended his 1953 epoch-making report on "Function and fields of speech and language in psychoanalysis" with the quotation from the Upanishads with which Eliot concludes the *Waste Land*.[10]

Like Lacan, and perhaps Freud, Eliot seems to have viewed history as a fickle feminine agency which has to be passed on by a more comprehensive tradition founded on the symbolic realm of paternity and language. Like them, he could only arrive at this insight by a deep, painful, and personal meditation on male and female hysteria. This is obvious in "Gerontion," in which a feminine History deceives with her "cunning passages, contrived corridors / And issues . . ." Such a hystericized version of history thrives on the perpetual mismatch of two temporalities, the cyclical time of myth and seasons and the linear time of Revelation. They must be shown to intersect in the concept of "tradition." For, since the incarnation of "Christ the tiger" is constantly betrayed by the "flowering judas" of a lush Maryland Spring, the male subject is left speechless as the *Verbum infans*, "word within a word, unable to speak a word." The feminine flow of words and sexual desire always threatens with absorption. The early prose poem "Hysteria" adumbrates in a nutshell the progression of *The Waste Land*, and depicts how the fear of being swallowed by a woman's laughter ("I was . . . lost finally in the dark caverns of her throat, bruised by the ripple of unseen muscles") can lead to a Jonah-like rebirth but only through a careful reordering of fragments ("I decided that if the shaking of her breasts could be stopped, some of the fragments of the afternoon might be collected . . .") A similar interaction of loss and rebirth is staged in "Marina." But the place where this drama came to be played out was the theatrical stage – a stage which is never very far from the Freudian notion of the "Other Scene" (*ein anderer Schauplatz*) of the Unconscious.

TRADITION: A "FAMILY REUNION," OR THE META-METAPHYSICS OF EUROPE

Many stray remarks on the unity of European culture are better understood when one realizes that Eliot fundamentally aims at a unification of experience, private and collective spheres being caught up in a general gathering of people and authors who are to be seen as members of one huge family. "The primary channel of transmission of culture is the family: no man wholly escapes from the kind, or wholly surpasses the degree, of culture which he acquired from his early environment . . . Even in relatively primitive societies this is so." (*NTDC* [London], p. 43) Once more, Eliot uses an anthropological model to overcome the limitations of the nuclear family. The example of primitive societies helps us understand the core of childhood memories indispensable to the writing of poetry. In fact, the notion of family seems merely to have been superimposed onto the concept of tradition: "But when I speak of the family, I have in mind a bond which embraces a longer period of time than this: a piety towards the dead, however obscure, and a solicitude for the unborn, however remote." (*NTDC* [London], p. 44). Such "piety" can produce clashes between private and public moralities similar to the basic dilemma of *Antigone*. As we learn from Eliot's first real play, the "family reunion" does not preclude ironies and betrayals.

The etymological bifurcation of "tradition" into "translation" on the one hand, "betrayal" on the other, is significant. It informs Eliot's relationship with "knowledge" in general. If he did not continue his philosophic studies for many personal and contextual reasons, it was also from a dissatisfaction with the role of philosophy itself, which proved unable to think tradition in a valid and lasting way. For Eliot the real and only role of philosophy was to weld faith and intelligence, belief and knowledge together. He meant to bring philosophy closer to other modes of utterance, and to this end he at first sought models with which to subvert it, in oriental mysticism with a Buddhist slant and then in the mainstream of the European metaphysical tradition. Even at the time of his most "relativistic" position, Eliot knew that one could not avoid metaphysics. One might hope to "analyze," but not to "overcome" metaphysics: "Of course one cannot avoid metaphysics altogether, because nowhere can a sharp line be drawn – to draw a sharp line between metaphysics and common sense would itself be metaphysics and not common sense" (*Letters* I, p. 80). (The insight remains a crucial one in Heidegger's philosophy.) Since it is impossible to "draw the line," one may still draw the conclusion that "men cannot get on without giving allegiance to something outside themselves" as the essays after 1928 repeat. The decentering of subjectivity by an Absolute already looming huge in Bradley's system finds an exact counterpart in the wish to be as "catholic" as possible and "re-twine as many straying strands of tradition as possible" in his poetry (*UPUC* [London], p. 85).

The gap between a "relativist" first Eliot and an "absolutist" second Eliot may be bridged if one sees that he has only varied strategies in order to come to terms with a given set of values bequeathed by a communal history, or with the culture of Europe as absorbed by someone who felt both part of it and a foreigner. *The Waste Land* is fundamentally a poem about Europe (if we leave aside the important confessional theme), although the word "Europe" is only given in German and in the notes. In fact, Eliot is close to Husserl's notion of Europe[11], in recognizing that cultural wholes are living organisms which develop of their own, without any conscious modification brought about by individuals:

> The persistence of literary creativeness in any people, accordingly, consists in the maintenance of an unconscious balance between tradition in the larger sense – the collective personality, so to speak, realized in the literature of the past – and the originality of the living generation.   (*PP* [London], p. 58)

This thought recurs in many essays, such as "The Social Function of Poetry" which alludes to "that mysterious social personality which we call our 'culture'" (*PP* [London], p. 23). Towards the end of "What is a Classic?," Eliot identifies Europe with an organism vivified by the two bloodstreams of Latin and Greek. (*PP* [London], pp. 69–70) The organic image is taken up in "The Three Voices of Poetry" (*PP* [London], pp. 97–101), when Eliot elaborates on Benn's theory opposing an "inert embryo or 'creative germ'" as the kernel image on the one hand, and Language on the other. This should be connected with the earlier description of the "auditory imagination" as a feeling into language, "penetrating far below the conscious levels of thought and feeling, invigorating every word; sinking to the most primitive and forgotten, returning to the origin and bringing something back, seeking the beginning and the end." (*UPUC* [London], p. 119)

The personal exhaustion Eliot evokes when describing the experience of the poet who has completed a lyrical poem ("he may experience a moment of exhaustion, of appeasement, of absolution, and of something very near annihilation, which is in itself indescribable" (*PP* [London], p. 98) – although already sketched in the pages of "Tradition and the Individual Talent" devoted to "personality" – seems very close to a mystical experience of death and rebirth. By a strange conceptual echo, such an "exhaustion" also takes place at the level of pure language when this vanishing, fading subject happens to be a Classic as well. A classic poet, Eliot claims, exhausts not only a form, but the language of his time (*PP* [London], p. 65). In a sense, this fits very well with Mallarmé's ideal of poetic disappearance. But is Mallarmé a Classic? One may want to argue about this, although most of us could agree that Eliot now stands as a true Classic of our time in that he urges us to realize that this time is haunted by a transcendent exteriority, inhabited by the ghosts of all the dead whose words still echo in our ears.

NOTES

1 Fritz Senn, "Book of Many turns," *Joyce's Dislocutions, Essays on Reading as translation* (Baltimore: Johns Hopkins University Press, 1984), pp. 127–36. For helpful discussions of Eliot's lifelong struggle with the term "tradition," see Sean Lucy, *T. S. Eliot and the Idea of Tradition* (London: Cohen & West, 1960), Richard Shusterman, *T. S. Eliot and the Philosophy of Criticism* (London: Duckworth, 1988), ch. 7, "The Concept of Tradition: its Progress and Potential"; and Erik Svarny, *The Men of 1914: T. S. Eliot and early Modernism* (Milton Keynes: Open University Press, 1988), ch. 7.

2 Charles-Louis Philippe, *Bubu de Montparnasse* (Paris: Garner-Flammarion, 1978), p. 53. The translation is mine.

3 Ezra Pound, *The Spirit of Romance* (New York: New Directions, 1968), p. 6.

4 See Charles Baudelaire, "Le Peintre de la vie moderne," *Oeuvres complètes* (Paris: Pléiade, Gallimard, 1966), pp. 1152–92. Eliot's aesthetics can be read as the prolongation of Baudelaire's definition of "modernity."

5 Ezra Pound, "The Tradition," *Literary Essays* (London: Faber, 1964), p. 92.

6 Emile Benveniste, "Deux modèles linguistiques de la cité," *Problèmes de linguistique générale* (Paris: Gallimard, 1974), vol. II, pp. 272–80.

7 See A. D. Moody, "The Christian philosopher and politics between the wars," *Thomas Stearns Eliot: Poet* (Cambridge: Cambridge University Press, 1979; new edn. 1994), pp. 319–26.

8 Remy de Gourmont, "La dissociation des idées," *La Culture des idées* (Paris: Mercure de France, 1900; 1964), pp. 68–69.

9 T. Stearns Eliot, *Syllabus of a Course of Six Lectures on Modern French Literature* (Oxford: Oxford University Extension Lectures, 1916), reproduced in Moody, *Thomas Stearns Eliot*, p. 43.

10 See Jacques Lacan, "Hamlet," *Ornicar?* 24 (Automne 1981): 7–31, and *Ornicar?* 25 (Rentrée 1982): 13–36. English translation by James Hulbert of part of this seminar, under the title "Desire and the Interpretation of Desire in *Hamlet*," Shoshana Felman (ed.) *Literature and Psychoanalysis* (Baltimore: Johns Hopkins University Press, 1982), pp. 11–52. See also Lacan, *Ecrits, A Selection*, Alan Sheridan (trans.) (London: Tavistock, 1977), pp. 104, 106–7.

11 Edmund Husserl, *La Crise de l'humanité européenne et la philosophie* (lecture given in Vienna in May 1935); the French translation is reprinted from the *Revue de métaphysique et morale* 3 (1950), (Paris: Paulet, 1968), p. 234.

16

BERNARD SHARRATT

Eliot: Modernism, Postmodernism, and after

Few readers would disagree that Eliot the man has been as much a puzzle as Eliot the poet. Two small books, with others, have now begun to clarify that puzzle.[1] The chief contribution of biography is to present relevant personal facts, and Ms. Gordon's patiently assembled facts have pointed, very pertinently, to how readers might have erred in their puzzlement over Eliot by not recognizing what might now be considered obvious: that Eliot's work represents a series of efforts, each trying to make sense of a persistent moral dilemma. The œuvre of T. S. Eliot will appear to us differently if, instead of treating the whole *Collected Poems* as due to Eliot's "impersonal" aesthetic, we perceive his poetry as negotiating intractable personal material which persists even in the final form.

We now know, in some detail, that there was indeed another woman in the life of the man, and that much of the work of the poet can be seen as full of some emotional and moral matter which the writer would not expose to light, and could not go away from. Since the only way of negotiating a moral dilemma is to find an objective situation which corresponds to that specific dilemma, it may be that Eliot's problems were such that the very *données* precluded objective resolution. And the alternative to resolution, in anyone who knows what it means to endure a situation one wants to escape from, may indeed be a form of madness, perhaps less the intensity of insanity than the desperate role-playing of the apparent *poseur*. We need, to be sure, a great many more facts in Eliot's biography; we should like to know, for example, whether, when and in relation to what personal crisis, he read Milton's *The Doctrine and Discipline of Divorce*. Certainly his animus towards Milton can seem in excess of the verse as we know it.

That was a way of putting it. Not very satisfactory. There are two elements at work in this passage. One concerns the claims of some recent scholarship on Eliot's life, which has established something like the following account of the relation between the work and the life:

Eliot was in love with Emily Hale. He married Vivienne Haigh Wood. The marriage was an appalling disaster. *The Waste Land* reflects the state of mind brought on by the marriage . . . In 1934 and 1935 Emily is in England. Eliot and Emily visit Burnt Norton. From that comes *Burnt Norton* (what might have been . . .) In 1939 Eliot and her brother have Vivienne committed to an asylum. *The Family Reunion* reflects (on) the guilt of possibly killing a wife, together with the more buried theme of infanticide.

I offer this simply to suggest the kind of account now possible, even plausible. The accuracy or credibility of these emerging accounts is not at issue here. What is significant is that, in a considerable shift of emphasis, we can now read Eliot's work in quite radically personal ways, if we wish. And this is, of course, to go directly contrary to Eliot's own critical stipulations and the orthodoxy of a generation: that our concern should be with the poetry not with the poet, that there is a disjuncture between the man who suffers and the man who creates. Certainly Eliot himself would have found my opening paragraph profoundly unacceptable. But the fact of the matter is that "T. S. Eliot" is constructed and reconstructed according to the ways in which his work is received.

The second problematic element in that paragraph is the deliberate echoing of Eliot's own essay on "Hamlet and his Problems." Is the relation between my text and Eliot's a matter of quotation, or of pastiche, or even parody? In what sense might the use of Eliot here be seen as an attempt to authorize my own text – to borrow a kind of authority for it by transposing his account of *Hamlet*? (But how authoritative is that account anyway?) Or is the echoing of Eliot serving simply to get my own writing under way, by taking Eliot as model for a certain kind of critical writing, a shadow voice I can adopt (but how persuasive, now, is that very tone and mode of writing, and with it Eliot's own criticism?). I pose the issue in that way because central in various reactions to Eliot over the years has been the role of quotation, allusion, and different "voices" in his writing. We can initially outline these reactions as a way into tracing a certain trajectory from Modernism to Postmodernism in the reception and construction of Eliot.

FULL OF HIGH SENTENCE

At its simplest, Eliot's use of quotations in both the poetry and the criticism can be taken as a sign of erudition, therefore as a mark of élite authority. Many students react this way, either in awe or hostility. Faced with the final lines of *The Waste Land* or even the epigraph to *Prufrock*, such readers may enjoyably succumb (the poetry *can* communicate before it is understood), or they may blankly decline to proceed or else reach defensively for a copy of

Southam's *Students' Guide to the Selected Poems of T. S. Eliot*. Eliot's characteristic mode and tone in his critical essays can seem similarly gnomic or
hermetic, superciliously dismissive of readers struggling to become even pre-
liminarily acquainted with the range of English literature: "The poetry of
Donne (to whom Marvell and Bishop King are sometimes nearer than any
other authors) is late Elizabethan, its feeling often very close to that of
Chapman . . ." The aspiring reader, apparently obliged to master both every
local echo and the overall mapping of how every author relates to every
other, can feel him or herself left in barbarian outer darkness.

Such responses might simply signal the passing of an era, the demise of
any adequate readership. Eliot's own *The Waste Land* and its notorious
notes can be cited in evidence: what else was *The Waste Land*, in its original
appearance in the first issue of *The Criterion*, than a complaint that the
great tradition of European culture had dwindled to a few disconnected
fragments, a case of battered books, which would not cohere any more than
the poem itself would. If the poem were to be received with incomprehen-
sion (requiring notes – though not for the élite subscribers to *The Criterion*)
that very reaction would reinforce its own case. The comically wide-ranging
notes reinforced awareness of cultural fragmentation with their barbed and
brittle playfulness. In such a situation, if one wanted to be a poet after one's
twenty-fifth year, one would grimly have to sweat for it in the library –
while acknowledging, of course, that Shakespeare had gained more from a
perusal of Plutarch than most men would get from a lifetime spent in the
British Museum. Literature was now an austere and full-time profession, an
impersonal task of storing up words and phrases, of becoming an ever-more
finely tuned catalyst, a precision instrument of feeling, the minimum qualifications being a feeling for the whole of European literature in one's very
bones. Few readers could hope to follow into that sacred wood. The temptation might be to burn it down instead.

However, another way of accounting for Eliot's proliferation of quotations and quasi-quotations is indicated by Eliot himself, in speaking of
how certain images can become personally charged with significance and
remain rather mysteriously in the memory to be evoked years later in the
poetry: the sight of an old white horse in a meadow, or six ruffians at a
window (*UPUC* [London], p. 148). We can then begin to read even the quotations in the critical essays as resonant with personal emotional investment
rather than with impersonal judicious authority, as saturated fragments of
Eliot's own psyche rather than fine placings of comparative merit. Thus the
motif of lost or even murdered children might be registered in the use of
passages from *Hercules Furens* in "Seneca in Elizabethan Translation" (an
essay he sent to Emily Hale), echoed also in the epigraph to *Marina* (with its

poignant "O my daughter.") The comments that Tennyson gives no evidence of having known the experience of violent passion for a woman and that the ravings of his lover on the edge of insanity in *The Princess* sound false might be linked as much with Emily's 1935 visit as with any considered judgment on Tennyson. The singling out of Yeats's lines about having reached forty-nine with only a book, not a child, to show for it might resonate onto Eliot's use in his poetry of Hieronymo's madness (at the murder of his children) or the fate of Ugolino in the tower (condemned to eat his own children). The choice of *Ion* as silent structure for *The Confidential Clerk* would go alongside Vivienne's addition to *The Waste Land* manuscript: "what you get married for if you don't want children?" The repeated citing of the sufficiently unfamiliar passage on "the poor benefit of a bewildering minute" might be set alongside that "awful daring of a moment's surrender" perhaps recorded most honestly in the original draft of the published lines "Your heart would have responded." Read along these converging lines Eliot's critical impersonality dissolves into as ᵣ ·sonal and emotionally porous a medium as the poetry.

A third and even more demystifying way of reading the quotations would be in terms of a simple serendipity, not just the occasional conjuncture of Spinoza and the smell of cooking, but the storing up of words and phrases as the regular by-product of the endless miscellaneous reviewing Eliot undertook to make ends meet in the early years of the marriage.[2] What seems like formidable erudition often derives from happening to be reading several different kinds of book at once, producing the accidental crossconnections and fortuitous juxtapositions familiar to any working writer. A simple example would be to trace how Eliot's close reading of Aristotle for his work at Oxford provided an epigraph for section III of *Tradition and the Individual Talent* while the same rather peculiar passage of the *De Anima* (book 1.4) fed into the composition of "Gerontion," a poem shaped by reaction to his father's death which had itself occurred in the same year that he undertook to review *The Problem of Hamlet*. Given also the anonymity of much cultural review work in those years, a tone of authoritative omnicompetence was easily available as cover for a young man's ignorance, inviting tonal camouflage for hair-raising audacities of arbitrary judgment. Eliot's "impersonal" critical style may then be compared to Addison's construction of an urbanely "a-political" prose persona: a neat resolution of an individual career dilemma, generalizable and imitable as the mode of a generation or the style of a discipline.

Eliot's status as American exile in England suggests a further element in his use of quotations, a matter of nervous anxiety rather than of aloof omniscience. His recently available letters show how linguistically precarious he could feel. We can sense him articulating his American English with an alien care. In 1914 he describes his boarding house filled with European exiles speaking several tongues; he transcribes what he calls "brilliants" – fragments of overheard British speech and odd sayings. His correspondence adopts a variety of styles and voices, reflecting an unusually dispersed set of simultaneous social locations. His poems in French already reflect this: "En Amerique, professeur," etc. Rather than being in awe of Eliot's multi-voiced ventriloquism as an index of ironic impersonal control, one can as easily see an anxiety of identity at work, deeper than Prufrock's though in continuity with it.

As with later writers in exile (especially in Paris), there is a tendency in Eliot to erect a whole theory of language from this denaturalizing experience of how words can fail to work for one. Being unable to say just what one means, or facing a roomful of people telling one that that was not what they meant at all, were real social experiences for Eliot during those early years in England. His letter of June 17, 1919 to Eleanor Hinckley (*Letters* 1, pp. 304f) is a hilariously painful account of the social complications of meaning and report possible in the politely vindictive world of literary London. In *The Waste Land* language itself is seen as having fallen, even from the first intelligible sound that broke the animal silence: that primitive imitation or quotation of the thunder's "Da" is already a deeply ambiguous and enigmatic syllable. Language is to fall again, in the seventeenth century, as a mysterious dissociation of sensibility allegedly "set in", like a nervous breakdown in the culture.

But to be unable to say exactly what one feels or to find a formula for a precise emotion may be a matter of personal social awkwardness rather than evidence for a cultural diagnosis. To resort to other men's words, for a word within a word when one is unable to speak a word, may be the linguistic equivalent of reaching for a mask, a socially acceptable persona. Numerous other American visitors have, after all, registered an unexpected muffling and peculiarly annoying opacity in the language they had thought they shared with their English hosts. And now that even that Anglo-American tongue has transmuted into the flat international "English" of cross-cultural conversations in airport lounges, satellite-linked television studios, and multi-national conferences, even the native speaker can feel irredeemably alienated from the unusable riches, resonances, and resources of the language. Eliot's own carefully constructed speaking-voice can then seem like both a delicate negotiation of a personal linguistic uncertainty and a paradoxical anticipation of the thin air of current English. A discourse constructed from quotation and allusion may be only a shade away from a discourse consisting entirely of sound-bites.

However, a more profound level of anxiety is also at work, in the problematic relation between contextual structure and local quotation. Necessarily, a quotation involves taking a phrase or formula from one context into another. But what legitimates the new context itself, the structure into which the displaced allusion fits? Eliot had a tendency to take even the skeletal framework of a new work from another source: what he called the mythic method in Joyce and which he uses himself, in the deployment of Jessie Weston and the Grail legend in *The Waste Land* or the appropriation of Greek tragic plots and/or West End theater forms in the plays. However, once the accommodating structure is itself registered as only another quotation a dizzying instability threatens.

The underlying problem is apparent in Eliot's repeated discussions of the complex relation between an artist's appropriation of dominant cultural thought frameworks and a reader's acceptance of such frameworks, putting in question the very possibility of poetic response and belief. The essays on Shakespeare, Dante, and Blake rehearse these issues of philosophical credibility, conceptual coherence and poetic suspension of disbelief; while the essays on Bradley and Leibniz reveal that for Eliot himself no metaphysical system, as such, could claim more than provisional credibility or coherence. In the essay on Bradley he characteristically puts the emphasis on Bradley's *style*. His radical epistemological skepticism is unusually explicit in an early letter to Norbert Wiener (January 6, 1915, *Letters* I, p. 79). From *Prufrock* to *The Hollow Men* a similar skepticism is at work concerning any underlying psychic structure, since, as "Tradition and the Individual Talent" acknowledges, the point of view Eliot was struggling to attack was indeed related to the metaphysical theory of the substantial unity of the soul.

Arguably, Eliot's only successful resolution of these interrelated problems was to construct an idiosyncratic form of spiritual autobiography sustained by the device of intra-textual self-quotation. In *Four Quartets* he may have begun by taking over the form of a Beethoven quartet but the subsequent quartets, in both structure and endlessly layered local echo, primarily relate back to and interweave with the previous quartets in the overall poem, and beyond that to Eliot's own œuvre, his own previous words echoing thus in our minds as we read. *Four Quartets* thereby becomes brilliantly self-sustaining. Only an occasional flatfooted assertiveness perhaps acknowledges a continued tension between epistemological skepticism and dogmatic authority: the hints and guesses may somehow be Incarnation but they nevertheless remain only hints and guesses. That elaborately appealing poetic solution could not be surpassed or even repeated. Indeed, in the post-conversion prose the omnicompetent tone of the earlier criticism returns as a kind of arrogance mitigated only by pseudo-humility: ostensibly tentative notes lead only to *the* definitive delimiting of culture and alternative notions can be only summarily dismissed. If Eliot did indeed move beyond the modalities of Modernism in his own lifetime, it is salutary to register where he moved to.

AFTER MODERNISM

I am not suggesting that Eliot was or was not a Postmodernist but rather that Eliot's work initiates a logic which can illuminate current notions of postmodernism, and that his ways of negotiating his particular cultural situation pre-echo some features of what is currently meant by postmodernism. The term is notoriously tricky, but the specifically architectural, and arguably still most influential, use of the term emphasizes precisely the deployment of quotation, the relation and dissociation between structure and facade in the design of buildings: while the undergirding skeleton may be the product of the latest technology, the cladding or appearance is constituted by a variety of essentially optional historical masks.[3]

Of immediate relevance to Eliot would be the example of exhibition architecture: the temporary buildings erected for various world's fairs and great exhibitions, offering artificially concentrated doses of the world's cultural styles. The classic American example was the Chicago Columbian Exposition of 1893. Stuart Ewen quotes a description of a central feature of that fair:

> The Midway in effect formed a colossal sideshow, with restaurants, shops, exhibits, and theatres extending down a huge corridor, six hundred feet wide and a mile long . . . Here the Beaux-Arts neo-classicism of the Court of Honour gave way to Barnumesque eclecticism, refined order to exuberant chaos. Fairgoers threaded their way on foot, or in hired chairs among a hurly-burly of exotic attractions: mosques and pagodas, Viennese Streets and Turkish bazaars, South Sea Island huts, Irish and German castles, and Indian tepees.[4]

In 1904 St. Louis, Eliot's boyhood hometown, was the site of the Louisiana Purchase World's Fair, with its construction of an entire artificial "Philippino" city. The sixteen-year old Eliot certainly attended the St. Louis Fair, but since his father was the President of a brick manufacturing company it was in any case unlikely that the young Eliot escaped awareness of the mechanics of balloon frame architecture. St. Louis was once singled out, by Giedion, as providing impressive nineteenth-century examples of severely functionalist architecture, a proto-Modernism abandoned before its time.[5] One might then see in the widespread American adoption of surface architectural imitation and facade quotation a loss of confidence in American civic culture's having a style of its own. Pound's ransacking of Provencal, Chinese and Renaissance Italian materials can then seem not so distant from Mellon's stone by stone transportation of a medieval French abbey facade to his Pittsburgh museum, or the artificial creation of the New York Cloisters or, finally, Disneyworld itself.

Eliot's recursive recycling of past literatures to create a modern literature can be seen as a similar strategy arising from similar problems. His construction of a pan-European poetic structure, incorporating vividly compressed fragments of Wagner, Verlaine, Augustine, and Ovid, can seem remarkably akin to the polycultural displays of the Midway. These suggested similarities are not only, in true postmodernist fashion, surface affinities but also structural. For the deeper superficialities of postmodernism are already at work in Eliot's construction of history as essentially a matter of literary taste. If a dissociation of sensibility can be so culturally devastating yet so evidently a matter of critical construction, then not only the blithely anachronistic collages of Hollywood or Great Exhibition representations of past and future are factitious and arbitrary, but the very narrative of history itself is merely a matter of organizing fragments of quotation, a textual reshuffling of an endlessly expanding but unreliable archive with no verifiable validity. If so, then even the worst examples of Heritage history, as a pattern of essentially timeless moments, styles and motifs, are merely indicative of a deeper abyss: that History may be neither servitude nor freedom, but unavoidably Disney. It simply depends on who creates and controls the taste by which that past is not only enjoyed but actually constructed. For when the cultural past is only another country to be exploited for commercial tourism then constructing either canon or criterion becomes critically impossible. Eliot's main cultural presence might then be only as the librettist of *Cats*. Perhaps we should now await the virtual reality version of *The Waste Land*, offering personalized interviews with the Sybil and a chance to interactively rewrite the ending.

It is time to re-examine the inherited notions of Modernism, and to consider how it was constructed and how Eliot became a key to its canon. As Raymond Williams has emphasized, what now constitutes "Modernism" is a highly selective construct.[6] The basis for that selection was, in part, another temporal contingency: the coincidence of "Modernism" with the emergence and development of "English" as a respectable academic subject. What such "difficult" writing as that of Eliot, Joyce, and Pound potentially offered was justification for claiming the status of a "discipline" for "English" in the first place. The function of quotations in this context was twofold: to validate the notion that genuine learning was required and to reinforce a claim for necessary training in close and practiced attention. However, the merits of Modernism were not, of course, immediately endorsed by the academic community. Roughly, three phases can be outlined in the assimilation and construction of "Modernism" in English criticism.

In the first period, from say 1922 to 1945, the "new bearings" suggested by Eliot's critical preferences and poetic practice were established as canonical, shaping the curriculum into a remapping of the highpoints of literary history so that Eliot and his generation were seen as the appropriate culmination. But by the time this effort was successful the Modernist moment was already history. After 1945 another generation of critics emerges, in the increasingly professionalized and institutionalized field of "EngLit." Especially in the United States a generation of well-trained elucidators produced an impressive body of scholarly commentary, with ever-more specialized studies of every aspect of the Modernists. Eliot's own erudition was thereby emphatically highlighted, while the poetry risked disappearing into the accumulating apparatus of the knowledge industry. Student "Guides" such as Southam's were then doubly constitutive of the canon: effectively delimiting it to those texts chosen for exegetical commentary and implying a virtue in sheer density of allusion.

Arguably, the problem facing the third generation of, say, 1968 onwards, was both that the elucidatory work upon Modernism had been largely completed (they had been the students for whom the guides were already written) and that the redefining of the canon had been almost too successful: no group of writers later than the Modernists could claim anything like their established prestige, measurable by the groaning library shelf-load. For the aspiring professional critic not content to be the acknowledged expert on the comma in later Henry James, the strategic problem was how to tackle the same terrain as before but with a different critical emphasis: how to say something new about the monstrous bibliographical construct that was now "T. S. Eliot" or "Joyce."

One initially successful strategy was to find new theoretical ways of revalidating the already established valuations. The various retheorizings of literature and/or criticism or the several forms of deconstructive reading tended in that respect to be professionally productive. An alternative, more high risk strategy was simply to expand the canon to the point where canonical considerations were entirely surpassed and "literature" dissolved back into textuality and rhetoric, whether Black/Woman/Working-Class writing, Government texts or advertising copy. The copresence of both strategies necessitated a complex reformulation of value (as whatever yields pedagogic surplus?) and simultaneously induced a strained sense of professional over-load: too much requiring to be read and too diverse a range of competences to be called upon.

In this phase Eliot's status was deeply ambivalent. As both unquestion-ably eminent and now reasonably teachable (compared with Joyce or Pound) Eliot's work figures increasingly as exemplarily canonical, yet for the same reason was imputed with a double discredit: as ur-draughtsman of the critical orthodoxy to be deconstructed and as archetypal white male élitist conservative literary icon. Surprisingly little work attempted to reclaim Eliot as, say, proto-structuralist (layering myths upon each other) or precursor of linguistic constructions of illusory subjectivities (Prufrock on Lacan's couch). Instead, even in this era of authorial death and disso-lution, Eliot's complicated, and exploitative, relations to women were increasingly subjected to biographical and psychoanalytic scrutiny; the "personal" reading even of Eliot's previously erudite quotations became plausible precisely as a contribution to the necessary ideological dethronement.

One way of placing "Postmodernism" is then as the next (1980s?) generation's nominal resolution of a shared professional impasse (the term itself has all the marks of such a career move). "Postmodernism" in this context refers to the fourth phase in the critical reworking of "Eng.Lit" (now a whole repertoire of cultural studies) in which the awesome job description of required expertises was made tolerable by a countermove: all previous phases of the discipline were now to be taken as providing only provisional overall structures, fabricated framings and mappings, them-selves now available as material for reflexive analysis but all under equal epistemological erasure. In this phase Eliot is a somewhat neglected figure, but aspects of his own career might be plausibly offered as allegorical or exemplary. As in Eliot's own development, "postmodernist" criticism com-bined a kind of intellectual serendipity with a rhetorical mode that could mimic omnicompetence: the remorseless overproduction of critical publi-cation combined with the speed of theoretical redundancies confronted younger practitioners with a variant on Eliot's own early dilemmas. And as with the resolution offered by *Four Quartets*, some postmodernist (critical) writing tended towards self-sustaining structures, held up only by acts of intertextuality, a form of critical suspension of skepticism in which alter-native positions are treated not as statements open to refutation but as storehouses for competing quotations or simply as memories of once-held positions now available for autobiographical revision. The end term, as in Eliot's poetry, would presumably be a criticism composed of reflexive self-quotation.

AFTER POSTMODERNISM

As an academic *topos* "Postmodernism" was of course plausibly sustained by wider cultural developments. It may be, however, that the most frequently celebrated features of Postmodernism are now waning into a past: the period of Postmodernism (1979–89?) may itself be over. In the wake of world events of the early 1990s it now seems merely quaint to proclaim the end of metanarratives, the repudiation of overall histories and frameworks of interpretation, the demise of grand explanatory theories. As new world narratives popularly proliferate, from Kennedy's *The Rise and Fall of Great Powers* to Fukuyama's *The End of History*, it becomes increasingly plain that some central postmodernist motifs operated to undermine only certain kinds of grand narrative, those stemming from the generally "liberal" or "progressive" camps of the past decades. The appeal to "Postmodernism" provided a way of discrediting, or avoiding engagement with, those attempts at global coherence which both repudiated and offered to explain capitalist domination. "Postmodernist" was frequently simply code for "post Marxist."

However, the collapse of the Soviet forms of Communist organization in Eastern Europe has now removed the need for that stratagem. The more triumphalist apologists for the "West" are therefore only too ready to reintroduce grand narratives, with predictable epic heroes (Spirit of Free Enterprise, Genuine Democracy), and global perspectives: a New World Order is (once again) proclaimed and it is perhaps already possible to see what is likely to come after Postmodernism, at least at the level of political rhetoric. The somewhat unconvincing "Victorian values" of the 1980s have been revamped in 1990s America as the timeless shibboleths of Family, Nation, and Religion, while in an allegedly unified Europe these values reveal their nightmare forms: in wars fought in the name of ethnonationalisms and ethnic cleansing, in bitter religious contestations, in enraged racist conflicts. Some commentators already see Postmodernism as cultural precursor to a "soft path" fascism,[7] while others interpret the newly rampant fundamentalisms, whether Christian, Islamic, or Israeli, as paranoid reactions to the corrosive uncertainties celebrated in postmodernist positions.

Whereas the "Postmodernist" phase had at best an ambivalent debt to Eliot and no clear pigeonhole for his work, in this now-emerging post-Cold War period Eliot is clearly ripe for several possible new appropriations. His own move towards a reactionary and religious conservatism will perhaps makes him congenial and useful to some of the new currents of right wing thought. Both the various parochial nationalists and those who claim a new pan-Europeanism can legitimately cite his perspectives in support: either group can now quote *"Bin gar keine Russin, stamm' aus Litauen, echt deutsch"* with suitably different emphases. The renewed strength of religious ideologies leaves Eliot well placed for a certain resurrection: the *Idea of a Christian Society* might go down well in some circles, and any number of regressively conservative tendencies may seek support and comfort in Eliot's deliberately restrictive definition of culture. As increasingly the benefits of "democracy" are also questioned, in favour of an incremental authoritarianism, the more anti-democratic aspects of Eliot might again find a new lease of life.

It is, fortunately, possible to put this in more neutral terms. The issues treated in *Notes Towards the Definition of Culture*, of cultural community and identity, of the relations between region and nation, sect and cult, are clearly on the new European agenda. In considering these issues Jacques Derrida has even brought the neglected Valéry back into the debate.[8] Perhaps Eliot is now due for similar resuscitation. Eliot's version of Modernism emerged in response to the specific cultural dilemmas of his generation of Americans faced with post-World War European culture as a questionable and uncertain option rather than a dominant given; after the Cold War we may all be in an analogous position for a while, as exiles – of uncertain cultural identity – from an as yet undefined future "Europe." Eliot's soberly pitched voice may still be one of those we must attend to if we are not to develop merely a continent-sized EuroDisney. We may even find ourselves, squatting in the ruins of postmodernism, rereading *The Waste Land* afresh and rejoicing that once more we have to construct something upon which to rejoice.

A particular strand within Modernism may be due for revaluation. From Imagism to, say, Eliot's essay on Dante there is a concern with the possibility of a new kind of thinking in images, even a logic of images, more multi-dimensioned and popularly accessible than that of words. If political democracy in the television age necessitates a capacity for shared political discourse not dependent upon educational or linguistic differentiations, then these issues remain active. Eliot's attempt to devise, or revive, a form of passionate thinking may also be worth pondering: a world of ecological awareness may well be one in which we truly do need to have our modes of feeling directly altered by our reading and thought, in which to feel our thought as immediately as the odour of a rose may be a requisite capacity.

We can return here to the opening issues. A quotation operates in a double faceted mode: by quoting we seek authority from another, yet often it is the very act of quoting that endows that source with its putative authority. (Student essay-writers often face the dilemma of negotiating between mere appeal and appropriate support.) The authority of a quotation is always only provisional, dependent finally upon the force of our own case or context. We perhaps need to relearn that all authority is so delegated, however indirectly, from ourselves, and not from some pregiven superiority. It may be time to pursue further the basic insight of Modernism that even genius is a job, no more mysterious than turning the leg of a table. Insofar as the refined impersonality of Eliot's authority presided over, and shaped the agenda for, a whole era in literary criticism, the long-delayed demystification of both the man and the poetry in the mainly sympathetic light of new biographical readings may be the last and best contribution he can now make to a suitably disenchanted but open future.

NOTES

1 L. Gordon, *Eliot's Early Years* (Oxford: Oxford University Press, 1977) and *Eliot's New Life* (Oxford: Oxford University Press, 1988).

2 A useful list is in C. Behr, *T. S. Eliot: A Chronology of his Life and Works* (London: Macmillan 1983), pp. 95 120.

3 See C. Jencks, *What is Post-Modernism?* (London: Academy Editions, 1986).

4 John F. Kasson, *Amusing the Million*, quoted in S. Ewen, *All Consuming Images* (New York: Basic Books, 1988), p. 37.

5 S. Giedion, *Space, Time and Architecture* (Cambridge, MA: Harvard University Press, 5th edn., 1971), p. 393f; cf. pp. 200f.

6 Raymond Williams, "When was Modernism?," *New Left Review* 175 (May/June 1989): 49.

7 Dean MacCannell, "The desire to be postmodern," in his *Empty Meeting Grounds: The Tourist Papers*, (London: Routledge 1992), pp. 183–229.

8 J. Derrida, *L'autre cap* (Paris: Les Éditions de Minuit, 1991) – translated by Pascale-Anne Brault and Michael B. Naas as *The Other Heading: Reflections on Today's Europe* (Bloomington: Indiana University Press, 1992).

17

JEWEL SPEARS BROOKER

Eliot studies: a review and a select booklist

Readers coming to T. S. Eliot at the beginning of the last decade of the twentieth century will find no complete edition of his writings and no comprehensive catalog of unpublished materials. They will discover, moreover, that many important documents are sequestered in research collections in England and the United States and many manuscripts are sealed well into the twenty-first century. Readers venturing into the secondary writings will find a dark and tangled wood of opinions and counter opinions. The biographies that exist range from partisan to abusive; none are satisfactory, for no biographer has had access to Eliot's papers. Literary criticism fills several library shelves, but it often obscures the poet and his work or, in the interest of cultural politics, turns him into a straw man. Writings about Eliot range from excellent to useless, from reasonably objective to wildly subjective, and for the innocent reader (the non-specialist), it is difficult to know which is which.

Most Eliot manuscripts and papers are located in the United States and England. The most extensive American holding is the T. S. Eliot Collection in the Houghton Library at Harvard University. This collection, the gift of the poet's brother Henry, contains manuscripts, letters, and family photographs. The Beinecke Library at Yale University has a few Eliot items and will eventually receive the major collection accumulated by the poet's bibliographer Donald Gallup. The Berg Collection of the New York Public Library contains Eliot's early poetry notebooks, *The Waste Land* manuscripts, and other materials the poet had given to his patron John Quinn. The Ransom Humanities Research Center at the University of Texas has a major Eliot Collection, including manuscripts, letters, periodicals, and first editions. The Texas holdings are listed in Alexander Sackton's *The T. S. Eliot Collection at the University of Texas* (1975). Princeton University houses an important collection of Eliot letters, a gift of the poet's long-time friend and correspondent Emily Hale, but these letters will remain sealed until the year 2020. Most libraries holding collections of papers related to

Eliot's friends (Ezra Pound, Conrad Aiken, Allen Tate, Paul Elmer More, and many others) or to modernism also contain Eliot items.

The finest collection of Eliot materials in England, a gift of the poet's friend John Hayward, is at King's College Library, Cambridge. The Hayward Collection includes Eliot's early philosophical papers and his 1926 Clark Lectures. Typescripts of *Four Quartets* may be found in the Pepys Library at Magdalene College at Cambridge, and a cache of Eliot letters was purchased by the British Library in 1991. Valerie Eliot has a valuable private collection of letters; she also owns the poet's personal library and his business files, including those related to his editorship of *The Criterion*. Eliot papers can be found in smaller quantities in numerous institutions and in the libraries of his many friends.

The one indispensable guide to Eliot's published writings is the revised edition of Donald Gallup's *T. S. Eliot: A Bibliography* (1969). Virtually all of Eliot's published work is listed in this splendid catalog. Gallup describes books and pamphlets edited by Eliot, translations of his poetry and prose into foreign languages, and in an appendix, miscellanea. Gallup missed a few items, noted in addenda by George Monteiro (1972), A. M. Cohn and Elizabeth Eames (1976), and A. S. G. Edwards (1981), all in *Papers of the Bibliographical Society of America*. Important Eliot materials have appeared since 1969 and others are now being prepared for the press. Mr. Gallup is updating his work and will publish a final bibliography as soon as possible following the publication of letters and other primary materials.

Eliot's poetry and plays are published in a number of volumes, none of which contains the complete œuvre. Some of his literary essays are included in collections published in his lifetime, but many lie scattered in periodicals and manuscript collections. The same is true of his social and religious criticism. In Britain, the poetry and criticism are published by Faber and Faber, and in the United States, by Harcourt Brace Jovanovich. For the American market, the main verse collections are the *Collected Poems 1909–1962* (1963), the *Complete Plays* (1969), and the so-called *Complete Poems and Plays of T. S. Eliot: 1909–1950* (1952), which includes neither *Poems Written in Early Youth* (1967) nor his last two plays, *The Confidential Clerk* (1954) and *The Elder Statesman* (1959). In 1969, Faber and Faber brought out a more comprehensive *Complete Poems and Plays of T. S. Eliot*, unfortunately marred by its many misprints. The plays are available in England in *Collected Plays* (1962).

Most of the verse which Eliot himself wished to appear is included in Faber and Faber's 1969 *Complete Poems and Plays*. Perhaps the most interesting unpublished verse is that contained in his early poetic notebooks

(Berg Collection, New York). These workshop pieces, which include fragments, drafts, and poems which the poet excluded from his early collections, are being edited for publication by Christopher Ricks. The discarded drafts of *The Waste Land*, ably edited by Valerie Eliot, were published in 1971. *The Waste Land: A Facsimile and Transcript of the Original Drafts* contextualizes the poem and clarifies the collaborative roles played by Ezra Pound and by the poet's first wife Vivien (Vivienne). *The Composition of Four Quartets* (1978), edited by Helen Gardner, contains drafts of *Four Quartets* and describes the growth of the sequence. Gardner's detailed annotations, helpful in clarifying sources and meaning, make this volume as indispensable for students of *Four Quartets* as *The Waste Land: A Facsimile and Transcript* is for students of the earlier masterpiece.

Of Eliot's various collections of literary criticism, the most important are *The Sacred Wood* (1920, 1928), *Selected Essays* (1932, 1951), *The Use of Poetry and the Use of Criticism* (1933), *On Poetry and Poets* (1957), and *To Criticize the Critic* (1965). *Selected Prose of T. S. Eliot* (1975), edited by Frank Kermode, is a one-volume edition with selections from Eliot's published essays. Kermode includes a generous sample of the literary criticism and a few excerpts from the social criticism. His work in this convenient volume is, generally speaking, judicious; serious readers, nevertheless, will prefer their Eliot without ellipses.

Most of Eliot's early literary criticism appeared first in periodicals, and much of this material has not been collected. Much of Eliot's later criticism appeared as prefaces or forewords to books, and this material also remains uncollected. Valerie Eliot is editing these papers herself and in due time will release them. Eliot's Clark Lectures, given in spring 1926 at Trinity College, Cambridge, and his Turnbull Lectures, given at Johns Hopkins University in January 1933, are available under the title *The Varieties of Metaphysical Poetry* (1993). Edited by Ronald Schuchard, these lectures contain brilliant discussions of literary history and the dissociated sensibility.

In 1964, Eliot's doctoral thesis was published under the title *Knowledge and Experience in the Philosophy of F. H. Bradley*. His student notebooks and several substantial essays on philosophy and comparative religion have survived, and Valerie Eliot expects to publish all of these materials. They show that Eliot anticipated in his early work the most interesting currents of late twentieth-century thought and thus have much to offer the many critics now working at the intersection of philosophy and literary criticism. Eliot's published social criticism is found in *After Strange Gods* (1934 – never reprinted by Eliot), *The Idea of a Christian Society* (1939), *Notes towards the Definition of Culture* (1948), and various uncollected pieces beginning in the 1920s. The wide-ranging nature of his cultural, social, and political views is evident in his editorial column ("A Commentary") for *The Criterion*, the journal he edited in the stressful years *entre deux guerres*. In 1967, Faber reprinted *The Criterion: 1922–1939* in eighteen volumes, and thus this intellectual diary is available in many libraries.

Shortly before his death, Eliot gave his wife permission to publish his letters on the condition that she edit them herself. Valerie Eliot, who estimates that the letters will run to six volumes, has been working on this project for a quarter of a century. The first volume, covering the years from 1898 to 1922, appeared in 1988. The remaining primary materials include a few interviews and some recordings and films. The most substantial interview, conducted by Donald Hall, appeared in the *Paris Review* in 1959. Recordings of Eliot reading his poetry, including "The Love Song of J. Alfred Prufrock," *The Waste Land*, and *Four Quartets*, are available. A number of films have been produced using footage of Eliot. *The Mysterious Mr. Eliot* appeared soon after his death, and in the 1980s, several other documentaries appeared, including one in the US public television series on American poets, *Voices and Visions*. A list of readings, films, and musical compositions is included in Brooker, *Approaches to Teaching Eliot's Poetry and Plays* (1988).

In "The Function of Criticism," Eliot argued that literary criticism should consist of "the common pursuit of true judgment." Generally speaking, this definition is not descriptive of Eliot studies, although it must be noted that in the 1980s, the situation began to shift towards greater cooperation. The T. S. Eliot Society, founded in 1980 in St. Louis, sponsors an annual presentation of papers and in 1988 arranged an international centennial program. The growing sense of community in Eliot studies can also be seen in the other fine centennial conferences and publishing projects. Still, it must be noted that there is no institutional or geographical center for work on Eliot, no body of scholars who have been trusted to edit his papers, no reliable biography, no journal devoted to his work. The *T. S. Eliot Newsletter*, founded in Canada in 1974, had a brief history and was succeeded by the *Yeats–Eliot Review* at the University of Arkansas. The *T. S. Eliot Annual* no. 1, announced for 1984, did not appear until 1990 (Bagchee, 1990); no. 2 is expected eventually. A scholarly journal and clearinghouse for Eliot studies is much needed.

The history of Eliot criticism from the 1920s until the present can be charted dialectically. Major critics in the first generation (say, from the late twenties to the fifties) accepted Eliot into the canon and anointed him as the greatest poet of his age; many critics in the next generation (say, from the sixties to the eighties) rejected him and heaped contempt on his art, his literary theories, his religion, and his politics; a number of present critics, younger and trained in philosophy as well as literature, have returned to him with fresh appreciation and understanding. The negative criticism was part of a larger reaction against modernism and the New Critics, but the attacks on Eliot went far beyond the attempt to historicize him and to judge him by standards other than his own. Attacks on Eliot and modernism abated in the 1980s; he is returning as a positive reference point in modern letters and his position as one of the century's finest poets is secure.

The vicissitudes of Eliot's reputation notwithstanding, critical literature on his life and work has steadily accumulated in the seventy years since the publication of *The Waste Land* (1922). Fortunately, there are a number of fine bibliographic guides. Most helpful are the bibliographic reviews. The first of two helpful book-length bibliographies is Robert H. Canary's *T. S. Eliot: The Poet and His Critics* (1982). Canary focuses on English-language scholarship of the 1960s and 1970s, assessing "the current state of Eliot criticism in addressing the central issues raised by his work." Chapters are devoted to psycho-biographical-critical studies, to Eliot's theories of language and art, to his social and religious writings, to his use of and place in the western tradition, and to his place in modernism. Canary's work is supported by an exceptionally full index, invaluable for the busy scholar. It includes not only the articles and books under review, but many others, topically organized in "Selected Additional Readings."

Canary's topically organized extended essay is by principle comparative. This is one of its strengths, but does make it cumbersome for those who wish a quick reference book. A second book-length bibliography, Sebastian D. G. Knowles and Scott A. Leonard's *An Annotated Bibliography of a Decade of T. S. Eliot Criticism: 1977–1986* (1992), on the other hand, is very easy to use and will be indispensable to serious scholars. This resource, volume II of *T. S. Eliot: Man and Poet* (National Poetry Foundation), lists 1,423 books, articles, and dissertations, annotating 304 articles and 136 books. Claiming their book represents "just the tip of the iceberg of Eliot criticism" in the decade from 1977 to 1986, the authors summarize and sometimes evaluate arguments, with longer annotations for more important pieces. This excellent resource ends in the mid-1980s, before the publications of the centennial year and its aftermath, but a few post-1986 items are added in a separate section at the end.

Chapter-length reviews of Eliot scholarship can be found in several books. Most notable are the two volumes of *Sixteen Modern American Authors*, edited by Jackson Bryer. The Eliot chapter in the first volume (1973), an exemplary survey of research and criticism by Richard Ludwig, covers scholarship from the 1920s to 1972; the fine Eliot chapter in the second, by Stuart Y. McDougal, from 1972 to the mid-1980s (1989). These chapters are divided into sections on bibliography, editions, manuscripts and letters, biography, and criticism. Together, these two essays form an invaluable commentary on Eliot scholarship from its beginning. A third chapter-length survey, Alistair Davies's *An Annotated Critical Bibliography of Modernism* (1982), includes 128 selected items of Eliot studies from the beginning to 1980. In addition to excellent annotations of Eliot materials, Davies provides a valuable survey of research in modernism. Finally, in this category, the "Materials" section of Jewel Spears Brooker's *Approaches to Teaching Eliot's Poetry and Plays* (1988) not only lists editions but also compares popular anthologies used for teaching Eliot. Brooker reviews scholarship, using the two-tiered approach of the MLA series with separate recommendations for students and for teachers. A brief guide to Eliot studies is also included in *Guide to American Literature from Emily Dickinson to the Present*, edited by James T. Callow and R. J. Reilly (1977).

The best resource for current scholarship is the annual bibliographic review. *American Literary Scholarship*, an indispensable critical survey of each year's work in American literature, began including Eliot (previously classified as British) in 1973 and from 1974 has included a full chapter on Eliot and Pound. Written by scholars, these essays review both articles and books under bibliography, biography, and criticism. *ALS* also includes reviews of the best foreign scholarship of the year, including work from France, Germany, Italy, Scandinavia, and Japan. The *Year's Work in English Studies*, similarly, features scholarly essays summarizing and evaluating the most notable work of each year in English, American, Commonwealth, and some Continental literatures.

Eliot scholarship is also served by a number of volumes which list and lightly annotate titles. The first is Mildred Martin's *A Half-Century of Eliot Criticism: An Annotated Bibliography of Books and Articles in English, 1916–1965* (1972). To Martin's list of 2,692 items, 1,300 are added in *T. S. Eliot Criticism in English, 1916–1965: A Supplementary Bibliography* (1977), compiled by Mechthild and Armin Paul Frank and K. P. S. Jochum. Another helpful compilation of secondary references is Beatrice Ricks's *T. S. Eliot: A Bibliography of Secondary Works* (1980), which brings the record up to the late 1970s, at which point the less comprehensive but far more detailed work of Knowles and Leonard (above) begins.

The periodical bibliographies, finally, provide the most comprehensive checklists. Most notable are the *MLA Bibliography* and its British equivalent, the *Annual Bibliography of English Language and Literature* (ABELL). *The Journal of Modern Literature* includes Eliot in its annual bibliography survey, and the *Yeats–Eliot Review* has items of interest. The

T. S. Eliot Society News & Notes began in 1992 listing dissertations on Eliot. The most current listings can be found in the quarterly *Humanities Index* or the monthly *Literary Criticism Register: A Monthly Listing of Studies in English and American Literature. Abstracts of English Studies*, a quarterly, is also useful for current scholarship.

One of the most serviceable resources, *Contemporary Literary Criticism*, comes from Gale Publications, the extraordinarily prolific house which produces the *Dictionary of Literary Biography*. This series contains key excerpts from articles and books on writers now living or who died after 1960. The first collection, published in 1973, and many subsequent volumes contain long blocks of Eliot criticism, and one can quickly get the drift of Eliot studies by reading the excerpts as they have appeared in this baggy but enjoyable compilation. Such cut-and-paste volumes are only a beginning point, but when intelligently selected and arranged, they can be a major resource for busy scholars.

Two multi-volume compilations of Eliot criticism have been published and another is forthcoming. The first is the two-volume *T. S. Eliot: The Critical Heritage* (1982) edited by Michael Grant. Intended to show the reception given a writer by his contemporaries, the Critical Heritage series includes much commentary, some familiar, some retrospectively amusing, some keenly insightful. Grant limits himself to Eliot's verse. A four-volume compilation, *T. S. Eliot: Critical Assessments*, edited by Graham Clarke, appeared in 1990. Although it is far more ambitious, it is less useful and more expensive than its *Critical Heritage* counterpart. The forthcoming compilation, a volume in Cambridge University Press's *American Critical Archives* series, will reprint (in full) early reviews of all of Eliot's book-length works. The Cambridge volume will focus on American responses and will include the reception of Eliot's prose.

Fifteen months before he died, Eliot added a note to his will stating that he did not want his executors "to facilitate or countenance the writing of any biography of me." In her struggle to honor this wish, his widow has been involved in a number of quarrels, from which several speculative biographies have sprung, the worst of which is *Great Tom: Notes Toward the Definition of T. S. Eliot* (1973) by T. S. Matthews. Speculative biographical essays on such topics as Eliot's first marriage and his sexual inclinations have appeared and need to be corrected. Mrs. Eliot is slowly releasing basic materials, and thus the plague of inaccessibility should diminish over the next decade. Much material is already available, of course, in the letters and papers of Eliot's friends and contemporaries. Virginia Woolf's *Diaries* and Bertrand Russell's *Autobiography*, for example, contain valuable pieces of the Eliot puzzle. Letters, memoirs, and even fiction by Ezra Pound, Conrad Aiken, Richard Aldington, Wyndham Lewis, and other friends add fascinating details to the picture. The closest approximation to a standard biography is Peter Ackroyd's *T. S. Eliot: A Life* (1984). Although he did not have access to Eliot's papers, Ackroyd managed a reasonably comprehensive account. He is weak on Eliot's American experience, and perhaps by choice, he remains close to the surface of this primarily interior life. A barebones outline and bibliography is available in *T. S. Eliot: A Chronology of His Life and Works* (1983) by Caroline Behr.

A number of hybrid works combining biography, psychology, and literary analysis have appeared. Lyndall Gordon's *Eliot's Early Years* (1977) and *Eliot's New Life* (1988) are the best of these. Gordon coordinates all the facts at her disposal with an autobiographical reading of the poetry. Her umbrella thesis is that Eliot's life and work were motivated by a search for salvation. John Soldo in *The Tempering of T. S. Eliot* (1983) also merges fact and psychological analysis in his study of Eliot's early life. In *T. S. Eliot: A Study in Character and Style* (1983), Ronald Bush combines an autobiographical approach to the poems with literary and psychological analysis in order to reveal the poet's "character" and to coordinate it with his style. Not all critics who combine biography and criticism make extended use of psychology. Eric Sigg, for example, in *The American T. S. Eliot* (1989), emphasizes Eliot's religious and family traditions in his historicist approach to the early poems.

Fascinating biographical and critical material can be found in various birthday symposia and memorial collections. For Eliot's sixtieth birthday, in *T. S. Eliot* (1949), Richard March and Tambimuttu assembled tributes from such friends as Conrad Aiken, Clive Bell, and Wyndham Lewis. Neville Braybrooke put together *T. S. Eliot: A Symposium for His Seventieth Birthday* (1958), an interesting and entertaining collection. The year after Eliot's death, Allen Tate edited *T. S. Eliot: The Man and His Work* (1966), containing brief and poignant remembrances from many friends and coworkers. Other memorial volumes are primarily scholarly in nature, including several occasioned by the 1988 centennial of Eliot's birth. *The Placing of T. S. Eliot* (1991), edited by Jewel Spears Brooker, *T. S. Eliot: The Modernist in History* (1991), edited by Ronald Bush, and *T. S. Eliot: Man and Poet* (1990), edited by Laura Cowan, are the most important of these. *T. S. Eliot* (1988), edited by James Olney, consists of new essays written for the fiftieth anniversary in 1985 of the founding of *The Southern Review*.

Among the studies of Eliot's work as a whole, the best of those combining scholarship and criticism are A. D. Moody's comprehensive interpretation of the poetry and plays, *Thomas Stearns Eliot: Poet* (1979, 1994), Martin

Scofield's introductory survey of the poems in *T. S. Eliot* (1988), and older studies by Hugh Kenner (1959), Helen Gardner (1959), Bernard Bergonzi (1972), Stephen Spender (1975), and Philip R. Headings (1982). More specialized studies are available, especially on *The Waste Land* and *Four Quartets*. Grover Smith's *The Waste Land* (1983), like his earlier *T. S. Eliot's Poetry and Plays* (1974), simply bulges with scholarly information. Marianne Thormählen's *"The Waste Land": A Fragmentary Wholeness* (1978) focuses on the structure of the poem. Anne Bolgan's *What the Thunder Really Said: A Retrospective Essay on the Making of "The Waste Land"* is the first study to take Eliot's philosophical studies into account. More recently, *Reading "The Waste Land": Modernism and the Limits of Interpretation* (1990) by Jewel Spears Brooker and Joseph Bentley provides a close reading of the poem using both Eliot's own philosophical studies and contemporary literary theory. Harriet Davidson's *T. S. Eliot and Hermeneutics: Absence and Interpretation in "The Waste Land"* (1985) takes Heidegger as a reference point. There are several useful collections of essays, including *"The Waste Land" in Different Voices* (1974), edited by A. D. Moody, and more recently, Lois A. Cuddy and David Hirsch's *Critical Essays on T. S. Eliot's "The Waste Land"* (1991), a gathering of the best commentary from the past seventy years. Keith Alldritt's *"Four Quartets": Poetry as Chamber Music* (1978) explores the much-discussed issue of musical form in Eliot's poetry. *Four Quartets* is a major reference point in J. P. Riquelme's *Harmony of Dissonances: T. S. Eliot, Romanticism, and Imagination* (1991). *Words in Time: New Essays on Eliot's "Four Quartets"* (1993), edited by Edward Lobb, contains studies of each poem and of the sequence as a whole. Jewel Spears Brooker's *Mastery and Escape: T. S. Eliot and the Dialectic of Modernism* (1994) contains several essays on both *The Waste Land* and *Four Quartets*.

Several books focus on Eliot's plays. One of the poet's collaborators in theater, E. Martin Browne, has provided an invaluable firsthand account, *The Making of T. S. Eliot's Plays* (1969). Two early studies, Carol H. Smith's *T. S. Eliot's Dramatic Theory and Practice* (1963) and D. E. Jones's *Plays of T. S. Eliot* (1960) are still useful. Randy Malamud's *T. S. Eliot's Drama: A Research and Production Sourcebook* (1992) includes much valuable material on the plays, including textual notes, publishing and production histories, and critical analysis. Virgina Phelan's *Two Ways of Life and Death: Alcestis and The Cocktail Party* (1990) is one of the few book-length studies of individual plays.

Eliot's intellectual development is at the center of a number of fine studies. Piers Gray's *T. S. Eliot's Intellectual and Poetic Development: 1909–1922* (1982) is an excellent survey of Eliot's graduate studies in philosophy, religion, and myth. William Skaff's *The Philosophy of T. S. Eliot: From Skepticism to a Surrealist Poetic 1909–1927* (1986) covers the same period with very little redundancy. Ronald Schuchard's "T. S. Eliot as an Extension Lecturer: 1916–1919" (1974) includes the syllabi Eliot designed for his courses. John Margolis's *T. S. Eliot's Intellectual Development: 1922–1939* (1972) focuses on the period during which the poet was editor of *The Criterion*. One of the best works on Eliot's philosophy is Jeffrey Perl's *Skepticism and Modern Enmity: Before and After Eliot* (1989). In *The Political Identities of Ezra Pound and T. S. Eliot* (1973), William Chace argues that an understanding of politics is important in reading poetry. Richard Shusterman also looks at the relation of art and politics in *T. S. Eliot and the Philosophy of Criticism* (1988). In *T. S. Eliot and the Poetics of Literary History* (1983), Gregory Jay helpfully brings contemporary literary theory to bear on literary history. The Indic materials which Eliot studied as a graduate student are dealt with in a fine book by Cleo McNelly Kearns, *T. S. Eliot and Indic Traditions: A Study in Poetry and Belief* (1987). The social theories which figure in Eliot's later prose writings are examined in some detail in Roger Kojecký's *T. S. Eliot's Social Criticism* (1971). Eliot's social and political views are treated sympathetically in Russell Kirk's *Eliot and His Age: T. S. Eliot's Moral Imagination in the Twentieth Century* (1984).

Eliot's relation to other writers has stimulated a substantial body of influence studies. Leonard Unger's *Eliot's Compound Ghost: Influence and Confluence* (1981) considers the influence of Milton, Conrad, and others. The influence of earlier writers such as Frazer and Bradley is surveyed in several of the intellectual biographies mentioned above. The Dante connection is analyzed in numerous articles and in several of the comprehensive studies, including those of Philip Heading and A. D. Moody. Stuart Y. McDougal's "T. S. Eliot's Metaphysical Dante" in *Dante Among the Moderns* (1985) shows that Eliot found in Dante a fusion of thought and feeling which served as an example for his own writing from "Prufrock" through *Little Gidding*. The best account of the influence of T. E. Hulme is Ronald Schuchard's "Eliot and Hulme in 1916: Toward a Revaluation of Eliot's Critical and Spiritual Development" (1973). Eliot's relation to Ezra Pound and Wyndham Lewis is examined in a number of works, including Timothy Materer's *Vortex: Pound, Eliot, and Lewis* (1979).

Eliot's early critics worked with assumptions which he himself had helped to create. Recent critics have begun to question his account of literary history by emphasizing modernism's continuity with nineteenth-century literature. The continuities were stressed as early as the 1950s by Frank Kermode in *The Romantic Image* (1957). George Bornstein maintains in *Transformations of Romanticism in Yeats, Eliot, and Stevens* (1976) that modernist poetry, including Eliot's, is a continuation of Romanticism. Edward Lobb in *T. S. Eliot and the Romantic Critical Tradition* (1981) and Jay in *T. S. Eliot and the Poetics of Literary History* see Eliot's criticism as continuous with Romantic thought. David Spurr's *Conflicts in Consciousness: T. S. Eliot's Poetry and Criticism* (1984) examines the tensions in Eliot's poetic consciousness. Other critics have focused on individual nineteenth-century writers. Vinnie-Marie D'Ambrosio argues in *Eliot Possessed: T. S. Eliot and FitzGerald's Rubáiyát* (1989) that the young poet's imagination was captured and shaped by the Rubáiyát. Robert Crawford makes the case in *The Savage and the City in T. S. Eliot's Poetry* (1987) for continuities with Victorian culture.

Much has been written about Eliot and modernism. The best guide in this area is Alistair Davies's chapter on Eliot in his *Annotated Critical Bibliography of Modernism* (1982). Two anthologies are particularly useful. The first is the Pelican collection of essays, *Modernism: 1890–1930* (1976), edited by Malcolm Bradbury and James McFarlane. The other, a collection of primary documents, is *The Modern Tradition: Backgrounds of Modern Literature* (1965), edited by Richard Ellmann and Charles Feidelson Jr. Recent analyses of modernism include Perl's *Skepticism and Modern Enmity: Before and After Eliot*, Sanford Schwartz's *The Matrix of Modernism* (1985), Louis Menand's *Discovering Modernism* (1987), and James Longenbach's *Modernist Poetics of History* (1987).

This review represents only a small part of the many fine articles and books published on the writings of T. S. Eliot and none of the extensive and significant scholarship in languages other than English. Eliot scholarship is international in scope and shape, a fact immediately evident from the rich bibliographies of Eliot studies in German, French, Italian, Japanese, and other languages. The vitality of his poetic language and the range of his ideas promise that the release of primary materials in the 1990s will lead to a renaissance in Eliot studies by the turn of the twenty-first century.

A SELECT BOOKLIST

Ackroyd, Peter. *T. S. Eliot: A Life*. New York: Simon and Schuster, 1984.

Alldritt, Keith. *"Four Quartets": Poetry as Chamber Music*. London: Woburn, 1978.

Bagchee, Shyamal (ed.). *T. S. Eliot Annual No. 1*. London: Macmillan, 1990.

Behr, Caroline. *T. S. Eliot: A Chronology of His Life and Works*. Macmillan Reference Books. London: Macmillan, 1983.

Bergonzi, Bernard. *T. S. Eliot*. New York: Macmillan, 1972.

Bolgan, Anne C. *What the Thunder Really Said: A Retrospective Essay on the Making of "The Waste Land"*. Montreal: McGill-Queen's University Press, 1973.

Bornstein, George. *Transformations of Romanticism in Yeats, Eliot, and Stevens*. Chicago: University of Chicago Press, 1976.

Bradbury, Malcolm, and James McFarlane (eds.). *Modernism: 1890–1930*. New York: Viking-Penguin, 1976.

Braybrooke, Neville (ed.). *T. S. Eliot: A Symposium for His Seventieth Birthday*. New York: Farrar, Straus, and Cudahy, 1958.

Brooker, Jewel Spears. *Mastery and Escape: T. S. Eliot and the Dialectic of Modernism*. Amherst: University of Massachusetts Press, 1994.

Brooker, Jewel Spears, and Joseph Bentley. *Reading "The Waste Land": Modernism and the Limits of Interpretation*. Amherst: University of Massachusetts Press, 1990.

Brooker, Jewel Spears (ed.). *Approaches to Teaching Eliot's Poetry and Plays*. Approaches to Teaching World Literature 19. New York: Modern Language Association, 1988.

(ed.). *The Placing of T. S. Eliot*. Columbia: University of Missouri Press, 1991.

Browne, E. Martin. *The Making of T. S. Eliot's Plays*. London: Cambridge University Press, 1969.

Bush, Ronald. *T. S. Eliot: A Study in Character and Style*. New York: Oxford University Press, 1983.

(ed.). *T. S. Eliot: The Modernist in History*. Cambridge: Cambridge University Press, 1991.

Callow, James T., and R. J. Reilly (eds.). *Guide to American Literature from Emily Dickinson to the Present*. New York: Barnes & Noble, 1977.

Canary, Robert H. *T. S. Eliot: The Poet and His Critics*. Chicago: American Library Association, 1982.

Chace, William. *The Political Identities of Ezra Pound and T. S. Eliot*. Stanford: Stanford University Press, 1973.

Clarke, Graham (ed.). *T. S. Eliot: Critical Assessments*. London: Christopher Helm, 1990. 4 vols.

Cohn, Alan M., and Elizabeth R. Eames. "Some Early Reviews by T. S. Eliot: Addenda to Gallup." *Papers of the Bibliographical Society of America* 70.3 (1976).

Cowan, Laura (ed.). *T. S. Eliot: Man and Poet*. Orono, ME: National Poetry Foundation, 1990.

Crawford, Robert. *The Savage and the City in the Work of T. S. Eliot*. Oxford: Clarendon Press, 1987.

Cuddy, Lois A., and David Hirsch (eds.). *Critical Essays on T. S. Eliot's "The Waste Land."* Boston: G. K. Hall, 1991.

D'Ambrosio, Vinnie-Marie. *Eliot Possessed: T. S. Eliot and FitzGerald's Rubáiyát*. New York: New York University Press, 1989.

Davidson, Harriet. *T. S. Eliot and Hermeneutics: Absence and Interpretation in "The Waste Land."* Baton Rouge: Louisiana State University Press, 1985.

Davies, Alistair. "Thomas Stearns Eliot 1888–1965." *An Annotated Critical Bibliography of Modernism*. Sussex: Harvester Press, 1982. 189–239.

Edwards, A. S. G. "Addenda to Gallup: T. S. Eliot." *Papers of the Bibliographical Society of America* 75.1 (1981): 93.

Ellmann, Richard, and Charles Feidelson Jr. (eds.). *The Modern Tradition: Backgrounds of Modern Literature*. New York: Oxford University Press, 1965.

Frank, Mechthild, Armin Paul Frank, and K. P. S. Jochum (comps.). *T. S. Eliot Criticism in English, 1916–1965: A Supplementary Bibliography*. Victoria, B.C.: Yeats Eliot Review, 1977.

Gallup, Donald. *T. S. Eliot: A Bibliography*. Rev. and extended edn. New York: Harcourt, Brace & World, 1969.

Gardner, Helen. *The Art of T. S. Eliot*. New York: Dutton, 1959.

The Composition of "Four Quartets." New York: Oxford University Press, 1978.

Gordon, Lyndall. *Eliot's Early Years*. Oxford: Oxford University Press, 1977.

Eliot's New Life. New York: Farrar Straus Giroux, 1988.

Grant, Michael (ed.). *T. S. Eliot: The Critical Heritage*. Critical Heritage Series. London: Routledge & Kegan Paul, 1982. 2 vols.

Gray, Piers. *T. S. Eliot's Intellectual and Poetic Development 1909–1922*. Sussex: Harvester Press, 1982.

Grove, Robin. *The Early Poetry of T. S. Eliot*. Sydney: Sydney University Press, 1993.

Hall, Donald A. "The Art of Poetry I: T. S. Eliot: An Interview." *Paris Review* 21 (Spring Summer 1959): 47–70.

Headings, Philip R. *T. S. Eliot*. Twayne's United States Authors Series. Rev. New Haven, CT: College & University Press, 1982.

Jay, Gregory. *T. S. Eliot and the Poetics of Literary History*. Baton Rouge: Louisiana State University Press, 1983.

Jones, D. E. *The Plays of T. S. Eliot*. Toronto: University of Toronto Press, 1960.

Kearns, Cleo McNelly. *T. S. Eliot and Indic Traditions: A Study in Poetry and Belief*. Cambridge: Cambridge University Press, 1987.

Kenner, Hugh. *The Invisible Poet: T. S. Eliot*. New York: Harcourt, Brace & World, 1959.

Kermode, Frank. *The Romantic Image*. London: Routledge & Kegan Paul, 1957.

Kirk, Russell. *Eliot and His Age: T. S. Eliot's Moral Imagination in the Twentieth Century*. 1971. Rev. Peru, IL: Sherwood Sugden, 1984.

Knowles, Sebastian D. G., and Scott A. Leonard (comps.). *An Annotated Bibliography of a Decade of T. S. Eliot Criticism: 1977–1986*. *T. S. Eliot: Man and Poet*: vol. II. Orono, ME: National Poetry Foundation, 1992.

Kojecký, Roger. *T. S. Eliot's Social Criticism*. New York: Farrar, Straus, and Giroux, 1971.

Lobb, Edward. *T. S. Eliot and the Romantic Critical Tradition*. London: Routledge & Kegan Paul, 1981.

(ed.). *Words in Time: New Essays on "Four Quartets."* London: Athlone, 1993.

Longenbach, James. *Modernist Poetics of History: Pound, Eliot, and the Sense of the Past*. Princeton: Princeton University Press, 1987.

Ludwig, Richard M. "T. S. Eliot." *Sixteen Modern American Authors: A Survey of Research and Criticism*, Jackson R. Bryer (ed.). New York: W. W. Norton, 1973, pp. 181–222.

Malamud, Randy. *T. S. Eliot's Drama: A Research and Production Sourcebook*. New York: Greenwood Press, 1992.

Margolis, John D. *T. S. Eliot's Intellectual Development: 1922–1939*. Chicago: University of Chicago Press, 1972.

Martin, Mildred. *A Half-Century of Eliot Criticism: An Annotated Bibliography of Books and Articles in English 1916–1965*. Lewisburg, PA: Bucknell University Press, 1972.

Materer, Timothy. *Vortex: Pound, Eliot, and Lewis*. Ithaca: Cornell University Press, 1979.

Matthews, T. S. *Great Tom: Notes Towards the Definition of T. S. Eliot*. New York: Harper & Row, 1973.

McDougal, Stuart Y. "T. S. Eliot's Metaphysical Dante." *Dante Among the Moderns*, Stuart Y. McDougal (ed.). Chapel Hill: University of North Carolina Press, 1985, pp. 57–81.

McDougal, Stuart Y. "T. S. Eliot." *Sixteen Modern American Authors: A Survey of Research and Criticism Since 1972*. Ed. Jackson R. Bryer. Durham, NC: Duke University Press, 1989. 154–209.

Menand, Louis. *Discovering Modernism: T. S. Eliot and His Context*. New York: Oxford University Press, 1987.

Monteiro, George. "Addenda to Gallup's *Eliot*." *Papers of the Bibliographical Society of America* 66.1 (1972): 72.

Moody, A. D. (ed.). *"The Waste Land" in Different Voices*. London: Edward Arnold, 1974.

Thomas Stearns Eliot: Poet. Cambridge: Cambridge University Press, 1979, rev. 1994.

Olney, James (ed.). *T. S. Eliot*. Oxford: Oxford University Press, 1988.

Phelan, Virginia B. *Two Ways of Life and Death: "Alcestis" and "The Cocktail Party."* New York: Garland, 1990.

Ricks, Beatrice. *T. S. Eliot: A Bibliography of Secondary Works*. Scarecrow Author Bibliographies 45. Metuchen, NJ: Scarecrow Press, 1980.

Sackton, Alexander (comp.). *The T. S. Eliot Collection of the University of Texas at Austin*. Austin: Humanities Research Center, 1975.

Schuchard, Ronald. "Eliot and Hulme in 1916: Toward a Revaluation of Eliot's Critical and Spiritual Development." *PMLA* 88 (October 1973): 1083–94.
   "T. S. Eliot as an Extension Lecturer 1916–1919." *Review of English Studies* 25 (1974): 163–72; 292–304.
Schwartz, Sanford. *The Matrix of Modernism: Pound, Eliot, and Early Twentieth-Century Thought.* Princeton: Princeton University Press, 1985.
Scofield, Martin. *T. S. Eliot: The Poems.* British and Irish Authors. Cambridge: Cambridge University Press, 1988.
Shusterman, Richard. *T. S. Eliot and the Philosophy of Criticism.* New York: Columbia University Press, 1988.
Sigg, Eric. *The American T. S. Eliot: A Study of the Early Writings.* Cambridge: Cambridge University Press, 1989.
Skaff, William. *The Philosophy of T. S. Eliot: From Skepticism to a Surrealist Poetic 1909–1927.* Philadelphia: University of Pennsylvania Press, 1986.
Smith, Carol H. *T. S. Eliot's Dramatic Theory and Practice: From "Sweeney Agonistes" to "The Elder Statesman."* Princeton: Princeton University Press, 1963.
Smith, Grover. *T. S. Eliot's Poetry and Plays.* Chicago: University of Chicago Press, 1974.
   "The Waste Land." London: Allen and Unwin, 1983.
Soldo, John. *The Tempering of T. S. Eliot.* Ann Arbor: University Microfilms, 1983.
Spender, Stephen. *T. S. Eliot.* New York: Viking, 1975.
Spurr, David. *Conflicts in Consciousness: T. S. Eliot's Poetry and Criticism.* Urbana: University of Illinois Press, 1984.
Tate, Allen (ed.). *T. S. Eliot: The Man and His Work.* New York: Delacorte, 1966.
Thormählen, Marianne. *"The Waste Land": A Fragmentary Wholeness.* Lund: C. W. K. Gleerup, 1978.
Unger, Leonard. *Eliot's Compound Ghost: Influence and Confluence.* University Park: Pennsylvania State University Press, 1981.

INDEX